SOCIAL & BEHAVIORAL SCIENCES   Sociology

36-3058
HT690   97-37532 CIP
Lett, Denise Potrzeba. **In pursuit of status: the making of South Korea's "new" urban middle class.** Harvard University Asia Center, 1998. (Dist. by Harvard) 256p bibl index afp (Harvard East Asian monographs, 170) ISBN 0-674-44595-3, $40.00

Lett contends that South Korea is a very status-conscious society, as exemplified by its new urban middle class. This status-consciousness generates all things related to the urban middle class. By design, Lett's study excludes people who would be classified as middle class by conventional sociological and economic criteria, i.e., education, income, and occupations. The South Korean urban middle class (estimated to be 36-60 percent of the early 1990 population in Seoul) represents non-kin managers of large conglomerates, white-color employees, administrators, professionals in government and business, and small to midsize business owners. Skilled laborers are excluded, regardless of income. This urban middle class possesses many upper-class characteristics not shared by their counterparts elsewhere. They maintain a many-faceted life style, with characteristics borrowed from their elite *yongban* model. They assert, solidify, and enhance these elite characteristics, including familism, through education, kinship, marriage, and association. Lett's book is based on 16 months of fieldwork in 1991-92 in Seoul, supplemented by mainly non-Korean publications. Suitable for general readers and undergraduates.—*H. T. Wong, Eastern Washington University*

IN PURSUIT OF STATUS

The Making of South Korea's
"New" Urban Middle Class

Harvard East Asian Monographs, 170

The Harvard-Hallym Series on Korean Studies

The Harvard-Hallym Series on Korean Studies, published by the Harvard
University Asia Center, is supported by the Korea Institute of Harvard University and by Hallym University in Korea. It is committed to the publication of outstanding new scholarly work on Korea in both the humanities
and the social sciences.

Professor Carter J. Eckert   Dr. Sang-Joo Lee
Director   President
Korea Institute, Harvard University   Hallym University

IN·PURSUIT·OF·STATUS

The Making of South Korea's
"New" Urban Middle Class

Denise Potrzeba Lett

Published by the Harvard University Asia Center
and distributed by Harvard University Press,
Cambridge (Massachusetts) and London
1998

The Harvard University Asia Center publishes a monograph series and, in coordination with the Fairbank Center for East Asian Research, the Korea Institute, the Reischauer Institute of Japanese Studies, and other faculties and institutes, administers research projects designed to further scholarly understanding of China, Japan, Vietnam, Korea, and other Asian countries. The Center also sponsors projects addressing multidisciplinary and regional issues in Asia.

Library of Congress Cataloging-in-Publication Data

Lett, Denise Potrzeba, 1956–
     In pursuit of status : the making of South Korea's "new" urban
middle class / Denise Potrzeba Lett.
        p.   cm.   -- (Harvard East Asian monographs ; 170)
     Includes bibliographic references and index.
     ISBN 0-674-44595-3 (alk. paper)
       1. Middle class--Korea (South)   2. Social status--Korea (South)
3. Korea (South)--Social conditions.   I. Title.   II. Series.
HT690.K8L48   1988
305.5'5'095195-DC21   97-37532
                                                               CIP

Index by the author

Printed on acid-free paper

08 07 06 05 04 03 02 01 00 99 98

To my husband, Bill

Acknowledgments

I have been very fortunate to have had an abundance of help from numerous individuals and institutions in the course of writing this work.

First, I thank my Korean informants; without them this work would not have been possible. To protect their privacy, pseudonyms are used in the text. Special thanks are due those individuals who went out of their way to aid me in my research, arranging interviews with their friends and family, including me in their daily and their special activities, and generally sharing their lives with me and enriching mine in the process.

The fieldwork I conducted in Seoul, Korea, over a period of fifteen months in 1991–92 for my Ph.D. dissertation constitutes the primary phase of research for this project. I would like to express my sincerest appreciation to Ajumŏni and to the woman I lived with during the better part of that period for their warm hospitality. I could not have had a more conducive environment, base of operations, and home in which to work and experience Korean middle-class life.

I thank Kim Kwang-ok and Lee Kwang Kyu of Seoul National University for arranging for SNU to be my institutional sponsor while in Korea. The support from Fred Carriere, Mrs. Shim, and the rest of the staff at the Korean-American Fulbright office in Seoul added to my sense of security and peace of mind while there. Financial support was provided by Fulbright and Social Science Research Council fellowships. From Laura Nelson I received emotional support as we shared with each other our concurrent fieldwork experiences in Seoul. Mary Mooney's interest in my research and her subsequent introductions to her students aided my work immeasurably.

Very special thanks are due Kim Hyun Mee, who freely gave her time both in Seoul and in the United States. Her readings of earlier drafts and her comments have provided me with insights into my data and Korean life that I might have missed otherwise. Her interest, her encouragement, and her emotional support are greatly appreciated.

Each of the members of my Ph.D. Supervisory Committee at the University of Washington aided me in different but complementary ways. I express my appreciation to Stevan Harrell for serving as my committee chairman. I also appreciate Noel Chrisman's enthusiasm and advice as a reading committee member. I thank James Palais for serving as my Graduate Faculty Representative and for showing such an interest in my work. Clark Sorenson shouldered much of the burden, especially in the last stage of writing the dissertation. For this and for his very constructive comments and advice in general I am very grateful. His assistance continued throughout the revision period. I am also indebted to him for allowing me to use an excerpt of his translation of an unpublished article. In addition, I wish to thank Robert Hill who, though not directly involved in this project, was very influential in developing my historical approach to anthropology while I was a student at the University of Texas at San Antonio.

The process of turning my dissertation into a book has also been aided by many people. Susan Hanley at the University of Washington read the manuscript from cover to cover, and her enthusiastic response and constructive criticisms helped me make the necessary revisions. Financial support in this period was provided by a Korea Foundation Postdoctoral Fellowship at Harvard University's Korea Institute in 1995–96.

The year at Harvard was an extremely stimulating one academically. I wish to express my thanks to Carter Eckert, Director of the Korea Institute, and to the members of its Executive Committee, including Vincent S. R. Brandt, Edward Baker, Yoon Choong-Nam, Milan Hejtmanek, and Anne Denna. The staff of the Korea Institute, especially Rose Cortese and Susan Lee, of the Fairbank Center for East Asian Studies, and of the Harvard-Yenching Library were not only very efficient but amicable and warm.

I am indebted to Ezra Vogel, James Watson, Laurel Kendall, and Roger Janelli, all of whom read through the manuscript and provided detailed written comments that were extremely useful. I am further indebted to Ezra Vogel and his seminal work on Japan's new middle class for my initial inspiration to undertake this project. Both Ezra Vogel and James Watson, no matter how busy, always found time to talk to me when I asked for their advice. I also thank James Watson for showing such an interest in my ideas on yang-banization, for calling to my attention the work of Japanese anthropologists in this area, and for allowing me to cite from his related paper.

I thank Laurel Kendall for encouraging me to examine even more closely my arguments and interpretations by presenting her views from a different perspective. I also thank her for permission to quote from her correspondence with me. I am also grateful to Roger Janelli for his insightful comments, and for permission to cite excerpts from these.

Jordan Sand and James Thomas also read through the manuscript and offered their comments. I thank them as well as Rubie Watson, Han Do Hyun, the participants in my colloquium, and all the scholars at Harvard with whom I had an opportunity to discuss my work.

Special thanks are due Han Do Hyun, whom I perceive as embodying all the positive attributes of the Korean sŏnbi. His assistance, which began at Harvard, continued in Korea. During my return visits to Korea in 1996 and 1997, he too always found time for me despite a very full schedule. I also appreciate his help in typing the Guide to Romanizations.

Funds for my month-long return visit to Korea in the fall of 1996 were provided by an Association for Asian Studies–North East Asia Council short-term travel grant. I also have used observations in Korea made during the first few months of a 1997 Korea Foundation Fellowship for Korean Studies. I also wish to thank the families I stayed with on these visits and their relatives who made the arrangements. I appreciate the logistical and emotional support of Mary Mooney and Ken Kahliher.

For their copyediting and proofreading, special thanks are due Elizabeth Gretz and Maria Duryea, respectively. Their work and enthusiasm are much appreciated. I also wish to thank Katherine Keenum, editor of the Council for East Asian Publications during my stay at Harvard, for her encouragement and assistance. Thanks are also due Linda Howe and John Ziemer, current editor at the Asia Center, for seeing that this work has been brought to completion.

I wish to thank very much my sister Lisa Potrzeba for turning my hand-drawn floorplans into professionally done, computer-generated ones. Additionally, with regard to my family, the support of my mother, Pauline Potrzeba, should not go unnoticed. It has been comforting to know that she has been behind me through all the years in whatever I pursued. In fact, I can say that of all my family, including my seven brothers and sisters and their families, and I am grateful. The encouragement my father, Walter Potrzeba, gave me in my studies in my youth remains strong in my memory.

Finally, but most important, I express my deepest appreciation to my husband, Bill Lett. By putting my interests before his, he has unselfishly allowed me to pursue this work in the most ideal circumstances possible. His sacrifices, his support, and his patience could not be surpassed or more appreciated.

D. P. Lett
Seoul, Korea
July 1997

Contents

IN PURSUIT OF STATUS

The Making of South Korea's
"New" Urban Middle Class

Introduction

South Korea is a very status-conscious society, and the assertion of status has become an important element in both the formation and the definition of its new urban middle class. My first real indications of this came in a personal way even before I left the United States for South Korea. "Don't even try to compete with the middle-class housewives in dress," a Korean colleague advised me, "for they spend much from toe to head to adorn themselves." If that did not alert me, the almost casual comment of my Korean-language tutor, "My sister will probably pick you up in a chauffeur-driven car," should have.

Indeed, the woman who met me at Seoul's Kimpo International Airport at her sister's request projected an image of some social standing. There was her stylish and impeccable attire. The chauffeur. The set of golf clubs in the trunk of the car. The woman's formal deportment, her hands properly placed on her lap as she sat very erect facing me in the back seat of the car.

This display of status was not pretentious. There was substance, I was to learn, behind the projection. Mrs. Hwang was well educated. With a master's of business administration degree in hand and with the financial backing of her family, she had built a successful taxi business. Her husband subsequently retired from his salaried job to take over the operation. I found this out not from Mrs. Hwang but, rather, from an admiring friend, Professor Lee. Mrs. Hwang preferred to emphasize to me that it was her husband who ran the company. As for herself, she was actively engaged in volunteer work with the church.

Mrs. Hwang and her former classmate Professor Lee presented a study in contrast. Although both of these women had earned undergraduate degrees from the same prestigious university in Seoul, their paths diverged from there. Professor Lee received her doctorate from an American university and married a man who was also an academic. Unlike her former class-mate, Dr. Lee spoke fluent English, had a ready laugh, and appeared very comfortable with me.

When Professor Lee came to pick me up at my hotel on my first day to show me the university, she arrived via public transportation and seemed quite familiar with the bus system as she introduced me to it. Dressed mod-estly, she did not display the wealth her friend did. Nevertheless, the deep bow, respectful language, and generally deferential treatment she received from a student on campus who knew her left no doubt in my mind that she was accorded high prestige as a scholar.

I had other doubts, however. Mrs. Hwang presented me with an image of one lifestyle in urban South Korea; Professor Lee with a radically differ-ent one. But were these two women both members of the middle class? I was left with a strong feeling, which was to be reinforced throughout my stay, that South Korea's middle class was somehow more upper class than America's. This ethnography of the everyday life of contemporary urban middle-class Koreans is an attempt to substantiate that feeling.

I will argue not only that South Korea's so-called contemporary urban middle class exhibits upper-class characteristics, but also that this is due to a culturally inherited disposition on the part of Koreans to seek high status, combined with a favorable political and economic climate that has made it possible for many Koreans in South Korea to actually achieve this status. Although Korea's Confucianist past is often blamed for Korea's late start in industrialization at the macro level, at the level of the family it is the Confu-cian legacy, or more specifically the legacy of the *yangban*, the aristocratic elite of Korea's former Confucian state, and especially their concern with status, that has been a driving force behind the development of South Ko-rea's new middle class and the nation's rapid emergence as a major player in the global economy.

In addition to inheriting the cultural need for status from the yangban tradition (see also Kim Kyong-dong 1994:102; Bourdieu 1984:1), Koreans, consciously or unconsciously, have been capitalizing on traditional ways of asserting high status, albeit adapted to meet today's requirements (see also Rozman 1991), in order to substantiate claims to status in the modern con-text (see also Bourdieu 1984:147). New ways of asserting status have also emerged as Korea has evolved from a "traditional" Confucian, agrarian, and largely closed and isolated society characterized as "yangban" to one that has become predominantly middle class, urban, industrialized, and exposed to and incorporated into the greater world community. All these ways of as-serting status constitute defining characteristics of South Korea's new middle class. Each of these will be explored in depth through examinations of occupation, family, lifestyle, education, and marriage strategies.

South Korea's New Middle Class: Theoretical Orientation and Definition

What comes out strongly and unambiguously is that class, however defined in detail, continues to be of the utmost importance in contemporary society. Class may be a 'contested' concept . . . but that does not mean . . . that it should be abandoned, only that it must be examined with the greatest care, and without too many preconceptions.

—Arthur Marwick (1986:167)

Preconceptions are exactly what I carried with me when I set off to learn firsthand about South Korea's new urban middle-class families. I took my initial definition of "new middle class" from Ezra Vogel's classic, *Japan's New Middle Class: The Salary Man and His Family in a Tokyo Suburb* (1963, 1991). "New middle class" as used by Vogel, and conventionally by sociologists (for example, Mills 1956), is primarily defined in terms of occupation and refers to the white-collar employees of the government bureaucracies and large business corporations, which developed along with urbanization and industrialization. In contrast to the small independent businessmen and landowners of the "old middle class," who are dependent on property for their income, members of the "new middle class," by this definition, rely solely on salaries for their livelihood. Associated with the "new middle class" is a lifestyle distinct from that of the "old middle class." The income of independent businessmen and landowners fluctuates with the economic climate, and time for work and leisure are blurred; salaried employees typically enjoy a guaranteed income with regular work hours and time off, without many of the anxieties and work connected with farming and independent businesses (Vogel 1963:4–7; Bestor 1989:261–265; Mills 1956).

When Vogel first went to Japan to study middle-class families, he did not distinguish them on the basis of occupation. In the course of fieldwork and analysis of data, however, the uniqueness and great importance in Japan of salary-man families over other types of middle-class families emerged and became the focus of his work. At the time of Vogel's research (1958–1960), Japan was the only non-Western nation to have reached a level of industrialization and urbanization comparable to that of the United States and of the advanced countries of Europe (Vogel 1963:3). Vogel found that because of factors such as income security and more leisure time, salaried jobs, which had emerged as a result of this industrialization and urbanization, were preferred far above others in Japan. By the time Vogel began his research, the salary man had become stabilized and clearly identifiable as a distinct occupation category in Japan, and it seemed to Vogel "an opportune time to examine the nature of his life" (Vogel 1963:5–6).

It seemed to me that the time had come to attempt a similar project in Korea. Although Vogel's research was conducted over thirty years earlier, it took place at a stage in Japan's development that was roughly comparable to South Korea's in the early 1990s. That is, South Korea had only recently reached the level of industrialization and urbanization that Japan had reached roughly three decades before (Tsuya and Choe 1991:11). Thus, in the summer of 1991 I went to Korea with the idea of conducting research on Seoul's middle-class families, in particular the salary-man's family, à la Vogel. What I found in Korea, however, was quite different from what Vogel found in Japan. As we shall see, "salary man" does not have the same significance in Korea as it does in Japan, and there are difficulties inherent in separating the "new middle class" from the "old middle class" in the context of contemporary South Korea. So how can we evaluate South Korea's class structure?

For the study of class in any particular society, Marwick (1986) suggests a general pragmatic historical approach. Although he does not reject the usefulness of micro- or macrotheories when they have analytical value (1986:6, 9), Marwick's view is that "it is more important to establish the particular forms taken by class in different societies than to establish some general model of class roughly applicable to all industrial societies" (1986:9). The first step, according to Marwick, is to establish the context that determines the particular shape that class and class relationships will take in a particular society. Among the elements that make up the context of class are history and tradition, levels of industrialization and the nature of industrial relations, and images of class as perceived from within the society itself "to see whether . . . there is any evidence within the society for envisaging it as being made up of several classes" (Marwick 1986:10, 11).

By using this pragmatic historical approach as well as Bourdieu's (1984:483) notion that class is determined as much by consumption or lifestyle as by relations to the mode of production, I attempt to produce "a rounded, and distinctive, model" of Korea's urban middle class, "firmly related to the particular historical context" of South Korean society, and in which both subjective and objective criteria are firmly integrated (see also Marwick 1986:13).

The Korean Development Institute (KDI) defines "middle class," or "*chungsanch'ŭng*" (literally, "middle-propertied strata"), according to four criteria: having the subjective feeling of middle class; having an income up to three times higher than the average urban household income; having an education past the middle-school level; and having a job among the self-employed, being an employer, or being a salaried worker. A survey by KDI using these criteria estimated the size of this population to be 36 percent of urban residents (*Seoul Daily News*, January 9, 1991, as reported in Kim Eunshil 1993:31; see also Moon Okpyo 1992). In popular usage, however, criteria are much more subjective and the term "chungsanch'ŭng" or "middle class" is very ambiguous. Government statistics show that by the early 1990s over 60 percent of the South Korean population claimed middle-class status (National Statistics Office 1991:307), and some other surveys as well as popular sentiment would consider this conservative. One of my informants, Miss Ko, a university graduate and account supervisor for a public relations company, explained this discrepancy in the following way:

The middle class is a very current and controversial topic in Korea today. Professors at Seoul National University debate the role the middle class should play politically. Several criteria are used to determine what is middle class. Middle class is the most desirable position to be. Many more people consider themselves to be middle class than actually are. There is a difference between perception and reality. Income level and occupation are determining criteria. But probably education is the most important. If a person is college-educated, even if they don't come from a middle-class family, they probably consider themselves to be middle class. Skilled laborers like construction workers or taxi drivers may make more money. But these and other "dirty jobs" are ones no one wants and are not considered middle class.

Then who are the middle class? Although this work addresses various markers of middle-class status, occupation, as one if not the most important indicator of class (Hong Doo-Seung 1990:7), provides a preliminary definition of middle class as used here. It is helpful in delineating both those who are and those who are not the primary subjects of this study.

This is an analysis of South Korea's *urban* middle class, in particular that of the greater Seoul metropolitan area of the 1990s. Thus agriculturalists who might be considered middle class are not subjects of this study. Manual laborers, even if skilled, are not considered middle class and are not included here. Moreover, in contrast to sociological convention, small-scale entrepreneurs are not included if their families did not earn enough money to support what Koreans themselves considered a middle-class lifestyle, the standards of which have been steadily increasing since the 1960s.

At the other end of the spectrum, as might be expected, the political and military elite are excluded from this study. So are the founder-owners and their kin who are managers of the *chaebŏl* or large business conglomerates such as Hyundai and Lucky Goldstar (now known as the LG Group). Included among the middle class, however, are all nonkin managers of chaebŏl, no matter how high their level. Finally, white-collar managers, administrators, and professionals in both government and business and small- and medium-sized business owners who were living at least a middle-class lifestyle are considered subjects of this study. In Korea, a woman's status is generally derived from that of her husband. As we shall see, though, a man's choice of wife and her choice of pursuits are also informed by subjective criteria of what is considered appropriate for those asserting middle-class status.

One final note on terminology. Because Korea did not have small independent businessmen classified as "old middle class" in the conventional sense much if at all before there were salary men in Korea, "new middle class" here refers to all those in Korea with middle-class status regardless of occupation. "Middle class status," nevertheless, is not an absolute category with clearly defined boundaries. Although there are those whose claim to middle-class status would not be contested, there are others whose status is debatable and is debated (see also Kim Kyong-dong 1994).

Methodological Approach and Setting

Through the end of the 1980s, village communities constituted the primary focus of Korean ethnography (Osgood 1951; Brandt 1971; Han Sang-bok 1977; Janelli and Janelli 1982; Chun Kyung-soo 1984; Kendall 1985a; Sorensen 1988). Today, as Kendall (1996:13) notes, "the sites for a possible anthropology of Korea proliferate." Recent studies have included those set in large corporations (Janelli with Yim 1993; Kim Choong Soon 1992), factories (Kim Seung-Kyung 1990; Spencer 1988), urban squatter communities (Cho Eun and Cho Oakla 1992; Thomas 1993), middle-class high-rise apartments (Kim Myung-hye 1993; Moon Okpyo 1990; Moon Okpyo et al. 1992; Yi Eunhee Kim 1993), ob/gyn clinics (Kim Eun-Shil 1993), and even "amidst the fray of social movements" (Abelmann 1996; Kim Hyun Mee 1995).

This ethnographic study of South Korea's new urban middle class is based primarily on fieldwork that I conducted in and around the capital city of Seoul from June 1991 through October 1992. A month-long revisit was made in the fall of 1996. A few observations have also been included from the early stages of a six-month period of research that began in February 1997. With few exceptions, which I point out, the descriptions and analysis contained herein appear to continue to apply to South Korean society as I found it in 1997. Although participant-observation and interviewing were the primary methods I employed, this work is not a classic community-based study as has generally been the case with Korean ethnographies to date and with ethnographies in general.

In contrast to the works already mentioned, a community-based approach would have been inappropriate in this instance. If I had restricted myself to a neighborhood or even several neighborhoods, for example, or if I had insisted that I keep to my original plan of concentrating solely on salary-man families, I would have missed essential features of South Korea's new urban middle class. I would not have captured the images of class as perceived from within the society itself to realize that South Koreans do not dichotomize what they perceive to be their middle class into "old" and "new" in the conventional sense. Nor would I have as fully appreciated how various middle-class factions as envisaged by Koreans are in part manifested in concrete differences in choice of lifestyle and consumption, including residential location and type of housing. Empirical observations across a large spectrum of South Korean society, rather than abstract theories about class, guided me in defining South Korea's middle class.

In her study of Korean weddings of first-generation working women in a "market town turned satellite city" of Seoul, Kendall presented personal accounts of her subjects, "a style of anthropological practice Lila Abu-Lughod characterizes as 'an ethnography of the particular' that resists the authoritative generalizations of an older ethnography to present its subjects" (Kendall 1996:20). Likewise, and in contrast to "traditional" anthropology, I present anecdotal evidence drawn from a wide range of informants when the diversity found among South Korea's middle class defies generalization. It is impossible to write simply about *the* Korean middle-class family, for example. This style is consistent with not limiting my study to a single community or to a particular occupational group in order to establish the particular forms taken by class in Korean society. How then did my actual fieldwork proceed?

When I first arrived in Korea and explained that I was interested in the middle class, Koreans invariably advised me to go to Kangnam, Seoul's "boomtown" area south of the capital's traditional southern Han River border and home to many of Seoul's new middle class. General participant-observation was thus first achieved by living in a middle-class, high-rise apartment complex in the Kangnam region. This particular complex, built about five years earlier, contained individually owned units that extended across the full range of sizes commonly found among the middle class, that is, from 22 *p'yŏng* to 55 *p'yŏng* (roughly 783 to 1,958 square feet; 1 p'yŏng = 35.6 square feet or 3.3 square meters). Middle-aged couples dominated the complex and especially the larger units. Younger couples with young children were also found here, however, some of them living with their parents.

Living in this complex, I was able to experience and make general observations of the amenities and activities in a typical urban, middle-class residential setting. I took note of such things as the on-site services available to the apartment dweller, including the daily early morning car washing in the parking lot, the thrice daily chantlike calls up and down the stairwell for dry cleaning by three competing local businesses, the regular door-to-door delivery of food items such as milk, juice, yogurt, bottled water, rice, and, from time to time, a catered Chinese dinner, the picking-up and dropping-off of children in a van operated by a taekwondo martial arts school, and the myriad of tasks from short-term baby-sitting to repotting of house plants that the guards stationed at each elevator entrance performed.

From my apartment vantage point I observed an occasional chauffeured car and the usual children's play in the parking lot. I listened to marchlike music blaring from the loudspeakers of the nearby government office building, where I came to know that government workers in white shirts, their suit coats removed, were out in their parking lot doing morning calisthenics. I watched older students who were preparing for the university entrance exams coming to, going from, and socializing in front of the private study facility located next door. I heard the sounds of piano and violin practice drifting from more than one apartment (and especially from the one directly above me, at 5:30 in the morning!). I ran into neighbors and their visitors and had short conversations with them. And I talked at length with the apartment guard, who surprised me by speaking fluent English.

I frequented the establishments in the adjacent small-business district, eating in the restaurants and shopping at the bakery, pharmacy, grocery, fruit stand, and newly built convenience store. I made note of the banks, hotels, tailors, video stores, *hagwŏn* (private educational institutions), and of the *norae bang* (places that provided individual facilities to practice singing, alone or with friends), which were springing up everywhere.

Before moving to this apartment complex in Kangnam, however, I had spent a summer in a dorm in the Kangbuk, or northern, region of Seoul, which allowed me to make at least basic contrasts between living in the older and newer sections of town, the former dominated more by enclosed, single-family residential compounds than by apartment complexes. After the move, I visited homes in and wandered around several other middle-class neighborhoods in and around Seoul, both north and south of the Han River and in residential areas that were dominated by houses or villas as well as by apartments.

I also visited places not necessarily residential, but where middle-class family members, as well as others, were apt to go. I was often accompanied by my regular Korean informants or met and became engaged in casual, one-time conversations with inhabitants of Seoul from all walks of life. I shopped at the markets and in small shops and modern department stores, ate at TGI

Fridays, Kentucky (Fried) Chicken, and other Western fast food places as well as Korean eating establishments, worked out in health clubs, went to the movies, and sipped the appropriate beverage at the ubiquitous (but expensive) tea- and coffeehouses. (I even had my fortune told at one of the newest, upscale coffee shops; it listed *"counseling"* on the menu, for 7,000 *wŏn* or about nine and a half U.S. dollars, along with its selection of drinks.

I visited universities, relaxed in parks, and attended cultural events. I spent time downtown. I hiked in the surrounding mountains, a favorite leisure activity of the citizens of Seoul. I ventured a bit further afield on occasion, contrasting Seoul with small towns, visiting temples, and taking in other sites popular to Korean and foreign tourists alike. I rode the crowded subways, buses, and trains. I got stuck in traffic. And I even drove a car by myself in Seoul. In short, I lived in Seoul, participating in and observing middle-class life as fully as possible.

Members from ten families in particular shared some of these and other experiences with me in varying degrees of intensity over extended periods of time ranging from six months to over a year. Another dozen met with me at least a few times over the same period of time. And then, in addition to the chance conversations already mentioned, I conducted over fifty one-time, formally scheduled interviews.

A look at how I came to know these people offers insight into Korean personal relationships and values. In so populous an urban area as Seoul, individual and family life tends to be less public than in a small community or village. Weddings and funerals, for example, are not community affairs open to all. One generally must be invited to attend. As a foreigner, it was impossible for me to simply "show up" and blend in. Networking, therefore, became my key to making contacts, just as it is for Koreans as they go about their daily lives.

Moreover, whereas Koreans may have various resources to offer one another, if I had anything to offer them, it was my native English fluency, something that Koreans tend to value highly. Although actual English-language abilities among the Koreans I met ranged from fundamental to fluent, I found the desire to have contact with Americans and especially with native English speakers quite pervasive in South Korean middle-class society. From the beginning, this desire, coupled with the normal process of networking, aided me in my research.

My first formally scheduled interviews, for example, were arranged by Mr. Oh, a mid-level government official who offered to help me with my research in any way he could just for the opportunity to practice his conversational English in the process. We were introduced by a former classmate of his who was the Korean language teacher of a Korean-American woman living in the same dorm as I. She had taken an interest in my research and put me in contact with her teacher. His friend, Mr. Oh, activated his personal network and called upon his colleagues at work and upon other classmates now working for private companies to allow me to interview them either in their homes with their families or in the teahouses or restaurants they frequented with their colleagues after work.

The Korean woman I came to live with had actively sought an American woman with whom to share her apartment. The apartment guard, who had learned English while working in Saudi Arabia, introduced me to a couple of families in the apartment complex who had asked him to approach me about English tutoring. The lady of the house of one of these families, Mrs. Baek, in turn introduced me to her former classmate and fellow church member, Mrs. Yu, who was living in a different neighborhood in Kangbuk, or north of the Han River.

Another example is Mr. Ch'oi, a white-collar employee of one of the large business conglomerates, who approached me on the subway, inquired about my reason for being in Korea, and then asked how he could help. In another instance, a university English instructor whom I met at a Fulbright lecture, upon hearing of my research, asked if I would be interested in interviewing her students. This led to introductions to still others (not to mention becoming chief judge of an English speech contest for an English club, or circle, as they are often known in Korea).

And so the introductions went on. Although at first it was difficult for me to make contacts, once the process started, it snowballed. My sampling of the families I met with repeatedly and of those I met with only once or a few times achieved a diversity representative of South Korea's urban middle class in terms of several factors, including, but not limited to, stage of individual and family life cycles, range of middle class (lower-middle through upper-middle), occupation, type of residence (apartment or condominium, house, villa), part of town (Kangnam, Kangbuk, or satellite city), family history (former social standing, what part of Korea the family originally migrated from and when, and so on), and religion.

Despite my efforts to reassure my Korean hosts that I was quite capable of acts such as using public transportation, eating Korean food, and sitting on the floor, logistics and a feeling of responsibility for me on the part of my Korean hosts remained a large obstacle to my being invited to participate in many family activities. In contrast to what one might expect in a village setting, everybody doesn't know everybody's business in the less personal setting of Seoul, with its eleven million people. Much more is required in the urban context to break through and become privy to the inner workings of a family. Nevertheless, over time I was privileged to be allowed into the homes and lives of my Korean hosts, to participate in and observe their daily activities.

In addition to the mundane (which was really quite exciting to me), I also attended or participated in a number of special events or activities, including wedding, funeral, and graveside ancestor worship ceremonies; a hometown visit to a small town to meet the parents and other relatives of one of my regular informant families, the Moons; a visit to relatives in the countryside with another of my informants, Miss Shim; a "homestay" with Mr. Ch'oi and his family in one of Seoul's satellite cities; and a three-day leisure trip with the Korean woman with whom I lived and three previously unknown, middle-class married couples from Seoul.

Finally, missionary and other accounts written by early Western observers, ethnographies, sociological studies, histories, and a geography of Korea published prior to my research have become ethnohistorical sources with the passage of time and are used here to reconstruct the process of change in various areas of Korean life. Ethnographies contemporaneous with mine that deal with South Korea's lower classes are used to contextualize and better define the middle class through contrasts and comparisons. Statistics are used whenever possible to illuminate certain trends and to demonstrate the degree to which my data are representative of South Korea as a whole.

South Korea's middle class itself is not a homogeneous group. The Koreans themselves, for example, make a distinction between middle and upper-middle class on the basis of criteria such as standard of living, lifestyle, and occupation. Moreover, this distinction is often but not always related to whether middle-class status is asserted primarily through the possession of cultural capital, such as education, or primarily through the possession of economic capital, such as property. These are not mutually exclusive, of course. It is through a display of a constellation of characteristics related to occupation, family, lifestyle, education, and marriage that middle-class status is asserted. And although transformations have occurred with changes in the political economy, historical antecedents may be found among the traditional elite, the yangban, for many of these characteristic ways of asserting status. Thus we turn first to the yangban heritage.

I

From Confucianism to Capitalism

Today all Koreans identify themselves with the lineages of yangban scholar-officials. Descendants of the "middle-people" (*chungin*), commoners (*sangin*), and even slaves (*nobi*) are indistinguishable from the descendants of yangban aristocrats. . . .

   With the rise of a rapidly industrialized and pluralistic democratic society, anybody can now become a *sonbi* [scholar]. I have met many Koreans who could identify famous scholar-official ancestors, but I do not recall meeting a Korean who could trace descent to a slave in the Choson dynasty.

—Fujiya Kawashima (1989:14)

One cannot consider South Korea's modern capitalist class system without taking into account its Confucian heritage, for Confucianism (more specifically, neo-Confucianism), adopted and adapted as state orthodoxy by the founders of Korea's Chosŏn or Yi dynasty (1392–1910) and upheld by the aristocratic yangban elite, served as a blueprint for ordering and integrating Korea's political and social life for over five hundred years. Capitalism, as Rozman (1991:19) comments, is not "as all-embracing a category for interpreting a country's development as many once thought. The historical slate is not wiped clean, and particularly in East Asia, its effects are becoming widely visible." He continues:

Not only is awareness rising of the continued significance of a country's heritage, there is also heightened acknowledgment that elements of that heritage can contribute to unusual dynamism in development. The way people interact at home, school, and their workplace, the way they view their government and their own society's place in the world, affects their rate of modernization. Even if, for a time, the foreign impact seems to be displacing more and more of the traditional behavior, a process of interaction is at work in which some elements of tradition may be reasserted and may guide modernization in new directions. (Rozman 1991:19–20)

I will argue that elements of Korea's traditional Confucian world order have reasserted themselves and become important elements in the development and definition of South Korea's contemporary urban middle class. Here I briefly describe pertinent elements of that tradition.

The Chosŏn Dynasty and the Yangban Tradition

Neo-Confucianism is a system of beliefs and practices that relies on self-cultivation and moral education (reinforced in practice with law and certain institutions) as a means of ordering society. The study of Confucian texts and the practice of Confucian ritual, especially mourning and ancestor worship, were the primary means through which Confucian norms were instilled in Korea during the five centuries of Yi rule.

At the core of this system are moral imperatives for ordering the five basic human relationships. Except for faithfulness between friends, the principles governing these relations are hierarchical in nature. Confucian principles of social relations stipulate that benevolence and filial piety should define the relationship between parent and child, that distinction should define the relationship between husband and wife, and that precedence should define the relationship between elder and younger siblings. The relationship between subject and ruler is modeled after those of the family. According to Confucian thinking, attention to developing proper family relationships also leads to the development of loyal and obedient subjects: "As it says in the *Analects* (1.2), 'Rare are those who are filial to their parents and deferential to elder brothers yet are fond of causing trouble to their superiors'" (Ebrey 1991:45–46). Loyalty and obedience in turn are expected to be reciprocated by benevolence on the part of the superior. Confucius explained the importance of proper family behavior to the state:

The gentleman's service to his parents is filial; the fidelity involved in it can be transferred to his ruler. His service to his elder brothers is deferential; the obedience involved in it can be transferred to his superiors. Self-disciplined at home, he can transfer his good management to official life. Through these means when his conduct is perfect at home his name will be perpetuated to later generations. (*Hsiao ching* 14; cited in Ebrey 1991:62)

Thus proper familial behavior was believed to be elemental to good government. Furthermore, good government was achieved through self-cultivation and moral education. Ideally, self-cultivated men, that is, men with superior benevolence and wisdom derived from the study of Confucian classics and tested by state examination, were recruited to serve in the government bureaucracy. Or, to look at it from the reverse perspective, to obtain a coveted position as a scholar-official, a man was required to demonstrate mastery of the Confucian classics by passing civil service exams (*kwagŏ*) and thereby prove his moral worth to govern others. Once having obtained a government position, a man and his family were expected to rule by example, adhering to the highest of Confucian norms, including those that governed family ritual and relationships (see also Deuchler 1992:120).

Although a meritocratic ideal was inherent in the Confucian system of recruitment of officials by examination, in Korea this ideal was tempered by a strict hereditary class structure whose origins predate the introduction of Confucian-based state exams and even the unification of the Korean peninsula by Silla in 668. Both the Silla (668–918) and the Koryŏ (918–1392) dynasties were ruled by a hereditary elite. In 958 a Confucian-style exam system was first instituted to recruit officials from among the hereditary elite, and status within this elite stratum became linked to government posts. The government gradually became organized into a rigidly hierarchical bureaucracy consisting of civil and military officials known as the yangban.

The beginning of the Chosŏn dynasty (1392–1910) marked the adoption of Confucianism as state orthodoxy. Despite the indigenous class structure, there were no legal class requirements to sit for the civil service exams, and many used the exams as a means of achieving social mobility. The combination of a well-developed class consciousness that "fueled the motivation for higher social status" and the Confucian meritocratic ideal with its associated ideas of social mobility led families to seek examination degrees and so-called yangban status, "yangban" being the Korean equivalent of an aristocracy (Haboush 1991:98). Encouraged by government policy, an increasingly larger segment of the population aspired to and succeeded in obtaining higher social status, if only by passing the lower-level civil service exams. Although a smaller, hereditary elite maintained power at the highest levels of government (Deuchler 1992:12), an increase in the number of successful exam takers at the lower level meant that a higher percentage of the educated population had no hope of obtaining a government position (Haboush 1991:98; see also Palais 1975:8).

By the middle of the Chosŏn dynasty, to protect their positions of power and prestige, members of the established ruling elite had effectively placed a hereditary requirement on future exam takers. Thus, while in the beginning of the Chosŏn dynasty yangban status was not automatically inherited but generally had to be revalidated through success in the state exams, by the middle of the dynasty yangban status came to be ascribed to agnatic descendants of former yangban. One had to prove one was a descendant of a former successful candidate in order to be eligible to sit for the exams. The assertion of such status became a primary concern.

In effect, yangban status had become hereditary and Korea's government officials were theoretically recruited only from the yangban stratum. Korean society had thus become dichotomized between the yangban, who as the ruling elite enjoyed status and prestige, and the lower classes. The latter included the *sang'in* or *yang'in*, that is, the "good people" or commoners (who were mainly peasants but also included a few merchants, fishermen, and artisans), often referred to as "middle class" in the writings of early Western observers of Korea, and the *ch'ŏnmin* or lowborn (slaves and those in low-status occupations such as butchers). (See Deuchler [1992] for an in-depth study of the Confucian transformation of Korean society; see also Palais 1996.)

The yangban "had many of the attributes of an aristocracy, [and] maintained itself by legal and de facto inherited status privileges, landholding, officeholding (in the central bureaucracy) and utilization of Confucian orthodoxy for the legitimization of status and economic interests" (Palais 1975:4–5). The lowborn and commoners "had virtually no privileges and [the commoners had] all the burdens of taxation" (Palais 1975:6), with no real middle class in between (Bishop 1970 [1898]:446–448; Moose 1911:99; McGrane 1973:24; Yoo Seung-won 1988:97). With the equal service reform of 1750, which marked the end of a protracted debate over the reform of military service and taxation, the yangban were ensured privileged tax-exempt status. "Equal" obligations provided for in Confucian tradition applied to the lower classes only. Interestingly, opponents of taxation of the yangban also used Confucian doctrine in their arguments to uphold the strong indigenous Korean tradition of social status distinction and privilege:

There is no great difficulty in understanding why some officials opposed yangban taxation on class grounds: they wanted to preserve their advantageous positions of wealth and prestige. Some extracted the notion of status distinction (*myŏngbun*) from the Confucian tradition and converted it into a cardinal principle of faith. For them, any lessening of the rigidity of status distinction threatened the collapse of the social and moral order, for hierarchy was the basic principle of the hallowed Confucian five relationships. To them, egalitarianism was anathema, for how would people be able to distinguish between what was noble and what was base, or, in other words, what was fine and worthy of emulation and what was beneath contempt and deserving of derision? (Palais 1975:95)

Although the yangban made up perhaps no more than 10 percent of the total population (Deuchler 1992:12), they held a hegemonic leadership position during Korea's Chosŏn dynasty, with the Confucian worldview of the yangban, the dominant class, becoming the "common sense" of the society as a whole (see also Eckert 1990–91:135; Gramsci 1971). Although there were countermovements, such as Buddhism and shamanism, the yangban world-view was so pervasive in Korea during the Chosŏn dynasty that the society as a whole is characterized as having been "yangban": "Precisely because it was this *yangban* class that directed the government, economy, and culture of Yi dynasty, it may fittingly be designated a *yangban* society" (Lee Ki-baik 1984:173; see also Deuchler 1992:12). Thus a Confucian ideological hegemony was attained in Korea through yangban hegemonic leadership, and to speak of Korea's Confucian tradition or legacy is essentially to speak of the tradition or legacy of the yangban. Social status distinctions were an elemental component of this tradition and were manifested in multiple ways.

In addition to its division into the ruling class and the non-ruling classes, Chosŏn society, borrowing from Confucian views of social organization, was divided into four large, hierarchically ordered occupational status groups or estates; in this scheme, economic status was considered secondary to social role (see also Kuhn 1984:25). The scholar-officials recruited from among the yangban were at the top of this hierarchy. Landholding, however, which was concentrated in the hands of the yangban, provided the economic base of the aristocratic elite (Palais 1975:64): "The salaries connected with the various of-fices were small, and the official was expected to look out for his living from the people" (Moose 1911:181), that is, from those who worked the land that the official held. "Squeezing," Bishop called it (1970 [1898]:448, 451). Officials commonly used or abused their positions and their landholding rights, prac-ticing extortion, bribery, and other corrupt means to enhance their economic standing (Hulbert 1969 [1906]:45–68; Chung Young-Iob 1984:41–43).

Following the scholar-officials in descending order of status were the farmers, merchants, and craftsmen. There was an additional intermediate oc-cupational group in Korean society just below the higher-ranking scholar-officials called *chung'in* or the "middle people," composed of both members of a hereditary group of chung'in lineages and members of offspring of yang-ban fathers and concubine mothers. The "illegitimate" sons of yangban, so-called *sŏja,* did not inherit the same rights of eligibility for high public office as their half-brothers whose mothers were the legitimate wives of these yang-ban. They were, however, eligible, along with the hereditary chung'in, to serve in positions as government clerks and functionaries. These were spe-cialists such as medical officers, translator-interpreters, astronomers, meteor-ologists, accountants, statute law clerks, and scribes.

Farmers formed the largest segment of Korean society, as noted by the missionary Moose, whose ten-year residence in Korea coincided with the final decade of the Chosŏn dynasty: "Our village farmer belongs to a very large and withal a very respectable class. Korea is preeminently a farming country. The large majority of those who work at all are engaged, at least part time, in farming" (1911:127; see also Chung Young-Iob 1984:25). In this precapitalist, Confucian society, businesses were small in scale and merchants were accorded low status: "Next to the official class stands the farmer, and next to the farmer stands the merchant in the social scale. There are many merchants, though many of them do a very small business, and they would not rank as merchants at all in a country like the United States" (Moose 1911:143; see also Gale 1975 [1898]:188). Bishop, an astute observer and chronicler of Korean life between 1894 and 1897, noted: "Even in Seoul, the largest mercantile establishments have hardly risen to the level of shops" (1970 [1898]:446; see also Chung Young-Iob 1984:26).

Confucian attitudes toward capital accumulation in the precapitalist era stunted the growth of both business and industry. The establishment of tributary relations with China in 1392 with the founding of the Chosŏn dynasty may actually have led to the decline of industry as the royal household increasingly met its needs through the import of luxury goods that were obtained in exchange for tribute in China (Amsden 1989:30; see also Hulbert 1969 [1906]: 273; Chung Young-Iob 1984:22, 39). Foreign trade overall was both very limited and tightly controlled by the Korean government. Outside of tributary relations with China, some illicit private trade at the Sino-Korean border, and a small amount of highly regulated trade with Japan, Korea, by its own choice, had no other trade relations or any foreign relations of any kind (save that of the Japanese invasions in the sixteenth and seventeenth centuries) until the end of the nineteenth century (see also Chung Young-Iob 1984:26).

Domestically, the basic commercial system was one of supplying the ruling elite. There was no free-market economy. In the countryside, "farmers maintained household industries solely to meet their needs and to fulfill tributary obligations to landlords. Although independent artisans produced handicrafts for others' use, the high degree of subsistence meant little market activity" (Amsden 1989:31; see also Chung Young-Iob 1984:26). In the capital city of Seoul, government officials granted monopoly rights to merchants in return for an agreement to supply needed merchandise at nominal prices (Amsden 1989:31). At the same time, officials continued to rely on their ties with their kin or landholdings in the countryside to supply them with foodstuffs and household goods (Bishop 1970 [1898]:60; Lee Hyo-jae 1971:17; Lee Ki-baik 1984:207–208).

As already noted, the craftsman was accorded even lower status than the farmer and merchant: "Our village mechanic belongs to a somewhat lower strata socially than that to which the farmer belongs. I do not understand the reasons for this," Moose admitted, "but the fact remains just the same that one who makes things in this country must take low rank in the social scale" (Moose 1911:137; see also Gale 1975 [1898]:188; Bishop 1970 [1898]:388).

The low status attributed to both entrepreneurial activity and manual labor had a legal basis. During the Chosŏn dynasty yangban were prohibited by law from participating in either entrepreneurial activity or manual labor. The penalty for engaging in business or menial labor was loss of yangban status, not only for the individual but also for all his descendants. Among its consequences, loss of yangban status effectively meant loss of prestige as well as loss of access to civil service exams and government office; an individual would also become subject to various taxes and military and corvée labor (Yoo Seung-won 1988; see also Chung Young-Iob 1984:28). Avoiding "unsuitable" labor was more important to maintaining yangban status than having material wealth (Moose 1911:54).

There was one exception to this prohibition against manual labor: farming. "A gentleman of the purest blood can engage in farming without soiling his escutcheon, but to be a merchant or manufacturer or broker would be beneath his dignity. Agriculture is so dignified an occupation that it stands quite alone among Korean industries" (Hulbert 1969 [1906]:269).

Outside and below this Confucian-derived system of dividing society into four large, hierarchically ordered occupation status groups or estates— namely scholar, farmer, merchant, and craftsman—was a stratum in Chosŏn society known as the ch'ŏnmin, that is, the base or lowborn. Though composed primarily of government and private slaves, the lowborn also included those groups engaged in hereditary occupations that were considered impure or polluted. These so-called paekchŏng were outcastes much like the "untouchables" of India and the eta or burakumin of Japan (Passin 1955, 1956–57).

The occupational categories included in the group of lowborn varied, if only slightly, from time to time (Chung Young-Iob 1984:23; Passin 1956–57). Passin (1956–57:205, 206) divided the ch'ŏnmin into public and private sectors. Those in the public sector consisted of persons who were in service to governmental institutions and included the kiseang (public entertainers); servants in government service, such as messengers and cleaners; those who worked in the government travel stations and rest houses; jailkeepers; public slaves; and fugitives, criminals, and the like. Ch'ŏnmin in the private sector included monks and nuns; messengers; chaein (actors and entertainers); shamans; executioners; shoemakers; and the paekchŏng. The paekchŏng proper were a settled, if not also segregated, group who engaged in servile and so-called polluted occupations, including basketry, butchering, leather-work, and straw-sandal making (Passin 1956–57:211–212).

Although commoners were distinguished from the yangban, commoners in turn set themselves off from the lower class of "base people" (ch'ŏnmin): "Membership in all these status groups was ascribed by birth rather than acquired by achievement, and the law as well as social custom guarded against infringement of social boundaries" (Deuchler 1992:13). However, although "Chosŏn society constituted a hierarchy of three distinct status groups that were based on hereditary and occupational criteria: the sociopolitical elite or the yangban; the commoners who did not belong to the ruling elite; and the slaves and other base people," the major dividing line in Chosŏn society was the distinction between the "noble" (*kwi*) and the "base" (*chŏn*) (Deuchler 1992: 302–303; see also Palais 1975:95, 1996) or the honored (*chon*) and the despised (*pi*) (Deuchler 1992:378, n. 32), based on a purity that is distinct from that implied by any opposition to the "base" or "impure" occupations of the lowborn:

In other words, the society of Chosŏn Korea was first of all perceived as forming two major groups largely defined in terms of "purity," that is, the elite on the one hand and all the other social groupings on the other. This division was never used synonymously with the distinction between the commoners (*yang*), that is, those who were not base, and the base people (*ch'ŏn*), that is, slaves and those who pursued impure occupations as shamans, butchers, and leatherworkers—a distinction some modern Korean historians see as the most important dividing line. The elite always stood above such categorization. (Deuchler 1992:302)

"Noble" and "base" "were subjective terms that denoted the dominant inequalities within the Korean society, and were clearly not used as generic status labels. Rather, they indicated the yangban's purity versus all the others' impurity, and . . . it is evident that they point to the perfect social order within which everyone occupies the position to which his (inborn) capacities entitle him" (Deuchler 1992:300–301). (See Deuchler 1992:341, n. 89.) Passin (1955:257) explains the relationship between birth or ancestry, occupation, and virtue:

Korean Confucianism made the basic assumption of all rigid hierarchical systems, especially of the Orient, that there was, in the nature of things, an inherent distinction between the upper and the lower orders. The upper orders were born to rule, to practice virtue, and to cultivate enlightenment and learning. The lower orders were born to obey and to serve; they were inherently ineducable and incapable of understanding the Confucian ethic. The upper classes were not only richer, more respectworthy, and better educated, but they were also more virtuous.

There was thus already inherent in the early Confucianism of Korea a predisposition to consider that the lower the occupation, the more immoral, or lacking in virtue, it was. (Passin 1955:257)

Although more important than economic gradations in Chosŏn's social organization was the Confucian-based dichotomy between those who labored with their minds and those who labored with their hands, we see that by the late Chosŏn dynasty this dichotomy was manifested in distinctions made between the hereditary yangban elite on the one hand, and commoner and lowborn on the other, the former ascribed by matter of birth to be "pure" and the latter to be "base." Most yangban, in fact, never passed the civil service exams; fewer became scholar-officials in the central government. The hereditary yangban elite were themselves basically divided between career bureaucrats in the capital, along with their close relatives who were eligible to sit for the exams, and local elites, either landlords, landowners, or simple tenants in the countryside who may or may not have passed civil service exams, but who had ancestors that had held office in the past.

Because ancestry constituted the main basis of elite status, patrilineage took on greater importance for the yangban. In contrast, it was not considered important for commoners or the lowborn to maintain links with their ancestors, none of whom presumably had been officials in the government. Accordingly, commoners and lowborn did not, in fact could not, form lineages, nor did they keep genealogies (*chokpo*). What may appear as "commoner lineages" can be explained, according to Deuchler, as impoverished segments of elite lineages, although, unlike Chinese lineages, Korean lineages as a rule did not segment internally on economic grounds (Deuchler 1992:10, 302, 378 n. 330; see also Janelli and Janelli 1978, 1982):

Therefore, . . . most notably [for reasons of] its genealogical orientation combined with acute status consciousness, a Korean lineage can be expected to be a socially homogeneous entity that did not cross social status boundaries. Lineage organization in Korea was "by definition" an upper-class phenomenon that preserved its vitality for such a long time precisely because of its social, if not economic, uniformity. In this point it differed sharply from the Chinese lineage, which accommodated members of diverse social background but tended to split on economic grounds. Korean lineages did tolerate considerable economic differences among their constituent parts, even though economic competition may have led to conflict among different segments. In the end, prolonged poverty and the consequent inability of certain segments to keep close ties with more influential kinsmen could cause downward mobility and a loss of yangban status (likely coupled with elimination from the genealogical records). What ultimately may have looked like a "commoner lineage" was in fact the result of downward mobility. (Deuchler 1992:302)

Thus in Korea lineages primarily were expressions of status and prestige in contrast to Chinese lineages that were primarily built on property (Deuchler 1992:289; see also Janelli and Janelli 1982:133). Genealogies became vital for establishing one's credentials and ensuring access to an appropriate social, political, and economic position in society. Because Korean lineages constituted the pool from which government officials were recruited, lineage organization, found by definition only among the yangban, was directly connected with the political process (Deuchler 1992: 8,10).

There were also status distinctions made between lineages within the yangban stratum itself. Members of a lineage had a common interest in advancing, or at least maintaining, social standing. Lineage ancestor rites, which were initially required to be conducted by officeholders, gradually became a symbol of prestige as more and more elite practiced them; they thus also became a major mechanism for asserting status (Janelli and Janelli 1982:130, 133; Haboush 1991:110). Asserting status in such ways was particularly important for those descendants of officeholders who had no hope of obtaining a government position (Haboush 1991:109). But other ways of asserting status existed as well.

Because commoners did not form lineages, their kinship system was less complex and less ritualized (Deuchler 1992:13). For this reason and because commoner and lowborn families (and even some yangban families) generally did not have the resources to maintain extended families, large patriarchal and patrilineal families were indicative of elite status. This elite Korean family system is characterized as corporate and stem, and the inheritance as partible but unequal.

Upon marriage daughters received a small dowry and transferred residence and membership to their husband's family. The eldest son remained a part of his parents' household. A stem family resulted upon his marriage. Choice of marriage partner was also a matter of status, as certain lineages tended to take spouses from other lineages of similar status in order to maintain the prestige of the line. Commoners, because they lacked recognized charters of descent, rarely were chosen by yangban for primary marriages (Deuchler 1992:13). Deuchler asserts that the yangban's refusal to take primary wives from status groups lower than themselves was a manifestation of the dichotomy of Chosŏn society as the yangban delineated themselves from the other two major social groups, the commoners and the lowborn, on the basis of the yangban inborn purity over all the others' impurity (1992:300–301):

The *sadaebu* [a term Deuchler uses synonymously with yangban; 1992:341, n. 89] were therefore a practically endogamous group whose membership was basically determined by the fact of birth. . . . It was not the men but the women who in fact preserved such exclusiveness. Consequently, only women whose agnatic kin belonged to the "noble" half of society could bring forth sons fully linked to their fathers' ancestral heritage. Conversely, sons of women originating from the lower ranks of society lacked the social purity to take over their fathers' ritual trust. . . .

. . . The selection of women as spouses was a critical instrument for delineating social status groups and accentuating their hierarchical ranking. A woman's social rather than her material endowment ultimately determined her value as a wife. (Deuchler 1992:301)

Despite the emphasis on the patriline in a Confucian world order, at least among the elite, the social background of a potential bride was thus an important consideration: "Most conspicuous was the continued strength of the maternal line of descent in determining and reproducing elite status. Women, as representatives of their respective patrilines, imparted the crucial hereditary essence that made their offspring full members or, if they lacked that essence, only half members of their husbands' descent group. For the elite, the reproduction of status remained bilateral" (Deuchler 1992:288).

Traditionally, the main household or "big house" (*k'ŭn chip*) went through a joint phase when younger sons married and brought back their brides. After several years, however, younger sons formally partitioned and formed a conjugal branch household or "small house" (*chagŭn chip*). At the time of partition younger sons received their inheritance, which was always less than what the eldest son received.

The eldest son was responsible for his elderly parents. Upon his father's death, he succeeded his father as head of the household and, inheriting the bulk of the property, became responsible for all members of the household as well as for conducting ancestor worship. After younger sons partitioned, they were required to go to the main house for these rites. An eldest son thus enjoyed a special status distinct from that of his younger siblings. His authority was recognized even before he succeeded his father and assumed his responsibilities. Deference was shown him by younger siblings, and even by his mother, from childhood: "All the boys in the same home do not have an equal chance, the oldest one always having the advantage of his younger brothers. His name is never called by his younger brothers, but he is addressed as 'my honorable elder brother,' this even when the boys are out at play. In the family circle he stands next to the father, and he lords it over his mother from the time he has the power of speech to command her" (Moose 1911:91). Because younger sons received lesser amounts of property, over time, in rural villages, "a nested structure of relatively prosperous main, and less prosperous branch, families tends to be created, perpetuating in following generations the status distinction between eldest and younger brothers" (Sorensen 1993a:106). Younger brothers would find themselves even more dependent on their eldest brother if their father died before partition, because it would then be up to the eldest brother to decide how much if any property was to be passed on to his younger brothers.

Status in Chosŏn society was also reflected in material ways, such as in housing, dress, and lifestyle: "Visually, the commoners were distinguished from yangban by different dress and by their simpler mode of life" (Deuchler 1992:13). In housing, there were certain elements basic to the Korean abode: "Every house has at least two rooms, the living room and the cook shed. For the latter always, even in the best houses, there is nothing more than mother earth for the floor. In the cook shed the fireplace is located, being nothing more than the entrance to the flues that run under the floor" of the living room, which is elevated above the level of the kitchen (Moose 1911:69). "A fire of brush and twigs is kindled [in this fireplace] under one side of the house, and as the chimney opens at the other side, the draft naturally carries smoke and heat through the flues, the floor becomes very hot, and the whole room is quickly warmed. The [kitchen] fireplace is built with pots for boiling the rice" (Underwood 1987 [1904]:4). Then "when the rice is cooked the fire at the same time heats the stone floor" of the other rooms (Moose 1911:69). "A room heated this way is called a *pang*," Hulbert (1969 [1906]:245) explains; "the system itself is known as *ondol*, and differs from the Chinese *kang* in no essential particular except that the latter occupies only part of the room and is raised like a divan, while the Korean forms the whole of the floor itself."

Beyond this basic plan, social distinctions were manifested in various ways, such as in the quality of materials used. For example, Moose noted: "Those who can afford it cover this floor with oiled paper" while the "poor man covers his floor with a straw mat instead" (1911:68–69). In their work on traditional Korean house furnishing, Wright and Pai (1984:116) remark: "The style, design, and size of a house were all carefully dictated by custom according to social position. The houses of the upper, middle, and lower classes were easily distinguishable from one another. By the end of the Yi dynasty, however, distinctions between the upper and middle classes [that is, commoners] had softened and rules relaxed so that there was much deviation from the original strict building dictates. However, the life-style [we describe] . . . was not something the lower classes would have had a chance to experience."

Size and complexity were two obvious distinctions. Larger houses and a lifestyle that included the service of servants and slaves often went hand in hand. Hulbert explains that a small house would contain only one pang or heated room, "with a kitchen attached and one or two storerooms; but a large gentleman's establishment, while built in the same general way, will contain perhaps a dozen or more such rooms and a long row of servants' quarters, making in all as many as a hundred and fifty or even two hundred *kan* [9,600 to 12,800 square feet]" (1969 [1906]:245–246).

Size also affected family relationships and behavior. Except among the poorest, a traditional house had separate quarters for males and females, but the actual degree of separation depended once again upon the occupants' status: "The well-to-do will have a large house, but always on the same plan. . . . It is built in a rectangle around an open court. . . . Every well-constructed house has its outer one for the men and the inner ones for the women" (Moose 1911:70), with all young children sleeping with their mother until boys and girls were separated around the age of seven or so. "Each dwelling is so arranged that the part of the house occupied by the women, which is called the *anpang*, or inner room, shall be screened from sight from the street and from those entering the gate—for every house has at least a tiny courtyard [*madang*], part of which is also screened off (either by another wall or by mats or trees and bushes) for the women's use" (Underwood 1987 [1904]:4). In more elaborate compounds with more than one courtyard, this inner courtyard belonged to the women of the household. The courtyard's various uses included serving as a playground for the children. Once they were old enough not to be under constant adult supervision, boys and girls were separated even in play, as Li Mirok, the son of a rich landowner, recalls his childhood: "Our house had several courtyards. The main building [the inner wing], consisting of six rooms, a kitchen, and a covered veranda [*maru*], was laid out in a circle around a large open space: the inner courtyard, where the women lived" (1986:4–5) and where his sisters and female cousins gathered to play various girls' games (1986:17).

"In front of the house," Li Mirok continues, "lay two more courtyards, separated only by a low wall with a door. The one on the righthand side, through which one reached my father's room, was called the well-yard, because of the deep well there; on the lefthand side was the outer courtyard, with a high gate and a number of guestrooms. We were allowed only in this courtyard" (1986:5). Here he and his male cousin played all day (1986:3), that is, until his father, being of an elite, wealthy, landowning family, hired a teacher for them "and opened a sort of domestic school in the outer courtyard" (1986:14) to which children from other families with yangban status were invited. (There were no public schools, and the education of children was the responsibility of the family. Commoners and the lowborn generally were uneducated. Thus education was also a status marker.) "The outer yard was not only our playground," Mirok adds. "There was also a vegetable plot, a shallow well without water, and a large barn" (1986:46). The courtyards were very much integral to the household activity, although the activity and courtyards were divided between male and female.

While the entrance to the women's quarters was inside a hidden courtyard, that of the men's opened either directly to the outside or, in more elaborate compounds, onto the men's courtyard: "Wherever it can be afforded, a *sarang*, or men's sitting [or reception] room, which opens directly on the street or road or upon the men's court, is a part of the establishment. Here any man may enter; male guests are entertained, and fed, and here they sleep. No men not members of the family or relatives ever enter the *anpang*" (Underwood 1987 [1904]:4–5).

"Absolute seclusion is the inflexible rule among the upper classes," Bishop emphasizes (1970 [1898]:340). "The ladies have their own courtyards and apartments, towards which no windows from the men's apartments must look," she adds. "Women of the middle class [that is, commoners] were not so secluded as those of the upper class," however (Hulbert 1969 [1906]:352). This was a function of economics and architecture. Hulbert explains that it was "far less common for a man of the middle class [that is, a commoner] to possess a general reception room, and the result is that relatives are much oftener invited into the inner rooms" (1969 [1906]:352). Thus "the degree of seclusion which a Korean woman enjoys depends upon the position she holds in society. . . . The higher her position, the more complete is her seclusion . . . women here pride themselves upon the fact that no male person outside the immediate household ever sees their faces" (Hulbert 1969 [1906]:350).

The seclusion of women from the public and the physical segregation of the sexes within the household into separate living quarters had implications with respect both to the division of labor within the household and to the roles and relationships among various household members. Within the household, the men and women generally slept and invariably ate separately. Whatever the size of the house, the simplicity of furnishings provided for flexibility in both sleeping and eating arrangements. Sleeping arrangements, for example, were not hindered by rigid bedsteads. On those occasions when a husband would sleep with his wife or a boy with his father, or should there be guests, lack or placement of beds was not an issue. Status, however, entered into degree of comfort: "It is not much trouble to get ready to retire in Korean style. The shoes are left outside the door on entering the room. The bed is always ready, since there is none except the floor. Those who are able to afford such luxuries have quilts which are spread on the floor when it comes time to retire. Absolutely nothing in the way of bedsteads or chairs is to be found in these houses" (Moose 1911:69).

Eating arrangements were also flexible. Small, portable tables, stored in the kitchen, were brought out as required. The "family dinner," though, did not exist. Men and women ate separately. The daughter-in-law served her husband and parents-in-law:

> She does not sit at table with him; she serves while he eats. It should be remembered that Koreans do not eat from a common table as we do, but from individual tables. But even then she does not have her table in the same room at the same time with her lord and master. If he wants another bowl of water or other article, he yells out: "See here, what-you-may-call-it, bring me some water." When his meal has been finished he yells for her again, and she appears and carries the table away. After all this service has been well performed, she eats her meal, often consisting of what has been left by the men of the house, out in the cook shed. (Moose 1911:115–117)

The seclusion of women led to a division of labor in which the men handled all business outside the home while the women concerned themselves solely with household matters. In his analysis of households living in traditional-style houses in a village in central Korea during the 1970s, Sorensen (1983) noted a relationship between the division of household labor, based on gender, and the physical arrangement of the traditional house. His analysis seems valid here as well:

> If we look at the male/female division of labor and at the arrangement of the Korean house, it is easy to see that an inside/outside theme is present. The house mistress lives in the Inner Room (*anbang*) of the Inner Wing (*anch'ae*) and takes care of the inside labor (*annil*); while the house master lives in the *sarangbang* of the Outer Wing (*pakkatch'ae*) and takes care of the outside labor (*pakkannil*). Moreover, the house mistress, although formally known as *chubu*, can colloquially be called the "inside master" (*an chuin*); while the house head, formally known as *hoju*, can colloquially be known as the "outside master" (*pakkat chuin*). (Sorensen 1983:70; see also 1988:134)

Sorensen adds that "the use of these metaphors goes beyond mere location, however, and reflects the sociological positions of the house master and house mistress within the household" (1983:70). In earlier times, the higher the class, the greater the seclusion of women, and thus the greater this division based on gender. Hulbert observes, "As we descend in the social scale, all restrictive laws and all inequalities between the sexes are toned down, so that when we reach the lowest classes we find that the relations are much the same as in our own land" (1969 [1906]:366):

> The middle class woman [that is, commoner] is more nearly on a level with her husband, she knows more about his business and has more to say in the management of the family affairs than the high-class woman. . . . The question arises as to whether a married woman has control of the wages which she may earn. In this respect the middle-class woman has the advantage of her higher sisters, for while a gentleman's wife

will invariably turn over the proceeds of her work to her husband, the middle-class woman may or may not do so. Every act of a high-born woman is subject to far closer scrutiny than in the case of the middle-class woman, and, as she can never go to a shop to buy anything, she cannot well use her money. (Hulbert 1969 [1906]:366–367)

The greater cultural need for higher-class women to remain more se-cluded precluded their ability to do other household chores in addition to marketing. They could not go to the stream, for example, to do their laundry, though perhaps they did not see this as a hardship. Hulbert writes that "as might be supposed, a descent in the social scale widens the field of the Ko-rean woman's work. The middle-class woman . . . may 'take in washing,' which means carrying it to the nearest brook or to the neighbourhood well-curb" (1969 [1906]:356). In Seoul, laundry was more often done by the lowest classes: "One of the 'sights' of Seoul is the stream or drain or watercourse. . . . There, tired of crowds masculine solely, one may be refreshed by the sight of women of the poorest class, some ladling into pails the compound which passes for water, and others washing clothes in the fetid pools which pass for a stream" (Bishop 1970 [1898]:45).

Social distinctions were also reflected in the quality of clothes (*hanbok*) members of a household wore. Differences in the quality of hanbok based on social standing were stipulated not only by economic ability but by law (Hong Sun-hee 1992:5). Type of material, color, and accessories distinguished the yangban's hanbok as Hong describes:

While commoners' wives were restricted by law as well as resources to cotton garments at best, "yangban" women used plain and patterned silks, and in warm weather, wore gowns of closely-woven ramie cloth or other high grade, lightweight materials.

As for color, the "yangban" could choose from a wide variety of bright colors while commoners tended to wear white and, if they did wear colors, they were dull shades of pale pink, light green, grey and charcoal.

In addition to high quality apparels, women in "yangban" households had their pick of colorful hairpins, pendants and pouch-ornaments. . . .

Meanwhile, accessories for men include beaded strings for the high horse-hair black hats and elaborately woven silken cords called "sejodae" worn around the chest just below the armpit around the coat as well as the golden, silver or amber buttons tied to the jacket worn just under the long coat. (Hong Sun-hee 1992:5)

Along with appearance, status could be asserted by "behaving as high-status people are supposed to behave. For one thing," write Janelli and Janelli (1982:132), "this meant keeping a strict sense of dignity and decorum." Avoid-ance of labor has already been mentioned. Carrying of funeral biers and pub-lic entertaining are other examples of behavior considered lower class. Janelli and Janelli continue: "Upper-class behavior was also expected to be righteous.

Moral worth became closely associated, if not equated, with social worth, and those competing for status and prestige could use moral qualities to support their claims or deny those of a rival. Filial piety and female chastity, including celibacy of widows, became particularly important indicators of a group's moral and social standing. A noteworthy activity in these areas by a lineage member or his wife affected the prestige of his entire kin group" (1982:133). Naturally the company one kept would also be expected to influence one's status either negatively or positively. Thus, housing, dress, lifestyle, and behavior in general along with literacy in Chinese, knowledge of the Confucian classics, passing civil service exams to earn a degree, holding government office, landholding, adherence to Confucian ethical norms (including those involving Confucian rituals and proper family behavior), an extended kinship system, marrying within elite lineages, the performance of lineage rituals, maintenance of genealogies, association with those with good social standing, and a life of leisure rather than one characterized by labor were all markers of high status and culture.

Not all yangban exhibited these features to the same degree. Depending on a family's assets, status was asserted in different ways, which often led to different lifestyles even among the yangban. For example, as mentioned earlier, the yangban were basically divided between the career government bureaucrats in the capital and the local elite in the countryside. Distinctions were found among the local elite as well, with a basic dichotomy between those who devoted their time to scholarship and those who were "unlettered" (see also Gale 1975 [1898]:186). Proper dress and behavior took on an added importance for those yangban who lacked the educational criteria for high status:

> For the unlettered gentry Chinese has no charm. They keep a few learned expressions at their finger ends, as a sort of bulwark of defence when hard pressed, but as far as possible they avoid the subject. Their life, since shut off from intellectual pleasure, consists of material pleasure, dress and enjoyment. This class of scholar is exceedingly common in Korea. In immaculate white he emerges from the holes and corners of every mud village. If he is an official of importance, he does not walk alone, but is assisted by the arms on each side. If he ventures by himself, it is with a magnificent stride that clears the street of indifferent passers, and commands only on-lookers. In one hand is a pipe three feet long, in the other a fan; over his eyes two immense discs of dark crystal, not to assist him in seeing, but to insure his being seen. (Gale 1975 [1898]:186)

Even for the "lettered" yangban, vast differences in ways of asserting status can be seen between those officials with government appointment in Seoul and those scholars, known as *sŏnbi*, who were not career bureaucrats and who generally lived in the countryside. In his study of sŏnbi in the Chosŏn dynasty and their heritage in modern Korean society, Fujiya Kawashima identifies the underlying principle of difference: "As I put together pieces of evidence from the society of the mid- to late-Choson dynasty, I begin to see a rough portrait of *sonbi* and their aristocratic peer group, and of their distinctive way of life, sustained by prestige rather than power and wealth" (1989:6). The prestige of the sŏnbi was derived from their scholarly lifestyle, perhaps seen as a life of leisure, rather than from an appointment in the central government and its associated way of life.

The sŏnbi are largely a product of the so-called literati purges between 1498 and 1545 "which drove many serious scholars out of the capital into the countryside where they followed the teachings of their fallen leaders" (Kawashima 1989:7; see also Wagner 1974). Essentially, those who were to become sŏnbi were often "critical of career bureaucrats who were dependent on the authority of their superiors rather than on the principles of government. The *sonbi* believed in loyalty to the throne, but their loyalty was conditional to such principles" (Kawashima 1989:11). Kawashima comments on these purges and their effect on the yangban dichotomy between the capital and the countryside:

Since the mid-sixteenth century, Choson politics became increasingly polarized between officials and their families in the Seoul region . . . and scholars and their families in the countryside. The former occupied important posts in the bureaucracy, while the latter stayed outside the officialdom as scholars of principle (*cho'osa*) or scholars of the mountain groves (*sarim shi sa*).

The social origin of the *sonbi* may be described here in terms of the social relations between officials and non-officials in early Choson society. Officials at the beginning of the Choson dynasty came mainly from aristocratic families that moved to the capital region from the provinces where their ancestors had lived for centuries. These families of officials distinguished themselves from the families that never produced officials by identifying themselves with their surname and place of family origin (*pon'gwan*). Marriage was arranged between the families of officials who belong[ed] to different clans (*ssijok*). These "official" families were united through the network of marriage and became a Seoul-centered aristocratic kin group. Members of this group were identified by the surname of their patrilineal ancestors, although they emphasized the importance of both patrilineal and matrilineal lines, as well as spousal lines. . . .

Beginning from the second half of the fifteenth century, the Seoul-centered aristocratic kin group branched out in significant numbers into the countryside. Many families acquired land outside the capital region through office-holding and in-law families in the countryside. By the end of the sixteenth century, their descendants became local landlords who were very conscious of their patrilineal "official" ancestors. They married only persons of similar family background and published their own branch genealogies to prove their connection with ancestors who were prominent officials. . . .

A majority of these families in the countryside did not take the civil service examination [to earn a degree] (mun'gwa) [*munkwa*] or hold a government office. As descendants of prominent officials, they studied and taught classics and called themselves *yuhak* ("student"). The common people referred to them as *sonbi*, and respected them for their scholarly lifestyle. Although they were not officials, they considered themselves equal to officials in scholarship, morality, and family background. (1989:7, 8, 9)

The sŏnbi derived his social status more from birth than from merit, Kawashima notes. He continues:

[The sŏnbi] believed that his lineage was superior to that of commoners because he belonged to a family that not only produced officials but also kept up its scholarly traditions for generations. He valued the maintenance of his proper kinship ties and ritually controlled conduct for the sake of his own, and posterity's well-being. His family took utmost care in the selection of marriage partners in order to maintain the family tradition.

On the other hand, the *sonbi* believed in the value of achievement, hard work, and scholarship, and his goal was to be employed in the officialdom because of his talent and ability. However, most *sonbi* ended their lives without realizing this ambition, and remained content to be local leaders and teachers....

Although some *sonbi* attained the lifestyle of a true gentleman, many were frustrated and unemployed in the countryside. Without a degree from the civil service examinations, their chance of practicing their ideals was limited, or nonexistent. They became experts in the study of genealogies (*pohak*) and family rites (*yehak*), which helped them to assure and preserve their special status.

Today all Koreans identify themselves with the lineages of yangban scholar-officials. (Kawashima 1989:11, 14)

Yangban status was thus asserted in various ways depending on a family's assets. (We will also see this to be the case with the modern-day middle class, at the same time that the members of this class model many of their ways of asserting status on traditional practices.) In general, career bureaucrats derived their prestige from, among other attributes, degrees gained in passing civil service exams, power from their official position in the central government, wealth from landholdings in the countryside, and residence in Seoul—as well as from the performance of ancestor rites and the maintenance of genealogies. The sŏnbi also performed ancestor rites and maintained genealogies, but derived much of their status from their literacy in Chinese, devotion to Confucian studies, high moral standards, and ethical leadership in the countryside. They may or may not have had much wealth in the form of land and slaves. Some families had not had a successful civil service examination candidate for generations and no longer had the economic means to support a lifestyle much different from that of the majority of the peasants. These sŏnbi were the most likely among the yangban stratum to take up farming themselves. It is estimated that "close to half of the numbers of households of putative yangban status hovered about the poverty line" (Palais 1975:65). Some "unlettered" yangban of the countryside, however, did own land and derived their status from land- and slave-holding and the conspicuous consumption that allowed (see also Deuchler 1992:11).

In various periods in history but notably toward the end of the Chosŏn dynasty, there were also those who tried to move up the social scale through various means, including forging of genealogies to "support" a yangban heritage, buying yangban titles and status, acquiring the trappings of yangban through accumulations of wealth, and even through registering as students in official schools and private academies (Palais 1975:99–101). It is not clear whether any of these were eligible to sit for the civil service exams and hold public office (Palais 1975:7). "Whatever their claim," Deuchler writes, "the established yangban were scarcely threatened" by these social upstarts because they lacked essential criteria for yangban status, including "a clear line of descent, a 'distinguished ancestor' (hyŏnjo)—'distinguished' meant, above all, scholarly reputation—from whom ancestry was traced and generally acknowledged, a clear geographic area within which such status was recognized, close marriage ties with other reputable lineages, and a special way of life" (1992:12).

Nevertheless, the fact that some tried to emulate the yangban is indicative that both the desire for status and the ideology of the yangban were shared by Korean society as a whole (see also Chung Young-Iob 1984:30). New opportunities to assert status were to come to many with the transformation of society, especially beginning in the second half of the twentieth century in South Korea. Rather than striving for yangban status, modern-day Koreans strive for middle-class status. However, just as with the yangban, there are those who claim middle-class status but, because they lack certain criteria, are not considered middle class by others. Moreover, as we shall see, there is more than one middle-class lifestyle, depending on the particular assets a family has and the particular ways status is asserted.

Transformations in Korean Society

Korean society began to undergo significant change toward the end of the nineteenth century when Korea's doors were forcibly opened. The year 1876 marks the beginning of Korea's emergence from isolation and of its embarkation on the road to modernization. It was in that year that Japan, itself having just recently come out of isolation, forced a trade treaty on Korea. This treaty was followed by others with Western countries in the early 1880s. It was this forced trade with other nations that led the Korean government to change its attitudes toward entrepreneurial activity, opening the way for yangban as well as others to legally participate in trade (Deuchler 1977a:127).

Although the traditional merchant class dependent on official patronage continued to dominate trade of Korean goods within the country for some time after the first foreign trade treaty in 1876, new types of entrepreneurs linked to new international commerce in export grains and imported manufacturers emerged (see also Eckert 1991, 1993). In the meantime, Japan's presence in Korea was becoming more pervasive and aggressive. It was the Japanese who pushed through the Kabo reforms of 1894, radically changing the nature of government in Korea. In 1897 Bishop enumerated some of the more pertinent reforms:

The most important of the changes during the last three years . . . may be summarized thus: The connection [tributary relations] with China is at an end. . . . The distinction between patrician [yangban] and plebeian [commoner] has been abolished, on paper at least, along with domestic slavery, and the disabilities which rendered the sons of concubines ineligible for high office. Brutal punishments and torture are done away with, a convenient coinage has replaced *cash*, an improved educational system has been launched, a disciplined army and police force has been created, the Chinese literary examinations are no longer the test of fitness for official employment . . . the pressure of the Trade Guilds is relaxed. . . . [And] the change from a land-tax paid in kind to one which is an assessment in money on the value of the land greatly diminished the opportunities for official "squeezing." (Bishop 1970 [1898]:450–451)

Furthermore, "superfluous officials unworthily appointed find that their salaries are not forthcoming; [and] every man entitled to receive payment is paid at the end of every month" (Bishop 1970 [1898]:449), these government employees becoming the first salaried employees in the modern sense in Korea.

In 1905 Korea became a protectorate of Japan, and in 1910 Japan annexed Korea. The Japanese colonial government concentrated on increasing agricultural production in Korea while discouraging the development of industry. The sociologist Hagen Koo (1987:170) notes that the Japanese were not necessarily interested in destroying the existing class structure, but only in slightly modifying it and then subordinating it to the Japanese colonial state bureaucracy. Even though the dominant landlord class was seriously undermined, the landlord class itself did not disappear. That is, many of the descendants of yangban, actually still referred to as yangban, were able to maintain some of their status vis-à-vis other Koreans during the Japanese occupation. But landholding itself became the basis of status.

The Japanese policy of excluding the Koreans from business and industry continued until a major uprising in 1919, from which time the Japanese loosened some of their most oppressive policies toward the Koreans and allowed, to the benefit of the Japanese themselves, a small layer of Korean entrepreneurs to develop. Business was becoming an acceptable occupation for the traditional elite as well as for the commoners: "Between 1910 and 1920, industry in Korea was altogether discriminated against by Japan in favor of agriculture. Then, after the 1919 uprising, a wafer-thin stratum of Korean capitalists was deliberately cultivated to further collaboration. With minimal assistance, an entrepreneurial class emerged, drawing its members from the yangban and from the commoner class. The new entrepreneurs were numerous enough to increase the variety of the indigenous elite, from landlord and scholar before the occupation to landlord, businessman, and intellectual after it" (Amsden 1989:331).

As a result of this change in policy on the part of the Japanese occupation government, many Korean merchants from the traditional commoner class as well as many yangban from the landowner class became entrepreneurs in the 1920s, and a number of Korean-owned enterprises came into being (Lee Kibaik 1984:359). After 1919 many of the Koreans who had made money in the rice trade began to transfer profits into industry, especially textiles, and thus contributed to the development of an industrial sector as well as of a proletariat or working class. Industrialization and proletarianization rapidly increased with the Japanese demand for military goods during the 1930s and 1940s. By the end of the colonial period in 1945, Korea had seen, along with a growing proletariat, "the emergence of a true 'sprout' of capitalism, a nascent bourgeoisie, a number of whose members . . . went on to become major business figures in South Korea" (Eckert 1993:99).

For three years after the end of World War II, the southern half of the Korean peninsula was under U.S. military control. During that time, the U.S. military restructured the Korean economy and pushed for land reform. The North Korean occupation forces carried out the land reform during the Korean War. This reform, coupled with the effects of the Korean War, enhanced the role of the bourgeoisie in South Korea's economy and society while having a devastating effect on the large landowning elite (Eckert 1993:100). Except for the few bourgeoisie, the playing field was leveled to a considerable degree, at least in an economic sense, making Korean society more egalitarian and fluid. With this destruction of the old class system based on landholding and with the social disruptions caused by war and massive migration, South Korea quickly transformed into a predominantly petit bourgeois society, with a "dense petite bourgeois desire for upward social mobility and a pervasive entrepreneurial spirit" (Koo 1987:175,171).

In laying the groundwork for later economic development, the adoption of a Western-style education system and curriculum among the masses as well as among the traditional elite was no less critical than changes in the economic system. Prior to the late nineteenth century, educational emphasis was almost solely on the Chinese language and Confucian classics. Although the chung'in ("middle men") could specialize in areas such as foreign languages, medicine, astronomy, law, and geography, because of the generally negative attitude toward anything other than Confucian studies and because Korea isolated itself from the rest of the world, it did not share in the development of science and technology that was occurring in the West and by then also in Japan.

With mounting pressure from Japan and Western powers for Korea to open its doors, however, some advocates of educational reform in Korea were heard. In 1881 the Korean government sent a group of observers to take a look at the effects Westernization was having on Japan. Another group of three went in 1882. Later that year, as a direct consequence of the latter trip, sixty-one Korean youth were for the first time sent abroad to Japan for modern studies (Lee Won-ho 1991).

In Korea itself, as a result of the 1876 treaty with Japan, the northern port city of Wŏnson was opened. The massive immigration of Japanese merchants that resulted concerned the local populace, and promising financial support, they petitioned their governor to open a modern school for Korean youth so that the Koreans could compete with the Japanese. In 1883 Wŏnson Haksa became the first school in Korea where a modern system of education prevailed. Although traditional Confucian studies and martial arts were taught, classes in arithmetic, physics, agriculture, sericulture, mining, and, later, foreign languages, law, and geography were also offered (Lee Won-ho 1991:24).

Further impetus toward modern education, as well as education for the masses, came when Christianity was officially allowed in Korea following the treaties with Western nations. The beginnings of Western medicine and the training of Korea's first doctors of Western medicine, for example, were directly attributable to missionaries. Other modern schools were built as well, many under the direction of the Japanese. Confucian schools, though, by no means disappeared. (The missionary Rutt reported their existence in the late 1950s [1964 (1957–58):79]; and the anthropologist Clark Sorensen came across one as late as 1976 during his fieldwork [pers. comm.].).

Many Koreans were initially unconvinced that the change from a Confucian to a Western curriculum was a good one (Li Mirok 1986:60–61), but the general perception that Confucianism was responsible for Korea's backwardness and inability to fight off foreign incursion at the end of the nineteenth century caused many to reject Confucian learning in favor of a modern, Western-style education. Education, regardless of content, continued (and continues) to confer status in Korean society. The change in curriculum contributed to changes in attitudes with regard to occupation (see also Mason et al. 1980:374–376). A Confucian education was pursued during the Chosŏn dynasty in order to obtain an appointment as a scholar-official, the only suitable position for the yangban. A modern university education is pursued not only to obtain a position in the civil service or as a scholar. Engineers, company managers and administrators, doctors, lawyers, and other white-collar jobs all became suitable occupations for those concerned with status. Opportunities for education spread among the masses as well.

During the Chosŏn dynasty, educational opportunities were essentially limited to the yangban. During the Japanese occupation, the Japanese, while setting up modern schools throughout the country, also limited education for Koreans, with relatively few exceptions, to the primary level. The purpose of the education provided by the Japanese was to benefit the Japanese politically, by converting Korean youth into loyal subjects, and economically, by training them for subordinate roles in both agriculture and industry. Koreans, however, took advantage of whatever educational opportunities were available.

After the failure of the independence movement of March 1, 1919, the spread of modern education was viewed by cultural nationalists as the only way Korea could regain its independence (see also Sorensen 1994:15). As Japan mobilized for war with China and saw the need to train Koreans for the munitions industry, access to primary education was expanded. By 1942, however, only 40 percent of Korean children were attending elementary school. As of 1945 only 2 percent of the Korean population over fourteen years of age had completed secondary school (Mason et al. 1980:344). The tradition of providing a Confucian education in Chinese and the Chinese classics in private homes continued among some of the yangban families during this time.

There was an attempt during the Japanese colonial period by the subjugated Korean government to provide for higher education by diverting funds raised to clear the national debt to the establishment of private institutes of higher learning. The effort was undermined by the Japanese, who regarded it as a serious challenge to their colonial rule. To nullify the Korean attempts at opening private institutes, Japan opened Seoul Imperial University, but two-thirds of its students were Japanese (Lee Won-ho 1991:29). A few Koreans did manage to go abroad, many of them to Japan, to pursue educational opportunities there.

During the five-year period immediately following the end of World War II, the United States invested heavily in South Korean primary education and in secondary-level vocational-technical (that is, nonacademic) schools, with little attention given to higher education. Between 1945 and 1947, attendance at the secondary level doubled (Sorensen 1994:16). The curriculum in schools controlled by the government was totally revised, with an abandonment of Confucian classics and the development of textbooks in the native Korean language. Much of the investment in education made after World War II, however, was destroyed during the Korean War (1950–1953). By its end, school enrollments in elementary, middle, and high schools and colleges for the corresponding age groups were 59.6, 21.1, 12.4, and 3.1 percent respectively (Mason et al. 1980:352).

Following the Korean conflict, more attention was given to academic high schools and tertiary education. Enrollments at all levels expanded rapidly. By 1965, 91.6 percent of elementary-, 39.4 percent of middle-, and 27.0 percent of high-school-aged children and 6.9 percent of those of college age (that is, those between the ages of eighteen and twenty-one) attended school. By 1975, enrollment increased to 107.6, 74.0, 40.5, and 8.6 percent respectively (Mason et al. 1989:352). (Children older than elementary school age who earlier did not have the opportunity to go to school now also enrolled in elementary school; thus the percentage is over one hundred.)

Changes in the educational curriculum, corresponding changes in attitudes toward occupation, and the spread of education among all levels of society prepared Koreans for the next phase of transformation, the rapid acceleration of modernization and industrialization that began after 1961.

The Emergence of South Korea's New Urban Middle Class

During the 1950s the South Korean government pursued an economic policy of import-substitution, which enjoyed only limited success. The society was highly educated, relatively egalitarian, but also poor. With the military coup of 1961, a new, outward-looking, export-oriented economic policy was implemented. As a result, in a very short time South Korea was transformed from a poor agrarian society into an urban, industrial nation with increasing wealth.

Although two-thirds of the work force in 1960 consisted of self-employed farmers and rural laborers, their numbers dropped to less than one-fifth of the labor force by 1990 (Yoon In-Jin 1993:17, 20). As the scale of the South Korean economy expanded, large numbers of people became wage or salary workers in both private corporations and government institutions. Production workers and manual laborers accounted for only 13 percent of the labor force in 1960. Their ranks increased to 22 percent by 1970, 28 percent by 1980, and 35 percent by 1990. And self-employed business owners, contrary to the predictions of their inevitable decline in industrial societies (Mills 1956), continued to grow in number during the 1960s and 1970s (Yoon In-Jin 1993:22). Of importance here is the concurrent rise in the percentage of white-collar workers. Professional, technical, administrative, managerial, clerical, and sales workers made up only 20 percent of the labor force in 1960. Their numbers increased to 27 percent in 1980 and to 36 percent in 1990 (Yoon In-Jin 1993:20).

In the course of the three decades leading up to the early 1990s, with the increase in both economic and educational opportunities, a new urban middle class thus emerged (see also Kim Kwang-ok 1993:5). In the 1970s a new term, *chungsanch'ŭng*, was coined by intellectuals and made popular by the media in the 1980s to refer to this new class (Kim Eun-shil 1993:31). Composed of both former yangban and commoner families, the middle class of the 1990s was a new and evolving class, in the process of developing defining characteristics. At the same time, those among this new middle class with yangban ancestry were seeking to maintain or retain some of their former elite status; those of commoner origins were seeking to acquire status (see also Kim Kwang-ok 1992:197). In this pursuit for status, members of both components of the new middle class, consciously or unconsciously, were capitalizing not only on new but also on traditional ways of asserting high status.

The anthropologist Kim Kwang-ok (1992:197) writes of a recent resurgence of interest in genealogies and ancestor worship by both descendants of the traditional elite "who perceive the presence of a 'new class' in the establishment as a challenge to their vested interests of access to social and political resources" and those of commoner background who want to achieve upward social mobility:

In order to exclude or minimize the advent of the new class, members of the traditional elite try to mobilize elite culture through refining and proliferating its content (Cohen 1983; Bourdieu 1988), thus attempting a symbolic construction of the cultural community (Cohen 1983). At the same time, members of the newly emerging middle class try to acquire the traditional elite culture in an effort to consolidate their status within the established cultural community. Redecorating ancestral graves and constructing ancestral shrines and memorial halls in the name of filial piety (*hyo*) has become fashionable. Activities for "exhuming" ancestors from historical anonymity and special programs to locate "roots" are organized by lineages old and new. Rediscovering family history is the aim of both sides to recognize their moral and cultural superiority. (Kim Kwang-ok 1992:197–198)

In this pursuit of status, members of the new middle class are doing more than reviving tradition in family ritual and genealogies. They have been influenced by the yangban tradition in other ways as well. The yangban legacy is seen in contemporary Korean attitudes toward status, occupation, family, lifestyle, education, and marriage. These aspirations are based partially on a yangban model that has been adapted to modern requirements. Confucian-

ism need no longer exist as a system of beliefs and practices nor need individuals be conscious of its impact for it to continue to serve as a guide. Rozman (1991:26) explains: "The true measure of [Confucianism's] impact is the
extent to which people's lives are guided by Confucian [or yangban] ideals.
Even if the point is reached at which consciousness of the Confucian roots of
particular attitudes has faded, the continued presence of such attitudes can be
taken as a sign in a single country or region that the tradition endures. It is
how individuals respond to family, school, community, workplace, and the
state that best informs us of their world view."

The resurgence of ancestor worship or other traditional elements in contemporary South Korea is not merely a return to the past. In discussing the
recent reassertion of Confucian tradition in East Asia in general, Rozman
(1991:23) writes: "Contemporary characteristics must be seen not as straightforward manifestations of the past, but as part of a changing historical context. Assertions about guiding attitudes should be supported with explana-
tions of how these attitudes came to be displayed in behavior." Part of the
changing historical context involves changing attitudes toward Korea's Confucian heritage, attitudes that, in turn, are a result of foreign influence and
the incorporation of Korea into a global capitalist community.

Korea's twentieth-century perspectives toward its Confucian heritage are
inextricably linked to the issues of modernization and nationalism. The efficacy of Confucian ideology was first questioned when the Chosŏn dynasty
was unable to keep its borders closed to foreign powers in the last quarter of
the nineteenth century. The attack on Confucianism became more severe
when the Chosŏn dynasty collapsed and Korea subsequently fell under Japanese rule. In this context, Confucianism was viewed as an obstacle to both
modernization and nationalism. Traditional Korean society's emphasis on
Confucian humanistic studies and its disdain of the military and scientific
disciplines left Korea unprepared, the argument went, to defend the incur-
sions of technologically superior military forces. Furthermore, even though
Confucian ideology had become quite Koreanized in its centuries-long hegemony in Korea, Korea's veneration of the Chinese foreign cultural system
and its subordinate status in the Chinese Confucian world order was blamed
by cultural nationalists for the lack of development of a strong national Korean identity (M. Robinson 1991).

After Korea's liberation from Japan in 1945, the attitude against Confucianism may have softened somewhat (Rozman 1991:2), but in the following
decades the South Korean government's attitude toward Confucianism was
often ambivalent. During the 1960s and 1970s the government led a modernization movement, encouraging the adoption of new lifestyles and elements of

foreign culture while denouncing traditional cultural elements as unscientific, irrational, impractical, and thus a hindrance to modernization. Later, though, the South Korean government reversed its position, appealing to Confucian virtues to its own end. Filial piety, for example, was touted as the basis of loyalty to the state, and history was interpreted in a nationalist manner. In the 1980s, at the same time that the government recognized such practices as ancestor worship "as part of the glorious cultural tradition," it encouraged the further influx of Western cultural elements, cultural consumption being regarded as "an act of proving the nation's achievements" (Kim Kwang-ok 1992:198). "Western" was often equated with "modern." Acquisition of certain Western cultural elements, then, along with the display of certain traditional elite characteristics, has also become a way of asserting status in South Korean society. Both indigenous and modern or foreign models have been employed, and an interaction between them can even be discerned as Koreans seek status.

With regard to the traditional model, South Koreans have revived interest in keeping genealogies and in performing ancestor worship, acts formerly indicative of elite status. Families of commoner background have even retroactively published genealogies to "support" their claim to "a good family background" (much as their predecessors did during the Chosŏn dynasty; see also Korea Annual 1992:353–356). In the past, the only people who were able to obtain an education were members of yangban lineages. Now a much greater proportion of the South Korean population is able to obtain an education. These educated people feel that they are entitled to the status traditionally conferred upon those with education. At the same time, because many records have been lost during the various crises the Korean people have suffered, it is possible to claim yangban ancestry without firm proof. For example, when asked, one young woman whose parents migrated from North Korea commented that the family genealogy (chokpo) had been left behind in North Korea along with most of the family possessions.

Koreans' attitudes toward their yangban heritage are very ambiguous, and the complex of subjective attitudes creates a tension among the people. On the one hand, there is an egalitarian ethic present, reinforced by government reforms aimed at providing more opportunities for all social groups (see also J. Robinson 1994:506; Brandt 1971), that makes it "politically incorrect" to stress yangban heritage. On the other hand, South Koreans still feel that people look down upon those without high social origins. The pressure is so strong to make the claim that one has yangban ancestry that most South Koreans do. At the same time in the South Korea of today, where status is no longer legally defined or inherited, status has also come to depend more on differences in wealth (see also Sorensen 1993b:144). Furthermore, because ancestry no longer constitutes the main basis of elite status, the patrilineage has taken on less importance and concern with status tends to be limited to the more immediate family.

The key to understanding South Korea's contemporary middle class and its development is the underlying drive Koreans have to attain status and prestige. In the closing years of the Chosŏn dynasty Hulbert noted "a passionate desire" among the Korean people "to ascend a step on the social ladder," as they tried in every way to insinuate themselves into good society (1969 [1906]:38). I found that characteristic to be as operative as in the past. Moreover, this desire to acquire status, coupled with new opportunities to do so, has been a driving force behind the development of South Korea's human resources in general, of its new middle class in particular, and ultimately of South Korea itself.

The new middle-class ideals have come to represent the aspirations of South Korean society as a whole. In a personal communication commenting on the question of who is the real middle class, the anthropologist Laurel Kendall wrote:

You are right that Sukcha's family are not "middle class" by Hong's [1990] attempt to reify categories, and your informants would certainly not recognize mine as kindred spirits. However, Sukcha's family and people like them are fueled by the belief that they are constructing respectable lifestyles on a middle class model, that they might one day own their own homes and send their children to college, that they are living in ways undreamed of by their parents. Their dreams are part of what makes the Korean economy tick. (Pers. comm.; see also Kendall 1996)

The following chapters examine various aspects of this middle-class model, of the everyday life of those who are realizing those dreams. The dreams themselves are continually evolving as the middle class itself evolves. Ways of asserting status may change. But status consciousness, the cultural need for status inherited from the yangban tradition, "surviv[ing] even the colonial rule which ironically reinforced it by a discriminatory policy excluding the Koreans from opportunities for education and status achievement" (Kim Kyong-dong 1994:102; see also Bourdieu 1984:1), remains the underlying principle behind the drive for status and the development of South Korea's urban middle class.

2

Occupations and Income

In the capital there are many people who have no business—that is to say, they are gentlemen of leisure. They are gentlemen, and gentlemen are not supposed to meddle with such sordid matters as manufacture and merchandise—no, not even office work, unless it be an office connected with the government.

—J. Robert Moose (1911:54)

With the establishment of trade relations with foreign countries and the adoption of a Western educational curriculum at the end of the nineteenth century, the range of "suitable" occupations for people of status to choose from gradually and greatly expanded beyond that of scholar and government official. Nevertheless, Koreans today no less than during the Chosŏn dynasty have very definite ideas about which occupations are suitable and which are not. These attitudes are informed by an interaction of traditional attitudes and modern influences.

3-D Pyŏng: "3-D Disease"

Our village gentleman is strictly opposed to undertaking anything that looks like manual labor. He may be ever so poor—yes, even dependent on others for his daily rice—but to get out and work is out of his line of business. It is not a disgrace for him to go hungry, but to engage in any sort of manual labor would at once lower his standing as a gentleman and ruin his prospects for future promotion along the lines which gentlemen are supposed to travel.

—J. Robert Moose (1911:101–102)

These words, expressing the disdain for and avoidance of manual labor by Korea's yangban elite of yesteryear and the implications for status that would result if one engaged in such activity, are just as applicable to South Korea's urban middle and upper classes of the 1990s. From the Korean perspective, by definition, manual laborers could never be middle (or upper) class. Although members of the middle and upper classes are no longer subjected to the same legal sanctions as their yangban predecessors (since status no longer has a legal basis), they nevertheless have avoided participation in blue-collar work or manual labor lest they lose their status. This avoidance of manual labor has been termed by critics as the *3-D pyŏng*, or "3-D disease," "3-D" being the label that Koreans have given to work that is dirty, dangerous, and difficult. The dichotomy of the South Korean labor force between manual and non-manual workers has remained as significant today as during the Chosŏn dynasty (see also Koo and Hong 1980:618).

The disdain educated Koreans generally have for the lower classes and for the labor in which they engage (see also Kim Hyun Mee 1995:93) is illustrated by the words, recorded by Kim Eun-shil (1993:173–174), of a woman with a high school education who thought it was beneath her dignity to engage in factory work. Kim Eun-shil's informant claimed to have come from a middle-class family. But because she had married someone who was unable to provide a middle-class lifestyle, she and her husband had moved into a working-class neighborhood on the outskirts of Seoul. The woman refused to work in a factory even though it would have helped her economic plight:

Jina's mother, a high school graduate, was staying at home as a full-time housewife and said that she was different from the women in the community. She said that she had worked as a secretary for a political party office and had dated reporters and political aspirants and came from a middle-class family. She described the *Yaksan* area in this way:

"My husband did not make money, so we moved into this area. This is a very poor neighborhood and all the women around here are working at factories. My daughter wondered why I did not work in a factory like her friends' mothers around here. Myself, I can't. I have never thought about working at the factory no matter what situation I am in. I cannot work in a factory to make money but I might work at a factory if I could work as an activist. When I first moved in here, I found out that the women in the neighborhood were ignorant and did not have the concept of hygiene. They were watching their children play in the dirty water mixed with chemical dyes overflowing from the drain. I cannot associate with any neighbors closely even though I have lived here for two years."

With regard to the feelings of the members of the working class themselves, Kim Hyun Mee (1995:78) reports: "The factory workers who lack outside resources to earn money other than by their physical labor power seem to feel class disparity from educated people who make money far easier, without disgraceful treatment." There is even a strong resistance by some laborers to identify themselves or their spouses as "menial factory workers" or as low class, as was the case with some of the women factory workers in Kim Hyun Mee's study (1995:108): "Even though their husbands also worked at factories, some women used the term company [hoesa] not a factory [kongjang] when I asked where their husbands worked."

Comparable to the situation in India both in the past and in the present and reminiscent of the hierarchy among manual laborers during the Chosŏn dynasty, where "commoners set themselves off against the lower class of 'base people'" (Deuchler 1992:13), distinctions have continued to be made within South Korea's lower classes today, with those higher up on the scale looking down on those below. The composition of the social ladder, however, has changed over the years. In the earlier years of industrialization in Korea, for example, young people from the countryside were the primary source of labor in the city after local urban women began to avoid "dirty and arduous work." In more recent years, however, the young labor force has almost been exhausted in the countryside in South Korea and, according to Kim Hyun Mee (1995:111), among women "marital status has become the important criterion of the division of labor at the factories or in various industries."

In her discussion of the shopfloor hierarchy at the factory of her informants, Kim (1995:104–109) explains that older, married women, regardless of their level of education, were not hired as line chiefs. These jobs were rather given to young, unmarried high school graduates who identified themselves as "managers" despite their low wages. These young female workers set themselves above, indeed, lorded themselves over the older, married women, treating them "as if they were slaves," though the hierarchical gap between the line chiefs and ordinary workers appeared minimal to Kim (1995:104–105). One union representative, who identified herself as a college drop-out, attributed the subservient behavior of some newly recruited middle-aged women workers to a "slave mentality." These women tried to curry favor with the line chiefs by bringing them lunch and snacks. This behavior was necessary, according to one of the older women, in order to ensure that they would receive permission to leave early when unexpected emergencies arose, as required by their roles as mothers and wives (Kim Hyun Mee 1995:106).

Thus as Deuchler notes, "consciousness of social status, deeply rooted in Korean society, has lingered on until recent times" (1992:13). Elitist attitudes displayed by South Korea's contemporary middle and upper classes, including a disdain for manual workers, as well as the attitude of the members of the working class about themselves and about those lower on the social ladder, have remained a feature of the South Korean social landscape. Further testimony that these attitudes have persisted is the severe shortage of manual labor workers. The Korea Annual reports: "By job category, blue-collar workers declined 7.8% in the third quarter of 1991 from the like period of the previous year, while white-collar workers and engineers rose 2.2%, *indicating Koreans increasingly shun manual labor*" (1992:227, emphasis added).

Increasing affluence has added to the problem. In 1987 the per capita gross national product (GNP) was US$3,110; by 1990 it had jumped to US$5,569: "'As people become more economically comfortable, making money is no longer a priority and they become more selective about what they want to do for a living,' said Yi Sung-Ki, deputy director of the employment policy division at the Labor Ministry" (cited in Chang 1992:42). Miss Han, a college graduate and office worker for a nonprofit organization, made note in a conversation with me of the negative attitudes held by Koreans toward blue-collar work; she also observed that those who pursued such work tended to come from lower-class families themselves, that is, there was generational continuity:

Some people in technical occupations, like electronics or construction, or taxi drivers, may make more money than the middle class. However, there is a shortage of skilled workers. No one wants the dirty jobs. There are technical and academic high schools. Necessity more than anything determines which one chooses. If a person comes from a poor family and has to work right after high school, he goes to a technical school.

Reminiscent of the yangban, to accept an "unsuitable" position has affected a family's status, so families have gone to great pains to secure suitable employment for their members. This effort begins with the high priority placed on education even before a child is of school age. As will be discussed in Chapter 5, middle-class families and those aspiring to become middle class make great sacrifices in trying to give their children what is necessary to qualify them for and provide them with a college education. For those entering the job market of the 1990s, a university degree was a prerequisite for most jobs suitable for middle-class status, including most salaried jobs as government officials and corporate managers and administrators, as well as for the professions, such as educator, doctor, and lawyer. Owning a business was perhaps the only suitable job that did not require a college degree, although many entrepreneurs were college educated as well.

Among the middle class, though the range of "suitable" occupations for people of status to choose from has expanded considerably as South Korea has modernized, I nevertheless found preferences expressed on the basis of several factors. Whether I asked a university-aged woman what she was looking for in a marriage partner or a man in the midst of his working life, there was quite a consensus on how various occupations were viewed.

Middle-Class Occupations

Scholars

University professor, the historical successor to the scholar of the Chosŏn dynasty, is among if not the most prestigious of occupations in South Korea today. The Confucian association of moral superiority with the highly educated has continued to be observed in the extreme deference shown to both male and female professors, not only by their students but by the public at large. This presumed moral authority of scholars is also manifested in their role of government critic, as certain (though, of course, not all) professors comment in the media on government actions and policies as well as on social issues. This media exposure on issues beyond a professor's particular academic expertise helps make him or her more of a public figure than what would generally occur in the United States and adds to the prestige South Korean professors in general enjoy. Some Ph.D.s become journalists rather than professors and are highly respected for their role as critics of government and society.

The doctor of philosophy or *paksa* degree is the modern-day counterpart to the degrees awarded during the Chosŏn dynasty for passing the high-level civil service exams. Many of these degrees are earned abroad, especially in the United States but also in Germany, France, and in a few other places (Yoon In-Jin 1993:28). Until 1981, the South Korean government strictly regulated the flow of students going abroad. The government controlled both the funds for overseas study and the selection of students through extremely competitive exams. Thus overseas study was a mark of privilege for those few who formed an elite corps (Hong Sah-myung 1991). Jobs in high positions awaited those with doctoral degrees, whether educated in Korea or abroad.

With the institution of an "open-door" policy by the government, however, and the growing number of parents who find themselves capable of financing such studies for their children, it is no longer the privileged few who are going abroad to study. Today the market is flooded with *paksa* or Ph.D.s, educated in both Korean and foreign institutes of higher learning. When I first arrived in Korea, I asked Professor Lee, who during my stay finally attained a permanent, full-time appointment after juggling four part-time teaching positions, which title was preferred, *paksa* (doctor) or *kyosu* (professor). She responded, only partly in jest, that in the past *paksa* was preferred. These days, however, with so many *paksa* being unemployed, *kyosu* was now preferred because it signified one had a job.

Whether or not one has a job, the *paksa* degree continues to confer high status. Moreover, not unlike the sŏnbi of the past, that is, the Confucian scholars without government appointment, professors are often considered and often consider themselves among the upper class socially, though most live a middle-class lifestyle economically. The salaries of professors, which do not generally match the high social status conferred on scholars, are usually supplemented by honorariums and royalties for special appearances and publications as well as by gifts in kind from students. Furthermore, professors may also enjoy income from other sources, such as property, as do most salaried workers. This will be discussed in more detail below.

Government Bureaucrats

Except perhaps for those at the very highest levels of government, government officials, whose historical antecedents were recruited from among the yangban elite, are classified as middle class today. Indeed, as noted in Chapter 1, government bureaucrats became the first salaried employees in the modern sense, and thus the first to be classified as "new middle class" in the conventional sense, with the enactment of the Kabo reforms in 1894.

In the minds of many South Koreans, "upper class" has negative connotations, as both the economic and the political elites in South Korea have lacked legitimacy. Although the situation may be improving, the legitimacy of the South Korean government has never been fully established since the military takeover of the country in 1961, and almost every government since the founding of the Republic of Korea in 1948 has had problems with legitimacy for one reason or another (see also Eckert 1993:128). One high-level Korean government official explained to me that he would rather be considered upper-middle than upper class, because those with upper-class status were always suspect. This would explain another high government official's self-introduction to me when he heard I was interested in South Korea's middle class. He said, "I'm upper class," and then quickly corrected himself, "Upper-middle class!"

Although other career choices have gained ground, a career in government remains one of the most preferred among Korean men. This is in contrast to the situation in Japan, where the prewar prestige and power of government positions were lost after Japan's defeat in 1945 (Vogel 1963:6; Lebra 1993:289). In Korea, the traditional prestige associated with government office has been one reason why civil service remains a popular career choice. However, that prestige remains in part because it has been reinforced by a constellation of other features, which include a guaranteed salary, the opportunity for advancement, a pension, usually quite regular work hours, and above all, job security.

In addition to these benefits, several informants cited the potential of receiving additional income above one's salary directly from citizens for services or favors as another bonus of civil service. This was especially true for those positions that involved contact with the public. I myself have knowledge, on the one hand, of a Korean citizen who was pressured to contribute so-called *ttŏk kap*, or "rice cake money," to the tune of several hundred dollars by a government official who not too indiscreetly solicited funds simply for doing his job. On the other hand, a middle-aged gentleman complained to me that, if stopped for a traffic violation, it was almost impossible to bribe the officer, now that regular traffic officers had been replaced by young men fulfilling their military obligations; they refused to accept bribes. Thus corruption can be seen in the attitudes of both government officials and the citizenry alike.

As discussed earlier, receiving income directly from the public was a common practice among the yangban during the Chosŏn dynasty and in fact was often the mainstay of their financial support. That such a tradition has continued among some government officials has been widely recognized and was highlighted by the arrest in 1995 of Roh Tae Woo, former Korean president (and the president during my tenure in Korea), on charges of accepting bribes. With the election of Kim Young-Sam in 1992 and his subsequent campaign to clean up government corruption, and especially with the arrest of Roh Tae Woo, it was expected that government officials would find it more difficult to supplement their income in this way. Reports of continuing corruption and of the failure of Kim Young-Sam's administration despite his efforts, however, proliferated in the media four years later in the fall of 1996 and the winter of 1997. Nevertheless, the temptation to accept bribes may be partially offset by increasing the salaries of those in positions susceptible to bribery to a level on which a government worker can support an appropriate lifestyle. Mr. Oh, the government official who offered to arrange interviews for me in exchange for the opportunity to practice his English, told me in a phone call in the summer of 1995 that he had received a substantial pay raise with his latest promotion and was now quite satisfied with what he was being paid.

With regard to the promotion process in civil service, favoritism based on region of origin has been a factor. This I learned the first time I met Mr. Oh. In our discussion about criteria regarding the interviewees, he inquired whether or not it made a difference where these families came from. I asked what significance he saw in this for my research. Using a map of Korea in his notebook, he explained that whether a family came from the southwestern or southeastern part of the country had implications for social mobility. Those coming from the southeast, he explained, "were more proud of themselves." "Three or four presidents," he said, had come from that part of the country. Those coming from the southeast had advantages over others when it came to such things as job advancement, Mr. Oh explained. Although he made no direct connection for me, I note that his father, who is also a government bureaucrat, came from Kwangju in the southwest.

Mr. Oh's perception about regionalism and favoritism in promotion is not unique. The existence of a deep-seated regionalism among Koreans and the fact that it has an effect on promotion not only in government service but in the military service and in business was a common sentiment among my informants. That this was a general perception is corroborated by Yoon In-Jin (1993:24):

People from Cholla Province, a traditionally agricultural area [in the southwest], tend to believe that they have been discriminated against in the important positions in government, business, and the army. Their pessimism has some justification because since General Park Chung-hee took power by a military coup on 16 May 1961, every subsequent president—Chon Too-Hwan (1980–87), Roh Tae-Woo (1987–92), and Kim Young-Sam, the newly elected and first civilian president since 1960 [who was elected just after I left Korea and thus of course after my conversation with Mr. Oh]— has come from Kyongsang Province [in the southeast], an industrialized area and archrival of Cholla Province.

Apparently region of origin was not the only basis of favoritism. Yoon In-Jin (1993:24) writes that, in general, "the low chance of social mobility [was] even more unlikely for those who have no connections with persons in important positions. Kinship, region of origin, and school ties still influence access to employment and prestige." Despite all this, a career in the government bureaucracy continues to be held in high regard. (Recall that there was much corruption in the government service during the Chosŏn dynasty, yet it was the most desirable and only suitable career, along with that of scholar, for a man of status to pursue.)

As a side note, shortly before I left the country Mr. Oh himself received a major promotion. In order to accept the promotion, he had to turn down an opportunity to study abroad for six months at government expense, an opportunity he earned just prior to this promotion through a competitive process in civil service. He subsequently received an additional promotion, already mentioned, and on top of that in the end he received his opportunity to study abroad after all. This may be a reflection of a decline of favoritism based on regionalism (if not also a reflection of the energy, enthusiasm, and competence displayed by Mr. Oh himself).

Corporate Salary Men

The benefits of employment in the government bureaucracy can be most appreciated when contrasted with those of employment in commercial companies, the other great source of salaried positions but often the least favored among the possible middle-class jobs. This is not to say that those in company positions were looked down upon or that such positions were not sought. On the contrary, competition for company positions, especially in the large business conglomerates, was stiff and usually only those who had performed well both at the university and on the company entrance exam were hired. The chaebŏl had a reputation for hiring the best from the elite schools, and many felt that their opportunities were limited if they were not among this elite group.

Although chaebŏl tended to offer more benefits than medium or small firms, there were several negatives voiced to me in regard to working for a company of any size in comparison with other middle-class jobs. We saw above that the occupation of corporate salary man became the ideal occupation in modernized Japan. In South Korea, although salary man has become one of the "suitable" occupations for the middle class, it has not necessarily become the ideal.

To begin with, though there was a guaranteed salary, that salary alone was insufficient to maintain any but the lowest of the middle-class lifestyles, and the potential for receiving ttŏk kap, or additional money in the form of bribes, present in many government positions, did not exist. One perceptive university student explained, "Having a good salaried position is not enough. You need assets as well." Her sister was married to a corporate salary man with a good job but no other assets, and they were constantly struggling financially. I have found this to be the case for any family trying to live on one salary alone. Thus, while the term "salary man" was not uncommon in South Korea, having a salary in and of itself did not bring the same prestige or distinct lifestyle that it had in Japan (see also Vogel 1963; Kelly 1986). The title *hoesawon* or "corporation man" was as likely to be used. It should be noted, however, that should one continue to advance to a senior executive position, promotions generally entailed an increase not only in social prestige but also in perquisites, such as an expense account and a membership in a golf club (which could be worth more than US$200,000), even if the salary increases themselves did not seem that large.

The long workday was another common complaint among corporate employees. Mr. Oh explained that as a government employee he probably had more time to help me than a man working for a company, because government employees had more regular work hours. He worked from 9 A.M. to 6 P.M., except during the winter months, when government employees only worked until 5 P.M., "to conserve energy," Mr. Oh explained. "Human energy!" he added, laughing.

Although what constitutes an actual working day is often left open to interpretation, South Korea is nevertheless known to have one of the longest work weeks in the world (see also Janelli 1993:203–210). Officially, the length of the average work week has declined since 1987, reaching 47.8 hours a week in the third quarter of 1991, down 2.4 percent from a year earlier (Korea Annual 1992:227). While most civil servants had specific quitting times, however, company employees did not usually feel free to leave before their bosses. That time was indefinite, often late, and not monetarily compensated for. Both government and corporate employees usually also worked a half day on Saturdays as well, although there were some changes under way in this regard. For example, some companies did not require their employees to come in one Saturday a month or required that they come in only every other Saturday.

On top of the longer working hours (or hours required to be at work; productivity is another matter), daily, after-work socializing (eating and drinking) with company colleagues until late at night was the norm among company men. Although peer pressure to do the same among government employees was also present, as a rule it did not appear to be as severe and government employees could return home earlier than their corporate counterparts.

Another complaint expressed to me by several company employees was that they felt a lack of control over their work and believed that even when they had good ideas, they went unappreciated at work. South Korean businesses generally are top-down oriented, being very authoritative, with decisions made at the top with little or no input from subordinates. This is in contrast to many Japanese businesses, where ideas may originate from lower levels, group consensus is sought, and modifications are made on the way up.

Perhaps the most significant difference I observed between South Korean government employees and corporate salary men, as well as between Japanese and South Korean salary men in the private sector, was that the Korean company man enjoyed no job security (or pension). In contrast with service in the South Korean government bureaucracy and in contrast to the Japanese situation (at least until recently), guaranteed lifetime corporate employment did not exist in South Korea for white-collar workers, a fact that weighed heavily both on the minds of young women looking for potential marriage partners and on the minds of company men in their thirties and forties anticipating a mid-career lay-off. The South Korean corporate structure has often been depicted as a pyramid, one which, in accordance with Confucian principles, generally has observed the age hierarchy, but which has fewer and fewer salaried positions as one goes up the ladder. Unlike many Japanese companies, South Korean businesses have not found quiet corners to maintain employees they do not want to promote. If salaried employees are not simply terminated, neither are they promoted. This has affected the attitudes and employment strategies of white-collar workers. One manager of a large business corporation explained the situation to me:

The promotion system is a big problem. As you advance, there is only one position for perhaps three or four people. Most people foresee that they will not be promoted and begin looking for another job, either starting their own business or with a smaller company who is looking for experienced people to help develop the company. Unless they are opening up a new department, it is very difficult to get a job with another large company because they have the same problem too. There are very few actual firings. If the company does not want to promote someone and that person has not already voluntarily resigned, they will give him nothing to do. The psychological stress of coming to work with nothing to do is so great that that person then usually resigns. There are also age limits for positions.

Although South Korean companies have tended to recruit recent university graduates as a group, some hiring has been done from outside. Thus while it has been possible for someone to move between companies, even from a small- or medium-sized company to a chaebŏl (something that would not have occurred in Japan; see Vogel 1963:8), this has also left even fewer positions available later on for those hired directly out of the university.

For those that have continued to advance, nepotism is increasingly a factor and at the highest levels of management, a difference in class positions between managers who were kin of the owners and those who were nonkin was discerned. Janelli (1993:96) observes:

Some intellectuals had begun calling the members of conglomerate-controlling families "capitalists" and "bourgeoisie" with even greater frequency after a major liberalization of the press in 1988. . . . Moreover, some of these authors also implied a distinction between this elite group and other managers by reserving for the latter the term *middle class* or *new middle class* (Christian Institute for the Study of Justice and Development 1988:150).

"New middle class" seems to be appropriate for nonkin managers and managerial-track employees, since some of their interests are congruent while others are opposed to those of the owning kin group (Koo and Hong 1980; Giddens 1981; Wright et al. 1989). Even the highest nonkin managers occupied contradictory positions, their interests partly aligned with those of the owners and partly with those of other classes. Though the higher a nonkin manager advanced up the corporate ladder, the more his total material rewards and power derived from the privileges of the dominant kin group, his interests never converged with those of the elite group. The higher his level, the more his chances for further advancement were blocked by the kin group's monopoly on most top managerial positions.

Just as among high-level government officials, the designation "upper class" in the corporate world had negative connotations. Because of historical circumstances, not a single extant enterprise that possesses large-scale production facilities made a start spontaneously with its own accumulated capital and expertise; rather, these enterprises were able to grow after Korea's liberation from Japan in 1945 under privileges and protective measures provided by those holding political power. Thus these economic elite have lacked legitimacy among the general Korean population, though this may be changing.

A survey of collegians conducted by the employment agency Recruit in 1997 and reported in the *Korea Times* (March 5, 1997, p. 3) found that students continued to favor public sector jobs as a stable career, although they saw little chance for advancing. Salaried work was ranked as one of the least stable careers, "evidence that [college students] are worried about [forced] early retirement and layoffs resulting from recent economic difficulties," the report concludes.

Janelli's (1993) and Kim Choong Soon's (1992) ethnographies of South Korean chaebŏl discuss corporate life in great detail.

Business Owners

Although I found that manual labor remained anathema for members of families concerned with status, participation in business, whether as a salaried employee of a company or as a business owner of a small- or medium-sized company, had become a "suitable" and even desirable pursuit. Though commerce was traditionally despised, attitudes have been adapted to fit the requirements of a modern capitalist economy. These changes in attitudes began with a proclamation by King Kojang in 1883 prompted by the trade treaties forced upon Korea first by Japan in 1876 and subsequently by Western countries in the early 1880s. The ban on entrepreneurial activity was lifted, opening the way for yangban as well as others to legally participate in trade:

Intensified contact with the outside world did not fail to have an impact on the Korean government's attitude toward domestic and foreign trade. A significant indication of the change was the official repudiation of the venerated concept that members of the yangban class should not engage in trade.... On February 5, 1883, King Kojang proclaimed that since foreign trade was beginning, yangban as well as commoners were henceforth allowed to "increase and circulate their wealth," that is, to engage in trade. Trade was officially recognized as an effective way of enriching the country. The best way to encourage trade, it was argued, was to outlaw the old institutions that had hitherto impeded its growth. (Deuchler 1977a:192)

Thus, "the government loosened its traditional control over trade and abolished the monopolistic rights it had granted to some select groups of traders. This policy liberalized trade as an economic activity and, as an occupation, made it socially acceptable to yangban who had hitherto been barred from it" (Deuchler 1977a:193).

As noted by Deuchler and elaborated on by Carter Eckert, enrichment of the nation, not personal profit, was the justification given for a change in attitudes toward entrepreneurial activity: "In Korea, capitalism was imported by the Confucian literati. They resolved the apparent conflict between Confucian attitudes of disapproval regarding the pursuit of individual gain and the profit motive inherent in capitalism by claiming that the central purpose of profit was to improve the general quality of life and ensure the nation's independence. Productivity and development were encouraged by the activities of hero-merchants, who were expected to subordinate their own interests to the nation" (Eckert as cited in Tu Weiming, Hejtmanek, and Wachman 1992:9; see also Eckert 1991, 1993).

Although it had been legally and therefore more socially accepted for yangban to participate in commercial activity since 1883, the stigma did not disappear among many yangban families overnight or, in some cases, for decades, as indicated by an anecdote related to me by one middle-aged Korean gentleman with yangban ancestry.

This gentleman told me of meeting another who had the same family name as he as well as the same family place of origin, signifying that they should be of the same lineage. However, when this gentleman looked for the other man's name in the genealogy, which most lineages of yangban heritage update and publish periodically to maintain a link with their elite past, this other man's name could not be found. This Korean gentleman was curious and went to ask one of his elders about it. The elder responded that one of the other man's direct ancestors sometime in the early 1900s had become a merchant. He and his descending branch were then permanently wiped out of the genealogy, because the other lineage members presumably no longer considered him or his descendants worthy of yangban status.

Thus even though legal sanctions were removed against commercial activity, yangban families could and did impose their own, perpetuating, even if to a diminished degree, the stigma against such activity. Over time, however, working in business became an acceptable occupation for people with status. Earning high profits, however, was still often scoffed at by those of high social origin if such success was not also accompanied by other more traditional ways of asserting status, such as higher education.

Even at the level of the individual, the stated motive for involvement in capitalist activities in the Korean situation was not profit, as in Western capitalist societies, but that capitalist activities provided a means of fulfilling the need for status—much in the way that obtaining high government office was for the yangban during the Chosŏn dynasty. The sociologist Kim Kyong-dong explains this perspective:

And in accordance with the Confucian values, achieving a high official status was not for personal glory but for the sake of the family and kinship group. The central importance of education, therefore, was conceived in terms of its role as the channel for status attainment and upward mobility. This tradition has survived even the colonial rule. . . . And in the process of capitalist development, afterwards, it was not the need-achievement of the pecuniary rewards as such that pushed the ordinary Korean people to be actively involved in capitalistic behaviour, but largely this status-achievement motive, inherited from the Confucian tradition. (Kim Kyong-dong 1994:102)

According to Kim Kwang-ok (1993:30), the members of the middle class, though criticized from below by the poor and by social activists for "living luxuriously and hedonistically on unearned income" and from above by the government for their "egotism and immorality," believe that they "have escaped poverty mainly through their [own] efforts, [and thus] they have a sense of pride regarding the path they have followed. Also these people have a strong sense of direction toward the idea that they have built the present economic prosperity and social stability of Korea through their sacrifices" and therefore "want complete justification for their experiences, and recognition of their position as a core element of history." Many found this reaffirmed in the church: "The middle-class parishioner gets a feeling of refreshment and confirmation of his blessed position when hearing a supporting sermon, which touts the importance of contributions of the middle class to the society. They confirm they are recognized truly in the sermons which define the middle class as the rich, successors and upper class, and encourage it to pray for the poor, failures and lower class" (Kim Kwang-ok 1993:30).

Many North Korean refugees, a significant number of whom came from the upper classes as well as a significant number of whom were Christian, chose the path of business as a means of reacquiring their status after losing everything with the division of Korea and the Korean War and their subsequent migration to South Korea:

Between 1945 and 1951, 1.2 million Koreans from the North made their way south to escape from political persecution, economic hardship, and downward social mobility under communist rule (Yu 1983:30). Disproportionately large numbers of these refugees were landlords, intellectuals, and government employees who had more to lose than did peasants and working-class people in the communist Democratic People's Republic of Korea. Christians also joined the South-bound exodus in large numbers

in search of religious freedom that was denied in the North. Christians thus constituted a large proportion of North Korean refugees. . . .

Despite their advantageous class backgrounds, North Korean refugees experienced
great hardship in establishing a solid economic foothold in South Korea because they
left all their wealth and social networks in the North. Although there has been no discrimination against people of North Korean origin in South Korea at the government
level, their having to start from scratch without social support networks put them at a
disadvantage in competing with South Koreans for wage employment in the private
and public sectors. As a result, North Korean refugees have engaged in commerce at a
higher rate than the national average. (Yoon In-Jin 1993:25)

Not all business owners were considered middle class. The manual/non-
manual axis of differentiation characterizing Chosŏn society has remained the
primary axis of differentiation in contemporary society and is one factor in
forming an opinion regarding class. Owners whose businesses required manual labor of themselves were generally considered lower class. Owners of those
businesses that were primarily nonmanual in nature could be considered middle class if the volume of business was sufficient to provide what Koreans defined as a middle-class lifestyle (see also Hong Doo-Seung 1990). The sector a
business was in was also a factor. For example, many of the successful business
owners were involved with import or export or upscale businesses such as
modern-style coffee shops.

Many Koreans expressed the sentiment that everyone wanted to own his
or her own business, everyone wanted to be his or her own CEO, that is,
chief executive officer. "Probably the richest people are those that own their
own business" was one informant's response when I asked which jobs were
most desirable. The potential for making more money than in a salaried position was there. Even though small businesses had a high failure rate, the belief was that if you had a good idea you would be successful. Furthermore,
while long hours as a salary man did not lead to additional income, the same
was not necessarily true when you owned your own business. The thinking
went: "If you're going to put in all those additional hours anyway, it is better
to do it in your own business where the potential to make more money exists." Finally, Koreans liked the freedom of being their own boss where they
could implement their own ideas.

It might be noted that although the large business conglomerates pre-
dominated in production and export, medium- and small-sized firms pre-
dominated in employment and in numbers. Moreover, most retail trade was
still in the hands of small merchants rather than Western-style department
stores (see also Macdonald 1990:205, 209; Ministry of Labor 1993:65). However, the "domestic retail sector remains primitive despite the industrialization efforts of the past decades" (Kwak Young-sup 1992:30). The boom of

24–hour convenience stores since their introduction into South Korea as multinationals in 1989 was expected to hurt the mom-and-pop stores even more (Kwak Young-sup 1992:30).

Although many business owners had university degrees and earned enough money to live comfortably, there were also many small business owners such as small shopkeepers without university educations or any other assets whose incomes did not allow them to live what Koreans have come to consider a middle-class lifestyle. These small shopkeepers may have been considered, and many considered themselves to be, among the lower rather than middle class. One indication that these small-scale entrepreneurs were not considered in the same class is their residence. The owners of the businesses that surrounded and serviced the so-called middle class inhabiting the high-rise apartment complexes generally did not live in these complexes, but rather commuted from elsewhere (see also Kim Kwang-ok 1993:6) or lived nearby in less expensive and less desirable housing. This is in contrast to the Japanese middle-class neighborhood studied by Bestor (1992:27), where "most shopkeepers, craftspeople, factory owners, and even professionals, such as doctors, dentists, or accountants, conducted business in small shops, workshops, or offices attached to their homes." I do not recall seeing any professionals, except for a pharmacist, "setting up shop" in the business district adjacent to the apartment complex in which I lived. Professionals were instead found in larger business districts.

My empirical observations regarding occupation and class and Hong Doo-Seung's analysis of class classification by cluster analysis support each other. On the basis of a survey using objective status, self-identification, and relations to the means of production, Hong (1990:23) found that "the old middle class such as whole-sale and retail traders and self-employed service workers are located in the middle of the new middle class and the working class, but closer to the latter." Moreover, "It should not be overlooked that independent tradesmen or working proprietors in service sector [sic] who are often classified as the old middle class show more similar configurations to those of the working class consisting of production/skilled workers than to the new middle class which forms the other half of the broad middle scale."

One finer but significant distinction that I would make concerns those business owners who were making sufficient profits to support at least a middle- if not an upper-middle-class lifestyle. Nowhere in Hong's scheme are these accounted for. He does detect, as I did, an upper-middle class distinct from a middle class: "The upper-middle class such as higher professional, administrative and managerial workers constitutes an isolated cluster distinct from any other class groups," which also included "self-employed technical workers" distinct from "self-employed production and skilled workers [who] are grouped together with self-employed shopkeepers and working proprietors in service sector" (1990:17). But there is no mention of other self-employed individuals who were not technical but who owned businesses, such as those in import/export, who were in many cases making more than those of salary-man families. Perhaps the term "small capitalists" would apply to these wealthy, small-business owners, though most would be considered upper-middle rather than upper class.

Thus I saw those in "old middle-class" occupations largely divided on either side of those with "new middle-class" occupations, that is, salary men. On one side were those shopkeepers, proprietors in the service sector, and self-employed production/skilled workers Hong identifies as being closer to the working class. On the other side were those making substantial profits who would thus be included in the "upper-middle-class cluster." (There were also those, of course, whose income in fact was comparable to that of the "new middle class" of salary men.)

Professionals

Although many professionals were employed in salaried positions, others constituted a special group of small business owners. These include such occupations as doctors, lawyers, architects, pharmacists, and dentists. Their counterparts during the Chosŏn dynasty were considered chung'in or middle men who were not eligible to hold more prestigious government positions. Today's specialists, however, referred to as professionals, require a higher education than those in most other contemporary, middle-class occupations and thus often ranked at the top of the middle-class occupational hierarchy in terms of income as well as prestige. Whether self-employed or salaried, their income was such that many were able to enjoy what is considered by many an upper-class lifestyle. For this reason, these professions were considered the most desirable of business occupations.

Religious Leaders

Religious leaders, including Catholic priests, Protestant ministers, and many Buddhist monks, were generally highly educated and well respected. For the middle class, according to Kim Kwang-ok (1993:26), a church represented its members' social position, and thus the church leaders' educational background was an important criterion in categorizing a church. The ministers of the large "high-class" churches in Kangnam that were attended by middle- and upper-class parishioners, for example, had studied abroad and obtained Ph.D.s; the deacons were engaged in professional occupations or were successful businessmen with some degree of personal fame (Kim Kwang-ok 1993:11). Among the Buddhists, too, it was preferable to have a Buddhist scholar or a professor of Buddhism for a religious leader (Kim Kwang-ok 1993:31).

These churches in general have provided new avenues of status assertion for lay people as well, as church members have sought lay leadership positions and thus status within the church. Especially among the Protestant denominations, which do not allow ancestor worship, positions in the church hierarchy have functionally replaced positions in elite lineages as a means of status assertion. Among the Buddhists, acts of giving and pilgrimages, which require financial means, effectively were also means of asserting status (see also Kim Kwang-ok 1993:23).

Nouveaux Riches

A somewhat more ambiguous status was held by those families who had only recently acquired wealth and by means other than work. Most of these made their money through real estate and money market speculation during the 1980s. An article in *Business Korea*, as well as general public opinion, attributed the emergence of this wealthy class to the development of the Kangnam area of Seoul south of the Han River, the development in turn partially spurred by preparations for the 1988 Olympics:

The Korean economy grew an average 12.8% annually between 1986 and 1988 and the demand for labor outpaced supply. The 1988 Seoul Olympics also had various side effects including real estate speculation and a construction boom. The Olympics created a new leisure class, the so-called overnight millionaires, who woke up and found that the land they were sitting on was worth a fortune. And since they had nothing better to do, they spent their new wealth at nightclubs and cabarets which caused the service sector to mushroom. (Chang 1992:42)

Although many had acquired the trappings of an upper-class lifestyle, the nouveaux riches were looked down upon by descendants of yangban families, who claimed the nouveaux riches had no culture and merely bought their status. Miss Ko described the recently wealthy, attributing to them middle- rather than upper-class status: "There are many nouveaux riches. The middle class is growing very rapidly. The boomtown area of Kangnam south of the Han River is where many upper-middle class—nouveaux riches—live. They are often criticized for the highly priced imports which they buy at stores which stock them in the Kangnam area. Apku-jŏng-dong along the Han River is the richest area in Kangnam. A small apartment there may cost about US$440,000."

Professor Lee explained that many who had been pursuing graduate studies abroad during the spiraling real estate market in the late 1980s missed out on these opportunities to accumulate wealth quickly, herself included. She revealed what I found to be a common attitude toward the nouveaux riches held by those with high social origins. When asked to define "middle class" in the Korean context, she mused, "It's difficult to say. Economically is one thing. Socially is another. If you happened to own a lot of land before the price of land went up so much, you became very rich. Many such people bought their status. They can buy anything. But they haven't earned their status socially." Others have simply said of the nouveaux riches, despite their undisputed economic status, that "they have no culture," that is, they lacked education, did not come from good (yangban) family backgrounds, and they displayed their wealth in conspicuously wasteful rather than culturally tasteful ways. More will be said about this lifestyle in Chapter 4. It should be noted here, however, that many nouveaux riches were reinvesting their economic capital into the education of their children in order to acquire the cultural capital associated with high status. By the mid-1990s, with tertiary education no longer being so rare (the percentage of the college-age population pursuing higher education surpassed the 60 percent mark in 1996), perhaps education was losing some of its prestige value. In 1997 a woman with both education and wealth commented to me that "it used to be that education was more important than wealth. But now an uneducated man can hire a college graduate." This woman explicitly attributed this shift in values to the country's shift to capitalism. Another educated and wealthy woman also told me that other criteria had been used to determine status, but that now money was the most important criterion.

Women and Work

Hulbert (1969 [1906]:355) described women's work at the turn of the century:

The Korean woman's main business then is wifehood and motherhood; but even so, there are many opportunities for her to help along the family finances and supplement the wages of a husband who is too often shiftless and dependent or even worse.

First, as to occupations open to women of the upper class. Strange as it may seem, the only kind of shop such a woman can keep is a wine-shop. Of course she never appears in person, but if her house is properly situated she can turn a portion of it into a wine-shop, where customers can be served by her slave or other servant. No lady would ever think of selling cloth or vegetables or fruit or anything except wine. Silk culture is an important industry, in which ladies take a prominent part, especially in the country. The care of the eggs, the feeding of the worms, the manipulation of the cocoons and the spinning of the silk afford means whereby the wife of the gentleman farmer passes many pleasant hours and adds materially to the finances of the household.

Sewing and embroidery are usual occupations of ladies, but they do very little of it for money. The vendible goods of this kind are made by a different class. Many Korean ladies of restricted means act as tutors to the daughter of their more fortunate sisters. They teach the Chinese character and literature, letter-writing, burial customs, music, housekeeping, hygiene, care of infants, obstetrics, religion, fiction, needlework and embroidery....

As might be supposed, a descent in the social scale widens the field of the Korean woman's work.

Except in a few professional fields such as teaching, medicine, and the media, as is typical in highly stratified societies, including Korea's traditional society, occupations in contemporary South Korea have been largely segregated by sex. Moreover, just as with men and just as in the past, a close link continues to exist in this very status-conscious society between family status and what is appropriate work for women (see also Papanek 1979). In addition, the more educated a woman is the less likely she is to work, at least in the formal sector (see also Yoon In-Jin 1993:17). (The informal sector includes such activities as money lending, property renting, private tutoring, commissions, and bribery; see also Koo and Hong 1980:613.)

Unless a woman had a professional job, I found, there was more prestige in claiming to be a full-time housewife, not only because the role of wife and mother continued to be valued highly in Korea but also because it implied that the family's financial situation was secure enough that a woman did not have to go out and work. Moreover, a woman who was a full-time housewife had more time to engage in status-production work (see also Papanek 1979). Nevertheless, many women were frustrated by their lack of choice in the matter. Miss Ko described the predicament of South Korea's contemporary middle-class women: "The educated, middle-class women are the most disadvantaged: there are no jobs for them. They are frustrated. Many who cannot find jobs marry, not for love, but because that is the only alternative they have."

At the end of the Chosŏn dynasty Hulbert (1969 [1906]:335–336) observed that there were many jobs that were beneath the dignity of a woman with high status. Nevertheless, there were many ways a woman could contribute to the household income. This situation persisted into the 1990s. Just as among men of the middle and upper classes, wage labor for women with such status was "unsuitable." Office work was acceptable, but generally only for young unmarried or recently married women. Except perhaps in the banking industry, which had taken steps to incorporate women in managerial positions, most white-collar positions in business held by women were clerical and secretarial. Very few management positions were open to women. One young college-educated woman in 1996 insisted that the situation was improving. In 1997 a newspaper reported that

according to a survey released this week, women face [a] difficult . . . time reaching the upper levels of private companies. The labor ministry surveyed 50 companies on the gender makeup of their management. They found 110,096 women are working in management—with only 729 in upper-level management positions, including 19 board members. Twenty-eight are department directors, 74 are deputy department directors and 608 are section managers, the survey found. Almost half of those high-level managers work for Samsung (235) or Lucky Goldstar (111).

Overall, the survey found, women comprised 11.3 percent of the college-educated work force in those companies in 1995. (*Korea Times*, February 27, 1997, p. 3)

Nevertheless, even women with university degrees were competing for secretarial and other positions that would be filled by high school graduates in the United States. Thus, this is one area in which the middle class in Korea held lower-status jobs than the middle class in the United States. For example, a university senior I interviewed was competing for a job as an airline stewardess or receptionist with Korean Air Lines just in case she did not get accepted to graduate school. She considered that position to be very desirable and competition for it stiff. Another young woman, a recent university graduate, had been hired by Korean Air Lines. She spoke fluent English (a requirement for the job) and was among the top students in her class. After starting to work, however, she became very disillusioned by the treatment she received. During my tenure in Korea, one of the large business conglomerates opened up fifty new positions for women in response to pressure against discrimination. The job title was "secretary."

Miss Ko, the account supervisor for a public relations firm for foreign companies, was the only woman I met whose position in a company was above secretarial. One day Miss Han, a friend of Miss Ko, and I were waiting at a fast-food place for Miss Ko to show up. Upon her arrival, Miss Ko promptly (and I think proudly) pulled out her business card. "Business woman!" Miss Han teasingly remarked. Miss Ko had been hired just two months earlier, and it was the first time the two friends had met since.

During the conversation, I asked Miss Ko, who had already reached thirty, the maximum desirable age for marriage, whether she intended to continue to work after she married. She said that she would like to because she had a great deal invested in her employment. She had not only earned an undergraduate degree but had put much effort into foreign language study afterward. However, Miss Ko said that in general it was very difficult for women to continue to work after marriage. For one, the place of employment could force a woman out. For another, if she worked outside the home, a woman had two jobs: one outside the home and one in the home. Husbands offered no help at home, Miss Ko explained. "Successful career women are single and have no children," she added. When I returned to Korea almost six years later, in 1997, I found that Miss Ko remained unmarried.

Even when young women engaged in office work after finishing school, most women were forced by the company if not also by their husbands and mothers-in-law to quit either upon marriage or after having children. Mrs. An, a woman who had worked as a secretary in a foreign national company, said she thought Korean companies forced women to quit after getting married and having children because they felt the women should be at home taking care of their families. This attitude was less likely the case with multinational companies, for which Mrs. An had worked.

Miss Shim, a schoolteacher and friend of Mrs. An, said there were three reasons why a woman would prefer to work for a foreign company rather than a Korean company: (1) the pay was better; (2) women were not forced to quit after getting married and having children; and (3) other Koreans thought that if a woman worked for a multinational company, she must be better educated, that is, there was more prestige for a woman to work for a foreign company than for a Korean company. Mrs. An agreed with Miss Shim, although she said, in fact, she did not know that she was actually better educated. Mrs. An added that though working for a foreign company might be better, there were still problems, which she did not elaborate on. (Kim Hyun Mee [1995], however, describes several problems working-class women had with at least one U.S.-owned multinational.)

Apparently women too found working for the government better than working for a company. Korean female government workers went home earlier in the day than their male equivalents, I was told. They were not forced to resign upon marriage and even had maternity leave. However, women for the most part were restricted to the lower ranks. In the executive branch, for example, on a scale of first grade through ninth grade with ninth grade being the lowest level of civil service, as of 1991, 92.1 percent of women were concentrated in the lower levels of seventh grade or below, and 26.4 percent of all female civil servants were in the ninth grade. Among the higher levels of fifth grade and above, only 1.5 percent were women (Korean Women's Development Institute [KWDI] 1991:45). Women were usually in special posts such as counseling and health care, which had limited opportunities for promotion. Of all the civil servants, one quarter were women, but 59.8 percent of them were teachers in public schools (KWDI 1991:46). By 1997, the situation had not much improved. According to a newspaper article entitled "Government Dragging Feet on Employment of Women" (*Korea Times*, February 27, 1997, p. 3), despite a government policy recommendation to increase the percentage of women in mid-level public administration and foreign service jobs to 10 percent in 1996 and 20 percent by the year 2000, "the government has a long way to go to hit the 1997 quota. There are only 634 women officials in mid-level government jobs or above, the [Ministry of State for Political Affairs in charge of women's affairs] says, about 2.3 percent of the total." The target for the year was 13 percent.

Teaching was considered a desirable job for a woman because there was more "free" time, though Miss Shim, a schoolteacher in a less affluent part of Seoul, said the pay was not very good and the prestige was less that what it had been in the past. The income of both male and female teachers, however, especially in the more affluent areas, was supplemented by gifts from the parents of the students, which could amount to thousands of dollars per year. (This is discussed at greater length in Chapter 5.) Teachers could also earn additional money by tutoring. Although it was illegal to hire those employed as schoolteachers to tutor students for the highly competitive university entrance exams, it nevertheless was common. One magazine article claims: "For many teachers, who can make $20,000 a month tutoring, the payoff is irresistible" (Emerson 1991:16).

Many husbands and mothers-in-law did not want their wives and daughters-in-law to work. At the time I met Mrs. An, she had just quit her job with the multinational company after working there for seven years. Although the company did not force her to resign, her husband and mother-in-law pressured her to quit after she became pregnant with her second child, especially as she was badly affected by morning sickness. Some men said they did not want their wives to work in an office because they knew how badly such women were treated (perhaps even by themselves).

Among the younger generation, most male university students whom I talked to expressed their awareness of the ideal that it was important that women also had the opportunity to develop their own interests and career, but most were also ambivalent about women working when it came to their own particular cases. When a mixed group of male and female university students was discussing the issue at an English club meeting, for example, one man acknowledged that it was important that his wife have her own career. When he added, "I'll *let* her work," the others in the group questioned this statement. This young man was betraying his "enlightened" outlook by expressing his assumed control and superiority over his future wife.

A few female university students volunteered that women themselves needed to change their attitudes if women were ever to be accepted in the business world. One such woman who had read a great deal of feminist literature said that she wanted to continue working after marriage and having children. However, she went on to explain, "Harmony is very important to me. Even though I am aware of the inequalities of the sexes and feel they are wrong, for the sake of harmony I will probably succumb to the pressures and conform to the traditional patterns."

Another university student told me that many women her age expected to continue to work after marriage. Her brother-in-law had told her that these women did not realize "social reality." It was at this time that this young woman told me that even though she was aware of the unfairness of men expecting obedience from women and "that men felt a certain pride just because they're men," she did not have the "bravery" or courage it took to go against tradition. This woman seemed almost resigned, if not saddened, regarding her situation. It is just these types of attitudes that one young woman said had to be changed. She reasoned that "if a company invests money in a woman's training and then she quits when she gets married or has a child, it doesn't encourage companies to hire women."

Professional jobs were one area in the formal sector where a woman might have a career even after having children. I asked Mrs. Soh what she would like her daughter to be when she grew up. "A doctor," was her prompt reply. "Why?" I asked. "There are three main reasons," she offered. "First of all, she would automatically become a professional. Secondly, as a doctor she would experience much less sex discrimination. And third, the money." Other positions such as professor, pharmacist, interpreter, and those in the media, such as in journalism and broadcasting, were also pursued by women. Nursing, sales, music, and clothing design were other possibilities.

Finally, owning a business was a very acceptable and often profitable undertaking for women working in the formal sector. It was not unusual for such a woman's earnings to exceed her husband's salary. Mrs. Hwang, the woman I met on my first day in Korea who had started a taxi business, is one such example. Mrs. Chung, another friend of Miss Shim's, is another. Mrs. Chung was concerned about her husband losing his salaried job with one of the large business conglomerates. Using "start-up" money provided by her family, she opened an up-scale coffee shop in the Kangnam area of Seoul. She now earned more than her husband. Miss Shim herself, a schoolteacher, expressed the desire to one day own her own business. Already beyond the desirable age of marriage, by her own admission, she faced the possibility of never marrying. Especially in such a case, owning a business could provide a better life for her than her low teacher's pay.

In my sample, only those few women who were in a profession, such as teaching, medicine, and entertainment, or who owned their own business, were employed in the formal sector after having children. Most women, however, were involved in some way in the informal sector. Cottage industry was one possibility, but one that was dying out. One university student's mother, however, still made Korean-style socks in her home. Tutoring English and other school subjects and teaching music were very popular as well as profitable occupations for middle-class women.

Although Miss Ko said that many women were frustrated because there were few jobs for women in the formal sector, she did add that "many, however, are involved in land speculation and stocks. In fact, their involvement in the informal economic sector is considered by the government to be a problem. A woman involved in land speculation makes a lot of money and can easily make more than a salaried man." In the anthropologist Moon Okpyo's (1990:36) discussion of the contribution women make to individual household economies, she writes:

> Although much has been said about the negative impact of such kinds of female activity on the state economy at large, few attempts have yet been made to examine the significance of these activities in terms of their contribution toward the economy of the individual household. In many of the households in our sample, however, both the husbands and wives are in general agreement that they would not have been able to enjoy their current economic standing if they relied solely on the husbands' salary, i.e., if it were not for the wives' independent efforts.

There were several types of money-making activities and sources of support besides jobs in the formal sector. These activities were not limited to women, though women more often than not managed the household's property and income (see also Moon Okpyo 1990), and are discussed in the following section.

Other Money-Making Activities and Unearned Income

Among my first observations regarding the life of urban middle-class Koreans was that salaries were low in comparison to the cost of living in Seoul, which was high. Salaries averaged less than US$20,000 per year, including bonuses. As an illustration of the cost of living, people whose salaries were around US$20,000 were living in condominiums worth over US$200,000, which they owned outright. There were no mortgages.

According to Ministry of Labor statistics (1993:280–281), in 1991 the average monthly income from salary (including bonuses) was 1,214,100 wŏn nationwide. (In 1991 this was roughly equivalent to US$1,660, where 730 wŏn equaled one U.S. dollar.) Total monthly disbursements, in contrast, amounted to 2,456,600 wŏn (or roughly US$3,365). I questioned how it was possible to support what Koreans had come to consider a middle-class life-style on such relatively meager salaries. One reply I received was that it was either from rental property or from ancestral property that the family had held on to. The situation was more complex than that, but it remained true that those families that relied on a single salary for their income struggled to maintain even a lower-middle-class standard of living.

Most middle-class families in general relied on a variety of sources of support. According to the same Ministry of Labor report cited above, total receipts, including salary, income from a "subsidiary job," "other" or unearned income, "other than income," and "carry over" amounted to 2,459,300 wŏn, just over the amount of total expenditures. This is the money that was reported. Money from "informal activities" can be expected to have been underreported or not reported at all and thus would not be reflected in government statistics (see also Koo and Hong 1980:613).

That families had to depend on multiple sources of income to support a middle-class lifestyle was apparently not new. In her survey of middle-class families in Seoul in 1967, Lee Hyo-jae (1971:44) found that a substantial portion of income came from unearned income, including, in the case of younger couples, assistance from parents. During the 1970s Spencer (1988:40) found that salaries needed to be supplemented by income from a combination of other sources in order to own a home, a common Korean criterion of middle-class status: "It must be said that Korean finances are complex in the sense that city dwellers, particularly those able to afford even a modest house, have several or many financial irons in the fire. To hold a job and maintain a family on a fixed or salaried income may be insufficient. The result is that a younger household head, particularly in the city, often has a series of ventures going on at the same time."

In the early 1980s the anthropologist Lee Kwang Kyu (1984:197) also commented on the fact that it took more than a salary to enjoy a middle-class lifestyle in the city. It was often the efforts of the wife that made the difference: "Even though a young man works hard, his salary is not enough to support his small family. If his wife's household management is poor, it is hard for a family to keep-up with the high cost of urban living."

Similarities in strategies used to support an urban, middle-class lifestyle are not only observable over the past two or three decades, however. Continuities also exist with precapitalist patterns in Korea. Contemporary middle-class South Koreans, like their yangban predecessors, derive their support from a combination of three main types of sources: occupation, property, and kin.

In earlier analyses, the industrialization of societies in general was expected to entail a shift away from dependence on property among an "old middle class" of land and business owners to sole dependence on occupation in salaried positions among a "new middle class." The axis of stratification then was expected to shift from property to occupation (Mills 1956:65). At the same time, traditional extended family systems were expected to transform into a conjugal family system as industrialization brought jobs and other opportunities that would allow individuals to support themselves independent of family resources (Goode 1982). This is basically what occurred in Japan (Vogel 1963, 1991; Kelly 1986). Korea, however, developed differently.

Although industrialization brought about salaried jobs in Korea, this generated no new middle *class* solely dependent on salary. Moreover, dependence on family for support among the middle classes in general remained high. Owning a business might in itself have been sufficient to maintain a middle-class lifestyle, but having only a single salary was not. A family might have gotten by on two earned incomes, such as two salaries or a salary and profits from a business. Some wives, as already noted, operated a business of sorts in the informal sector, such as tutoring, to supplement the household income. Even most of these households, however, along with all the single-salary households, had a variety of other "financial irons" in the fire. These will be discussed here. Support from family members will be discussed in the following chapter.

To begin, I found that some urban households received income from rural property that they owned, usually in the family's place of origin or hometown (*kohyang*). They might also have received income in kind, that is, actual produce from the land. A family member might have lived on and farmed the land or alternately the land might have been leased out.

Urban property provided a major means of increasing a family's wealth. Profit made by selling farmland that became incorporated into Seoul turned some families into nouveaux riches, as noted earlier. The real estate market in homes and apartments or condominiums was also lucrative, especially during the second half of the 1980s. From the mid-1980s, prices of condominiums in the boomtown area of Kangnam, for example, doubled every year. Mrs. Kim kept pointing out, however, that not everyone had benefited from the recent spurt in South Korea's economic growth. For those that did benefit, she attributed much of their success to luck. She cited herself as an example. She bought her 55–p'yŏng apartment, large by Seoul's standards, in 1987 at the beginning of sharp increases in prices; had she waited even a few more months to buy, with a 30 percent increase in price, she would not have been able to afford the unit.

The lucrative real estate market had been a result in part of a rapid increase in demand for better housing as families became more prosperous, coupled with an inability by housing construction to keep up with the demand, causing property prices to spiral upward. As a result of government policies aimed at halting the inflation, however, home prices in 1991 actually dipped 0.3 percent after having risen 21 percent in 1990 (Korea Annual 1992:181). If government controls remain effective, the real estate market will not be so lucrative, sealing off or at least limiting one of the major avenues people have been using to raise their economic status. If one was fortunate enough to buy a newly built apartment, however, one could obtain a hefty windfall under the *punyang* system of selling apartments or selling apartments by lots. Although the specifics for each construction project differ, basically the system works in the following way.

At least two years before wanting to buy, a person deposits the equivalent of a few thousand U.S. dollars in the Housing Bank. Interest is earned, but less than in other types of accounts. The amount deposited depends on the size of the desired apartment. When a construction project is announced, if certain criteria are met, a person who has deposited money in the Housing Bank can apply to be entered into a lottery of sorts. The odds of winning are set and stated in the announcement; twenty to one is common. In such a case, if one hundred units are to be sold, up to two thousand applicants will be accepted for the lottery.

Those who draw a lot make perhaps three or four installment payments over a period of a year or two while the apartments are being built. The apartment is paid in full before moving in. The cost (which is set by the government) is, however, less than the market value. After a short time, the owners can turn around and sell it for a profit.

In one case, a couple put the equivalent of US$4,000 into the Housing Bank in 1985. In the spring of 1992, they submitted their paperwork to buy a 48-p'yŏng apartment. Although the odds announced were twenty to one, because of the number of qualified applicants, the odds were actually eleven to one that they would win. The woman said they were very lucky: they drew a lot on their first try. Many try repeatedly without success.

This couple paid roughly 300,000,000 wŏn, or over US$300,000, for their apartment. It was in a good location, within walking distance of a mountain, considered good for its air and hiking, and very conveniently located to a subway station. The market value was roughly double what they paid. Overnight their investment doubled.

Much money was also to be made when condominiums were used as rentals. Most rentals were done on a *chŏnse* basis, which meant that the renter had to pay in advance key money, or a substantial percentage of the value of the property (usually between 40 to 60 percent), as a deposit of sorts that was returned at the end of the lease. In the meantime, the owner could purchase yet another rental or invest this money in other ways. Depending on the arrangement and based on the percentage of the value of the property the renter was able to come up with, the renter may or may not have had to pay an additional monthly rent in addition to the key money. In 1991 rent increases also leveled off, showing only a 1.6 percent increase, compared with 16.7 percent in 1990 (Korea Annual 1992:181). The money market, including stocks, bonds, and securities, had also been very profitable up to that time. But the stock market, too, in 1991 "was a disaster for investors, who saw stock prices plummet more than 10%" (Korea Annual 1992:183).

Another way a family could use its money to make money was through personal moneylending. Though illegal (the underground network is known as *sach'ae*, literally meaning "private loan"), these personal loans were in demand because it was almost impossible for an individual family to borrow money from a bank. It was even difficult to get small business loans. Interest earned on these private loans was high, 2 to 3 percent a month not being uncommon. A *Newsweek* article entitled "Too Rich, Too Soon: Is South Korea Living Beyond Its Means?" illustrates the obsessive pursuit of status that was perceived to be prevalent in Seoul:

[Schemes] of every conceivable variety are flourishing—schemes to get rich, get a husband, get into school, get ahead. The recent machinations of just one middle-class Seoul housewife, who insisted on anonymity, illustrate several of the more popular varieties. In 1989 she bought some land outside Seoul for 7,000 won per pyong (3.3 square meters), which she recently resold at nearly 600 percent profit. She now lends out the proceeds through a flourishing underground network, known as *sache* [sach'ae], which bypasses strict government limits on private borrowing. A kind of homegrown loan-sharking operation, without the heavies, sache offers investors hefty interest rates of 28 percent or more. (Emerson 1991:15)

Note that the article goes on to say that this woman paid "moonlighting teachers" $3,000 a month to tutor her son for the university entrance examination, yet she was still considered "middle class." Indicative of the size of the underground market and the concern of the government is the government's plan in 1997 to temporarily exempt people investing in small- and medium-sized companies and venture firms from tax payments and audits in an attempt to channel the tax-evading underground money into the formal or "productive" sectors of the economy. The underground money was estimated to be 10 percent of the gross national product. However, according to a least one report, there was doubt the plan would be very successful (Lee Chang-sup 1997).

Kye, or credit clubs, which have their origins in mutual aid societies in rural society, came in many shapes and forms and served various needs. Usually translated as rotating credit associations, kye generally involved members making contributions to a common fund and then each taking a turn in using the monies. Both men and women belonged to kye, even if the types of kye they belonged to tended to be different. Although most people would claim that the primary reason they belonged to a kye was social, there were usually economic benefits as well. People would participate in various kye in order to receive a large lump sum of money for a special event, such as a child's wedding, buying a home, taking a trip, or starting a business. These kye tended to dissolve after one or two years when everyone had had his or her turn at receiving a lump sum.

Certain other kye were long term and may have involved meeting a group of former classmates on a regular basis. (Some people did not call these types "kye" but would state that they were "something like kye.") Many men claimed that though the short-term purpose of these might be to have a night out with the boys, the long-term purpose was to build relationships so that in times of crisis, such as the death of a parent, they would receive aid, including cash, from the other members of the kye.

More often than not it is the women who, with a specific purpose in mind, participated in kye that dissolved after everyone received her lump sum. Men, on the other hand, were more inclined to be involved with ongoing kye. Mr. Mok explained it to me:

Nominally, the purpose of the kye is for fun. However, they are really investing in their future. They are developing strong ties. If one of the members has a hardship, the others would only be too glad to help. Many young housewives do not like kye. Women often organize kye to spend money on outings that a young housewife might consider a waste of time and money. Women get involved in kye for the present [that is, for a specific purpose]. Men invest in the future, not so much in money but in the connections they make. Let's say for example Mr. Soh becomes a banker. The bank has a limited amount of funds to give out [with respect to the number of businesses asking for it]. Let's say I have a business and need money. If everything else is equal, if I have developed a strong tie with Mr. Soh, Mr. Soh will give the money to me over others that have not developed that tie.

In 1997 a president of a medium-sized company told me kye were dying out. He looked to his wife for confirmation, and she nodded in agreement, adding that no one in their apartment complex participated in kye. When I commented that my landlady, whose husband worked in the *pudongsan* or real estate office in the market community I was studying, participated in kye, the company president remarked that the market people wanted to help one another.

In a later discussion with the wife of the company president, I told her upon further inquiry, I was assured by others that kye continued to flourish among white-collar members of the so-called middle class as well as among the small shopkeepers. She said that that could very well be the case; she herself, however, knew of no relatives or acquaintances, save one, who participated in kye. I offered that the reason might be that their economic status was high enough that they didn't need to resort to kye to finance such expensive items as a house or such big events as a wedding.

I then suggested that she might have been more inclined to engage in kye in her younger days, when her economic situation was not so secure. She replied that she had never participated in kye. Even before she married, she was able to get a bank loan to buy a small apartment. Surprised, I asked how that was possible, and she explained that she had been an employee of a foreign bank. In telling me this, she realized herself why others might participate in kye. Previously, she could never understand why. But now she saw that most people could not get bank loans. She had realized her case was an exception, but had never thought about what others without access to bank loans might do when large sums of money were needed.

Moon Okpyo (1990) writes of the social networking and gift exchange that women were engaged in and the contribution such activities made to enhancing the family's resources and status. We see here that such networking, though perhaps largely carried out by women, was not limited to them. And this was only one among various strategies employed by middle-class families to earn enough money to support a middle-class lifestyle.

Strategies and Case Studies

When I asked a civil servant what he thought distinguished the middle classes from the lower classes, he responded that middle-class families did not just live from day to day but planned ahead. When credit was hard if not impossible to obtain from formal financial institutions and costs for housing, education, cars, and weddings befitting middle-class status were high and generally had to be paid up front in cash, families had to rely on their own resources. They had to look at all the income-enhancing options available to them and develop long-term plans to maintain the middle-class status of the family.

In addition to the various sources of income, there were various strategies employed by families to increase their wealth and standard of living. For example, many salaried employees anticipated a mid-career lay-off and planned accordingly. Others found their salary insufficient and resigned. In either case, the most common option was to go into business for themselves. Many used their salaried positions as a means of accumulating capital and experience to prepare themselves for starting their own business.

Another strategy involved place of residence. This topic will be explored in greater depth in the chapter on lifestyle, but some general points about housing are useful here. Except for Western-style single-family homes, housing in the northern part of Seoul (Kangbuk) and in the satellite cities surrounding Seoul tended to be less expensive than in the Kangnam or southern region of Seoul. Moreover, the cost of housing tended to increase in the following order: older-style, single-family houses; duplexes and smaller villas; apartments (or condominiums); larger villas; and Western-style, single-family houses. Though representing a range of housing costs, all of these options were suitable for the middle class. Which one chose was at least partially a factor in the overall strategy a family adopted for the allotment of its available resources.

Several case studies demonstrate the complexity and diversity of household finances among typical South Korean middle-class families. (In fact, each case I cite may be even more complex than I present it, as I may not have been made aware of all sources of income or strategies.) These cases represent a variety of primary occupations, including business owners, government officials, corporate salary men, educators, and stockbrokers. For civil servants and company employees, both more senior (and more affluent) and more junior (and less affluent) examples are given. Strategies among these cases vary considerably, with various combinations of earned income and unearned income. These cases also represent generational differences and differences in family background.

Case: The Yu Family

Mr. Yu was originally from North Korea, "no more than a couple hours' drive from Seoul if it were allowed." Mr. Yu's grandmother, parents, and three siblings came to Seoul three years before the Korean War. They left almost everything behind in their home. Mr. Yu, an eldest son, related to his wife that his mother had put a pack of powdered rice around his waist and told him that if he should become separated from the family he should keep heading south. Mr. Yu was about nine years old at the time.

Starting from scratch, his father built a very successful business in Seoul. Mr. Yu himself started a subsidiary company exporting pipe to the United States. He and his parents had both lived in Western-style houses in Kangbuk, or the northern part of Seoul, in a neighborhood someone described as "almost, but not quite, upper class."

In its simplicity, the case of the Yu family represents the possibility of supporting a middle-class, in this case an upper-middle-class, lifestyle primarily on the profits of a business. It is also an example of a high-status North Korean family losing everything and choosing to go into business rather than compete with the South Korean in any kind of wage labor.

Case: The Baek Family

Mr. Baek and his wife were also a middle-aged, upper-middle-class couple, but living in a large, 55–p'yŏng condominium in Kangnam instead of a Western-style home in Kangbuk. They too were a success story from North Korea, although Mr. Baek got his start in the military, and his subsequent career path was quite diverse.

During the Japanese occupation, Mr. Baek's father had been a wealthy landowner in what is now North Korea near the Chinese border, his wealth having accumulated from a lucrative business in the silk trade with the Chinese. His father was educated in Japan. At the end of World War II, his family was living in China (Manchuria). The family lived two years under communism. During the Korean War, they left everything behind in North Korea and moved to Seoul.

In order to get an education, Mr. Baek applied to the military academies because they were free. He qualified for and graduated from the Korean Air Force Academy, which he said was much more prestigious in those days than now. Without acceptance to the academy, he might otherwise have had problems obtaining an education. His younger brother, for example, was unable to go to college, though Mr. Baek helped him to find a "suitable" job.

The Baeks had three adult children, a son and two daughters. During his twenty years in the service, Mr. Baek and his family lived rather simply on his small pay. Retired from the air force, he received a government pension. He also then worked for a salary for a Japanese company that imported large machinery. Along the line, as indicated by a plaque displayed in the living room and proudly pointed out to me on more than one occasion, Mr. Baek obtained a master's degree in business administration from Seoul National University, Korea's most prestigious institute of higher learning.

Once he started working for the Japanese company, Mr. Baek began to buy apartments and some stocks. Playing the real estate market, he gradually accumulated multiple rentals. Now he is also retired from the company as a salary man, but has continued to work for it on a commission basis and has been able to make good money. He said he liked this arrangement because he enjoyed control over both the amount of money he made and the hours he worked. He usually did not go to the office until late in the morning, although he frequently received business calls in the morning at home. Although his son of about thirty years was employed as an engineer for a company and his wife and daughter were musicians and earned money from teaching, Mr. Baek made a point of saying that he did not require other family members to contribute to household expenses.

Thus we see that Mr. Baek, conditioned by high social origins to seek status (Bourdieu 1984:151), sought ways to regain his status after his family members lost everything when they became North Korean refugees. Rather than starting a business as Mr. Yu did, Mr. Baek chose to obtain a higher education at the Air Force Academy and pursue a career as a military officer. Most of his wealth came from investments in the real estate and money markets, however, as well as from commissions from sales in heavy machinery for a Japanese company. Moreover, both Mr. Baek and his wife had balanced their economic capital with cultural capital: besides being college graduates, both were heavily involved in the church, he as a lay leader and she as a choir director.

Case: The Oh Family

Mr. Oh, in his thirties, and his father, close to retirement age and originally from Kwangju in southwestern Korea, are representative of those who chose the traditional prestigious career of government service. Mr. Oh's father's salary had been supplemented by his wife's income from a cottage industry in lace, which included employing other women to do piecework. Mr. Oh's mother, who has since died, had passed on the business to her married daughter a few years back. Cottage industries were dying out, however, and the daughter no longer was working at it. Yet twenty years ago, when combined with her husband's salary from the government, the income from the mother's lace business made it possible for Mr. Oh's parents to build a house in the northern part of Seoul. This was the house Mr. Oh and his family were living in when I met them.

Mr. Oh, his wife of eight years, and his young daughter had been living in an apartment of their own until recently when they had returned to his father's house. Before moving back, Mr. Oh's wife earned money teaching English at a *hagwŏn* or cram school. Now the Ohs used their apartment as a rental. Moreover, as described previously, Mr. Oh had been steadily moving up the career ladder; since his latest promotion the government provides him with a salary he is very comfortable with.

In both Mr. Oh's and his father's cases, the wives contributed to the household income. After moving back into his father's house, however, it was no longer necessary for Mr. Oh's wife to work outside the home. Although when I first met Mr. Oh he would have been classified as "solid" middle class economically, he was on the verge of becoming both socially and economically upper-middle class following his recent promotions.

Case: The Soh Family

Mr. Soh was a government official in his thirties, who rented an apartment on the far northern outskirts of Seoul. Mr. Soh's situation represents that of a government salary man struggling to maintain a middle-class lifestyle. Originally born in the countryside, Mr. Soh moved to Seoul with his family when he was twelve. His father was a pharmacist, still working and living with his wife in Seoul.

Mr. Soh's wife was a graduate of a prestigious women's university. Her major was chemistry. She had worked in a hospital for seven years from before her marriage and continuing until some time after their first child. They now had three children, all of preschool age. She said she would like to work, maybe later, when the children were all in school. "But how can I," she asked. " I have three children," she kept emphasizing. She participated in no activities outside the house. Mr. Soh participated in a kye, "an eating and playing kye." Mr. Soh met with six other friends once a month, and the meeting time itself was a social one of eating and talking. The money they put in was for "travel abroad." No one had cashed in yet, however.

Case: The Moon Family

The Moons were in their late thirties, slightly older than the Ohs and Sohs. They represent a couple in which the husband was a corporate salary man who was steadily advancing in the company, but planning for the possible loss of his job, and a wife who matched her husband's salary in the informal sector by tutoring English.

Though unknown to each other during their childhood, Mrs. Moon and her husband both grew up in the same area outside a small town. His father was a school principal, hers a government functionary. Presently his parents still lived in the same place, while hers had moved to an apartment in the town. Both families had sent their respective child to Seoul to go to college. Mrs. Moon explained that even though there was a university near where they lived, all parents wanted to send their children to Seoul. After graduating, both she and her future husband had returned to their hometown to work, she as a teacher in middle school and he for a branch of one of the large business conglomerates.

About eight years before I met them, Mrs. Moon and her husband met through a matchmaker and married, initially living with his parents. Mrs. Moon continued teaching for a short time in her hometown until her hus-

band landed a job with one of the chaebŏl in Seoul, at which time she resigned. Her husband's family put up the key money so that the couple could
rent a small apartment, and her family bought the furnishings. Eventually
they were able to buy an apartment in Kangnam but rented it out while he
was assigned overseas. When they returned to Korea, the lease was not up
and so they rented a duplex in the northern part of Seoul. This was where
they were living with their two young daughters at the time I first met them.

Mrs. Moon was then tutoring groups of middle-school students in her
home. Although her earnings rivaled that of her husband's, Mrs. Moon was
not particularly satisfied with her situation. One day, she said, she would like
to formally own her own hagwŏn, or school. This would require two or three
years of saving up the necessary capital and also improving her own English-
language ability. In the context of talking about the dependency women had
on men, I noted that if something happened to her husband, she, unlike
many other Korean women, at least had a way to earn a living teaching English. She, however, said there were many ways she was still dependent on her
husband. Medical insurance was one example she cited.

In addition to teaching in her home, Mrs. Moon participated in a kye or
rotating-credit association while I was in Korea. Although I do not know for
what specific reason she joined (perhaps she had buying her own hagwŏn in
mind), I know it was not for social reasons. Because she was busy teaching,
she said she did not have time for the socializing but rather just dropped the
money off.

According to Mrs. Moon, her husband was also contemplating going into
business. He had an opportunity to buy into a business with a friend, but decided against it because he still would not have total control. In the meantime,
he was advancing up the managerial ladder in the chaebŏl as a salary man.

Case: The Ch'oi Family

Mr. Ch'oi is a case of a married corporate salary man with few other sources
of money, save that which he, as an only son, may have inherited from his
father. Mr. Ch'oi, who in his own words was a somewhat rebellious son who
had antigovernment feelings, worked in a factory for one year before going
into the military for his mandatory service. He went to college afterward and
studied design engineering. Presently in his thirties, Mr. Ch'oi started off
after graduating from the university by working for a medium-sized firm located just outside of Seoul in one of the satellite cities. Here he bought an
apartment, where the housing prices were much lower than those in Seoul
proper. He had since changed jobs and was now working in sales for one of
the chaebŏl, commuting daily to Seoul. He had also recently contracted to

have a small apartment built in Seoul. His plans were to sell both of the apartments and buy a larger one in Seoul in a few years so that his daughter could attend school in Seoul. Mr. Ch'oi was also planning to quit his present job and go into business with a friend making and exporting electrical appliances. Mr. Ch'oi's wife, who was a high school graduate, did not work outside the home.

Case: The Bae Family

Mr. Bae's wife also did not work outside the home. Mr. Bae, however, an elementary school teacher in his forties, had many sources of income both from inherited property and from other investments. Thirteen years prior, Mr. Bae had bought a small villa in Kangnam. Because of real estate inflation, the house's value had now increased a hundredfold. But he was not interested in selling it. He had also inherited family property in the countryside about three hours away from Seoul. A nonrelative was living in the family house and farmed the land and took care of the ancestral graves. In addition to this property, Mr. Bae bought property he used for rentals. About eleven years earlier, Mr. Bae had also started investing in securities and had made a fair amount of money. He said he, unlike his friends, knew about securities and investing because his major in college was economics.

Mr. Bae used his earnings from the money market for traveling abroad. I asked Mr. Bae about traveling kye. He said, "Oh, yes." He heard about men doing that also, although he did not; he didn't need to. He did participate in "something like a kye," though. Every other month he met with high school classmates. On alternate months he met with college classmates. At each one of the gatherings, which were usually held at a drinking establishment, each member contributed 20,000 wŏn (or roughly US$25). From that they bought liquor and had a social evening. Everything left over was kept in a kitty. One member of the group was elected to hold the money. Mr. Bae did it for a while, but then gave it up to someone else, seemingly glad to be relieved of the responsibility. With the money saved, various things were done. If someone had a family member die, the other members of the group would bring that member about 500,000 wŏn (or roughly US$625). When asked, Mr. Bae said that his wife had participated in kye a long time ago, but that he had asked her to stop because he did not think it was a good thing to do.

Case: The An Family

The final example is of a young corporate salary man who resigned from a company to work in the financial market. Before getting married, Mrs. An's husband worked two years for one of the chaebŏl. Two years before his marriage, he became a stockbroker. Earlier, as a salary man, he could not save any money. Now he worked on a commission basis and was apparently doing quite well.

Mrs. An had attended a women's teachers' university in Seoul. For seven years, up until two weeks prior to my meeting her, Mrs. An had worked for a multinational company. Married five years, Mrs. An at that time had a three-year-old son and was pregnant with her second child. As mentioned earlier, since becoming pregnant, Mrs. An had been suffering from severe morning sickness, and her husband and mother-in-law pressured her to resign. At first she did not want to, but now that she had, she was glad she did. She claimed that she might go back to work after having her second child. The Ans were presently renting a 32–p'yŏng apartment in Kangnam on the chŏnse system. They had also put down a substantial down payment (more than 50 percent) on an apartment in the southern outskirts of Seoul in a government program; they were making monthly installment payments while the apartment was being built. The apartment was expected to be completed and paid for in a year and a half, at which time they would move in.

Thus we see that families employed various strategies and relied not only on occupation but on property in its various forms (rural land, urban land, stocks, bonds, cash savings for private money lending, investment in kye, and so on) as sources of income needed to support a middle-class lifestyle. Many also depended on support from other family members, including, minimally, parents and siblings from both sides of the family. Because bank loans were generally not available, relying on family and these other means was important. Moreover, if the real estate and money markets remained flat, thereby threatening two of the most important ways families have been able to make money quickly, opportunities for social mobility would be more difficult, widening and solidifying the gap between the middle and upper-middle classes. In the following chapter we will examine kin networks and the support individuals received from their families.

3

Family

A great and universal curse in Korea is the habit in which thousands of able-bodied men indulge of hanging, or "scorning," on relations or friends who are better off than themselves. There is no shame in the transaction, and there is no public opinion to condemn it. A man who has a certain income, however small, has to support many of his own kindred, his wife's relations, many of his own friends, and the friends of his relatives.

—Isabella Bird Bishop (1970 [1898]:446)

One of the major ways industrialization was expected to weaken the traditional family was by undermining its control over its members. Modern development, it was thought, would provide new types of jobs and opportunities that would allow an individual to make a living without depending on resources controlled by elders (Goode 1982:179–181). But as it turned out, the income from salaries in South Korea has been insufficient to support a middle-class lifestyle there. Credit from banking institutions for personal use, moreover, even for housing and cars (which must be paid for in full at the time of purchase) or for investment capital for medium- and small-sized businesses, has been minimal and for the majority unavailable. Thus, for the Koreans of the 1990s, dependence on kin and long-term planning were essential if a family was to maintain middle-class status. The price for dependence was a certain control by those one was dependent upon.

With ancestry no longer the primary determinant of status, the assertion of status had shifted from being largely a matter of lineage to an effort more narrowly though not exclusively confined to the more immediate family, including grandparents, parents, children, and siblings. Although status continued to be asserted by many through the performance of lineage rites and the maintenance of genealogies, the power of lineages over at least its urban-based member families appeared to have declined. Among those lineages that

continued to perform rites, however, urban males were expected to participate, even if this required them to travel to another part of Korea. One man
told me that if he didn't attend, he would later have to explain himself in a
phone call he would be sure to receive. Some lineages have formed large associations in Seoul. When I told some Koreans I was interested in Korean
families, the lineage organization is what first came to their mind. For example, the Moons thought it important that I visit the head of their lineage,
who lived in a provincial town. They took me there to meet him. A university
student introduced me to a friend of his whose father and father-in-law were
both deeply involved in lineage affairs. This friend also provided me with a
copy of a publication his father had had printed regarding the correct performance of rites according to their lineage tradition.

With some lineages, there were also other benefits besides status that
could be had. For example, a lineage might help support a member through
school. Assistance from a woman's natal family, such as start-up money for a
business, might also be forthcoming. Although the patrilineage and a
woman's natal kin undoubtedly were potential and often real sources of various types of support, more research needs to be done in these areas. This
chapter will focus on closer relationships.

Unmarried Adult Children and Parents

Except when military obligations for young adult males required otherwise or
when young men or women went abroad to study, unmarried adult children
whose families were established in the city usually lived with their parents
until they married. This was true even if they worked, and even if they did
not marry until they were thirty or sometimes even older.

Upper- and middle-class males did not usually marry until after they had
completed not only their three-year military obligation but also at least four
years of college. Middle- and upper-class women, who also often pursued
higher education, generally felt they were still too young to get married when
they first graduated from college and waited a couple of years, sometimes
working in the meantime. By 1988, as more and more women enrolled in
higher education, the average age of women at the time of their first marriage
had increased to 25.3, up from 21.6 in 1960; for men, the average age had increased to 28.4, up from 25.4 in the same time period (KWDI 1991:9). In contrast, the migrant working-class women in Kim Eun-shil's study (1993:210)
began living with their husbands at an earlier age than the average age of
marriage.

It is true that by the 1990s neolocal residence upon marriage had become
the norm today among all classes. But because the marriage age, especially

among the middle and upper classes, was much higher than in the past and because children in the city continued to live with their parents at least until they married, the children remained under the direct authority of their parents perhaps for even longer periods than in the past, even if that authority might not be as strong as it was formerly.

Those unmarried children who were the first generation of their family to migrate to Seoul, of course, may have lived with more distant relatives, rented an "officetel" or efficiency apartment, rented a room in a private residence or boardinghouse, or lived in a dormitory if attending college. Alternatively, parents might buy a condominium (apartment) for their children attending school in Seoul to live in. Most parents who lived in the city would not consider it appropriate for their unmarried children to rent a room or live in a boardinghouse, the only affordable options normally available to a young person trying to live on his or her own. Young people also had to bear in mind that when they did marry, they would need help with housing. If they moved out earlier against the wishes of their family, they could not expect that help.

Unmarried university graduates often did feel constrained living with their parents or relatives. One woman in her early twenties complained about her parents' nagging. Both Miss Ko, who was thirty-three, and her friend Miss Han, who was twenty-eight, were unmarried and lived with their parents. Miss Ko, though, added: "But I intend to move out soon. It is difficult to live with your parents when you get older, but it is difficult to move out" because suitable housing is so expensive. The schoolteacher Miss Shim, who was over thirty, moved out of her parent's home after I returned from Korea. She said it was difficult to leave, but her move may have been an acknowledgment on her part that she would probably never marry.

Living with more distant relatives could be just as difficult. Many Korean-Americans, including other researchers, found it difficult living with relatives while in Korea because they felt every movement they made was watched. One Korean high school student sent to live with his aunt in the United States found it unbearable, because his aunt never let him go out and insisted that he study instead.

It is expected that relatives watch over their charges closely. A woman in her fifties had her sister's daughter, a university graduate, live with her for a while because the young woman's grandfather had moved into her room at home while the grandmother was in the hospital. After the grandmother died, the niece continued to live with her maternal aunt for a short time. One day her aunt got a call from her own mother. Her mother scolded this middle-aged daughter because the niece had not joined the family that morning to visit the grandmother's grave. The niece was absent because she had been out partying until late at night. The aunt felt she deserved her mother's scolding: she should have been watching her niece more closely.

Parents even tried to keep track of their unmarried children who were the first generation to migrate to Seoul and who were not living with relatives. This was especially true for girls. One college student who roomed with her sister told me that her mother called them twice every day, once in the morning and once in the evening. She felt her mother wanted to make sure they were not spending the night out or not getting home too late. There were occasions, however, when one covered for the other. For example, when her sister was out when her mother called in the evening, she would say that her sister was already sleeping.

These first-generation migrants to Seoul also returned home on occasion, although the frequency decreased after their freshman and sophomore years in college. Alternatively, the mother may have visited, especially during stressful times, to help out. One student who commuted to the university in Seoul lived with her two brothers in a condominium her parents had bought on the outskirts of the city. During exams, the mother came to help with cooking and other housekeeping. Whether a child visited his or her parents back in the hometown or one of the parents visited a child, food, such as kimch'i, a Korean staple of spicy, pickled cabbage or radishes, was usually brought to Seoul as another way of helping out and staying in touch.

Married Children and Parents

Since the 1950s there have been a series of changes in family laws (see also Lee Tae-Yong 1991) aimed at reducing the authority and responsibility of the head of the household. Under current South Korean family law, however, the eldest son still succeeds his father as household head only upon his father's death. Until then, although he may live in a separate residence, he cannot register to form a new household, even upon marriage. In contrast, younger sons must now legally partition upon marriage and form a separate household. But in fact a younger son and his wife may continue to live with his parents for a time. The practicalities rather than the legalities are what are important to Koreans as they live out their daily lives. The following case illustrates the possible complexities.

As noted earlier, when I first met Mr. Oh, he, his wife, and young daughter were living in his father's house in the Kangbuk region of Seoul; they had just moved back there a couple of months before. He and his wife had been required by his parents to spend their first year of marriage living with the older couple but then were allowed to move into their own apartment. They were compelled to move back to his boyhood home, however, after his mother had passed away. In fact, Mr. Oh, who was the eldest of two sons and a daughter, said he was criticized for not having moved back earlier while his mother was sick.

Even though the father subsequently moved out of his own house for personal reasons after Mr. Oh and his family moved back in, Mr. Oh did not pay his father rent. Furthermore, when the heating system broke down, the son expected the father, who had not yet retired, to pay for the repair. After all, Mr. Oh explained, it was his father's house and he should want to take care of it.

Mr. Oh's younger brother, who was five years his junior and a salary man for a medium-sized company, had just gotten married. He owned an apartment but was leasing it out. Because he could not afford to pay back the key money, Mr. Oh's brother and his bride moved in with Mr. Oh and his family. I first met Mr. Oh the evening before his brother was to return from his honeymoon. Mr. Oh was very nervous. Mr. Oh had invited many people over for a party for his brother and new sister-in-law for the night of their return. One of his concerns was what was going to happen the next morning: "Who's going to cook breakfast, my wife or his? What about money for the food? Should we split it 50/50 because there are two families or should it be 60/40 because there are three of us and only two of them?" "How old is your daughter," I asked. "Six." "Well, then, . . . she doesn't each much." "No, but she makes a big mess over the whole house!" So the conversation went.

Although current Korean law now requires younger sons to partition, that is, to register as a separate household upon marriage, because these two families were living together and household expenses were shared, this is a rare instance of a de facto joint family. I pointed out to Mr. Oh that I thought it was interesting that even though he was the older brother, he was not registered as a household head (because his father was still alive), whereas his younger brother was. Mr. Oh said that he never gave any thought to those legalities.

Before I left Korea, the younger brother had moved out. Apparently there had been a great deal of conflict between the sisters-in-law. For example, Mr. Oh's wife was very meticulous about recording every expense; the younger sister-in-law spent freely. Moreover, the new sister-in-law cooked food that was spicier than everyone else liked. Mr. Oh thought she should make food the way her husband (that is, his brother) liked it. But this new sister-in-law had never learned to cook under the guidance of her husband's mother, her mother-in-law, because she had died before the marriage. Mr. Oh pointed out to me that his own wife treated her new sister-in-law harshly, using the least respectful language with her. Mr. Oh said that he himself couldn't do that but rather used polite language with her. Mr. Oh's wife was the mistress of the house and effectively lorded it over her sister-in-law, much as a mother-in-law might have done in similar circumstances, especially in times past.

Before I left Korea, Mr. Oh's brother and wife moved to a small place north of Seoul, but within commuting distance of his job. In the meantime, his bride was supposed to be looking for a job and Mr. Oh was trying to convince his father to move back into his own house. The younger brother did return with his wife to the house where his elder brother resided in order to perform ancestor worship for their mother. Thus we see in this case that although both sons benefited from being able to live in their father's house without rent, when a conflict occurred between the two wives of the brothers, it was the elder brother and his family who were able to remain in the father's house. The elder brother, Mr. Oh, was still legally a part of his father's household and would inherit the house should his father die, succeeding his father as head of the household.

For a young adult, getting married was an expensive proposition. Except perhaps in the case of doctors and lawyers, among the middle class it was typically the groom's family who provided housing and the bride's the household furnishings as part of her dowry. With the typical salary of a university graduate hovering around US$15,000 and suitable housing so expensive, young people were dependent upon their parents both for the cost of the wedding itself and for setting up a household.

There were several possible arrangements. The newlyweds could live with his parents. Whether the eldest son lived with his parents or not, because he remained on his father's household register, the family took the form of a stem family upon an eldest son's marriage. (If the grandfather was still living, it would already be in this form.) Patrilocal residence for at least a short time after marriage was not at all unusual for both elder and younger sons; that is, it was not at all unusual for a family to de facto go through a stem phase residentially as well. Alternatively the groom's parents could buy an apartment for the newlyweds or provide key money to enable them to rent. In either case, this required tens of thousands of dollars.

Dowries for daughters had also increased substantially in recent years (see also Kendall 1985b, 1989, 1996). A *Newsweek* article commenting on the likelihood a daughter could pay her own dowry illustrates the common perception regarding marriage costs: "An acquisitive spirit seems to animate even the search for a spouse. Ambitious young brides-to-be often must lay out a *hansoo*, or dowry, of at least 100 million won ($130,000) to land that perfect doctor or lawyer. 'For that amount we have to save our earnings for over 10 years,' complained a young university graduate, Hur Kwang Hwa, in a recent newspaper column" (Emerson 1991:15). Of course, most brides did not marry a "perfect doctor or lawyer," and the expenses may not have been that high. Moreover, many women did in fact contribute to their dowry. (Kendall [1996] discusses this issue and marriage practices in general in great detail.) It is expected that the less financially able the families, the larger the contribution from the efforts of the young couple themselves and the lower the standard of living the young couple would enjoy. Both the Ohs and the Moons, who were in their thirties and had been married less than ten years, commented that the cost of both weddings and housing was not as great when they had married. A marriage that I attended while in Korea illustrates the generational differences.

As we saw earlier, though the Baeks' adult children earned money and spent it on their personal needs, none of them was required to contribute to the household expenses, not even the thirty-year-old son who had been working as an engineer since graduating from the university and who had been living with his parents until shortly after his recent marriage. Although Mr. Baek's parents had not paid for his education (at the Air Force Academy) or for his wedding, he had footed the bill for all his children's education as well as all the expenses for his son's marriage. His son's honeymoon alone, which was to Hawaii, cost over US$3,000. The son did not contribute anything. Mr. Baek also provided housing for the newlyweds. He owned a 36–p'yŏng apartment in another neighborhood in Kangnam that he had been renting out. The apartment was worth about US$175,000. Mr. Baek needed to pay back the renters' key money, which ran over US$100,000. Citing taxes, Mr. Baek did not turn the title over to his son at the time. Even though he moved to a separate residence, Mr. Baek's son, as eldest son and according to law, remained legally registered as part of his father's household. The economic as well as social ties remained strong. Mr. Baek's son would only become head of a household when he succeeded his father upon his father's death. The legalities of whether or not the son formed a separate household were of no practical concern to Mr. Baek. He said he let the experts worry about that.

With regard to the apartment, Mr. Baek told me that his son even asked him to pay for the remodeling that was to be done. The father said he agreed to pay half, with the young couple and the bride's family picking up the other half. I asked Mr. Baek what his son did with his money. He said, laughing, "He spends it on his wife these days!" (Later, though, his son did contribute a substantial sum as a gift toward a new car for his father. Although the mother had a new car to drive around, the father was reluctant to spend money on a new car for himself and had been driving an older car that was beginning to have many problems.)

Mr. Baek's wife told me that the bride's family was responsible for furnishing the home. Among other things, this included furniture, appliances, blankets, and the like. The bride's family also furnished the groom's family with clothes for the wedding, including material for hanbok, the traditional dress, which the mother of the groom (and bride) wore for the wedding. Mr. Baek's wife thought that while she herself was busy with wedding preparations, the bride's mother was even busier. I jokingly asked if the bride's mother was busy sewing; she answered in the negative, saying that the bride's mother in this day and age was busy shopping.

Kendall (1996) provides examples of families not represented here which do not contribute to a young couple's marriage. It is expected that the fewer assets the family has, the less the family contributes: a range of contributions, rather than a dichotomy in practices between classes, exists. Among lower-class families with little or no property, kinship ties are less extensive; nuclear households are less dependent on their kin and therefore elders have less control over their progeny. This point is illustrated by the following story from Kim Eun-shil's comparative study of middle-class and working-class women:

In Juntae's mother's story, the couple were mad at the husband's father because they thought their wedding had nothing to do with the father; the whole expense of the ceremony had been covered by the couple. However, the father brought up the idea of the traditional marriage ceremony to the woman's family. Juntae's mother thought that the proposal could be ignored but her natal family tried to save face in order to secure their daughter's position in the in-law family. That this couple had not visited the husband's family for four years since the event showed that the family in *Yakasan* was quite independent from family networks compared with the middle-class families. Compared with middle-class women, comments [from working-class women] about in-laws were not mentioned frequently. (Kim Eun-shil 1993:223)

Effectively, these lower-class families were in a situation comparable to that of their historical predecessors who, in contrast to the elite yangban, were legally prohibited from forming corporate lineages. Deuchler wrote that "because commoners did not form [corporate] lineages, their kinship system was less complex and less ritualized" (1992:13). Resources, rather than law, now seem to be the overriding factor.

Children and Elderly Parents

In later years, an eldest son may find others dependent on him. The oldest son by law is responsible for taking care of his elderly parents, though others may in fact help. In the early 1990s, while many elderly parents did live with one of their children and especially with the eldest son, many elderly people preferred to live on their own if they were able. Such independence was not always possible, however. Homes for the elderly were for the most part non-existent and in any case were not considered an acceptable alternative. Yet after living in separate residences for many years, it was often difficult for elderly parents to move in with an adult child, as the Chos' story illustrates.

Up until now Mrs. Cho's parents had lived on their own. Both of them had become sickly, however, and could no longer take care of themselves. The parents did not want to leave their apartment. The mother did not particularly like her eldest daughter-in-law. She didn't "pamper" her as did her youngest daughter-in-law, nor did she use the most respectful language with her. The eldest daughter-in-law, unlike the youngest, did not want her parents-in-law to move in with her, but her husband, the oldest son, did. Because of that, the mother said she and her husband must move in with her eldest son; she did not want to cause any bad feelings between the brothers.

Mrs. Cho, if she was able financially and physically, did not want to live with her children when she became old. Many expressed this sentiment. The lack of alternatives, however, should they not be financially or physically able, may leave them with no choice. For this and other reasons, many couples still had a strong desire to have a son. The strong traditional concern for a male heir to carry on the family line and to perform ancestor rites was another motivation. I was told by Mr. Oh that Mr. Soh wanted very much to have a son, which he did have after two daughters. When I made the comment to Mr. Soh that it appeared that having a son was very important to him, he responded, in English: "Who will worship me [if I did not have a son]?" I asked if he had no son whether he would consider adoption, the standard solution during the Chosŏn dynasty. His response was that he never thought of that before and wouldn't like that. Other families, I found, were not as concerned with having sons. Mr. Oh said that his daughter could perform ancestor worship and if he had a son (which he did shortly before I left Korea), both of them could do it. Others with only daughters said that their brother's son could take care of their ancestor worship without the need for formal adoption.

Eldest Sons and Siblings

Although an eldest son will be responsible for conducting ancestor worship for his parents (assuming the family is not Christian), his younger brothers will be required to attend ancestor worship services for their parents at their elder brother's home. Younger siblings may also find themselves dependent on their elder siblings, especially the eldest brother, if the father dies before they themselves are married and even afterward. Changes in Korean family law have reduced both the responsibility and the authority of the eldest son, especially over younger siblings, but many still felt obligated to assume the responsibilities. Mr. Ho is one example.

Mr. Ho, in his forties, began his career working as a salary man for a company. He was the eldest of several children. As is traditional though no longer binding, he, as the eldest, felt a responsibility toward his younger siblings when his father died. His salary was not enough to help them as he saw fit. So he resigned from his salaried position and started his own business importing furniture. He paid for his siblings' education (70 percent of the cost for his brother who went to the United States to study) and helped one of his brothers buy an apartment. His youngest brother was still unmarried, and he expected to help him with the cost of the marriage. Lowering his voice so that his wife could not hear, Mr. Ho told me, "If your wife does not approve, you cannot help your family as such." In order to prevent his wife from complaining, he took her on trips to keep her happy. Women, too, may have depended on their elder brothers. Some college-age women indicated that they looked to their older brother for advice. In at least one case the woman received money from her older brother for school even though her parents were living.

It was not always the eldest brother who provided. One college student said her father, who was a tailor, often served as an eldest even though he was second eldest, both solving problems and helping out financially, because he was more successful in his business. In another case, an eldest son migrated to the United States, became a professor, and married an American, abrogating all his rights and responsibilities when he left Korea. According to Professor Pak, his family "quickly retrieved" his younger brother from the States "and made sure he married a Korean." The brother apparently had done well. The professor, by his own admission, was quite unsettled. Some of his family was upset because he was not supporting his parents.

Older sisters might also help younger siblings. For example, the university woman who lived with her two brothers in a condominium outside of Seoul had an older sister who lived in the same apartment complex. The younger sister and brothers often went to their married sister's home to eat. Miss Shim, the thirty-something schoolteacher, was asked by her parents to give money to her struggling younger brother's family. Siblings in general continued to pool resources and help one another out as situations required even as the gender and age hierarchy became more relaxed.

That the authority of elder brothers and of elder siblings in general had diminished from the past was reflected in language. Many university students told me that before they entered college they used the more respectful language with their older siblings. But now that they were in college, they used less respectful language. Their parents did not always approve; nor did the older siblings. The twenty-eight–year-old Miss Han, whom we met above, commented on changes in language: "Things are changing so rapidly. When I was growing up, we always used honorifics with our older brothers and sisters. But today . . . [pause] . . . I have two nieces living in our house. They are quite young: six and eight. But one day I heard the younger one use nonhigh form and they kept on talking! The older sister did not even get upset!"

When Mr. Oh's brother and wife were living with him and his family, I asked Mr. Oh about the dynamics between him and his brother. When asked, he said that he thought that it was good that someone was in charge, but in fact he asserted little if any control. One particular occasion illustrates the point. It had been a family tradition on New Year's Day to stay up late playing cards. However, his new sister-in-law had wanted to put an end to the evening and was making it difficult for everyone else, who wanted to continue. Mr. Oh thought his younger brother should have expressed his wish: if he wanted to continue playing, he should have told his wife they were going to continue and that she shouldn't interfere; if he wanted to stop, he should have expressed that to everyone. But his brother said nothing. Mr. Oh did not think it his place to assert control over his younger brother and his brother's wife and also said nothing.

Eldest Sons and Eldest Daughters-in-Law

Although there had been a diminishing of the rights and responsibilities of an eldest son, distinctions were still made. Some college women cited their mother or aunt as advising them not to marry an eldest son because of the obligations he had to his younger siblings as well as to his parents. Although an eldest son had these responsibilities, it was often his wife who carried them out. She would be the one who actually cared for the elderly parents and the one who organized and prepared all the food for ancestor worship. In such ways the wife of a first son, the first daughter-in-law, also remained distinct from other daughters-in-law. A family's harmony often depended on the character and skill of the wife of the eldest son. This is illustrated by an aberrant case.

Mrs. Pak complained of her eldest brother's wife. As wife of the eldest son in a "Confucian family" and living with her parents-in-law, "she should be the pillar of her husband's family," according to Mrs. Pak. Yet the husband, the eldest son, felt that his wife, who was in her forties and had two college-age sons, had never come to feel part of his family. He believed that she felt an alien in his family and that she was unpaid for the services she performed for the family. She continued to identify more with her natal family. Traditionally, according to Mrs. Pak, by the time a married woman was in her forties she had undergone a change in attitude and saw her husband's family as hers. Despite the fact that this woman had come from "good yangban stock," her sister-in-law did "not know her position." Mrs. Pak felt that it would only be to this woman's advantage to act in the way expected. Moreover, it was unfortunate her sister-in-law was this way, because she was the wife of the eldest son. For now, her elderly mother kept harmony in the family, but she didn't know what would happen once her mother was gone.

Marrying an eldest son thus carried certain expectations and responsibilities not associated with younger sons. There were also other considerations a woman might take into account when choosing a mate. One female university student indicated that her older brother was authoritative and that she did not want to marry an eldest son because they were too accustomed to giving orders. Another said that she did not want to marry an eldest son because her parents had no sons, and as the eldest daughter she felt it her obligation to take care of her parents in their old age and to conduct ancestor worship for them after they passed away. If she married an eldest son, she and her husband would be responsible for two sets of parents and that would be difficult. She also noted that it might be difficult to find a younger son, since these days most sons were eldest sons now that most people had only one or two children.

There were also many who did want to marry eldest sons. Some felt they were more responsible. In these days of high housing costs, moreover, they stood to inherit his parents' home. In-sook wanted to marry an eldest son and live with her in-laws for five or six years, because that would be a good way to get to know how to do the domestic work; she also believed it was important to become intimate with her in-laws. In-sook did not want to marry a non-Christian eldest son, however, specifically one that conducted ancestor worship. She saw how much work her mother had to do because her father was an eldest son and they were responsible for ancestor worship. She did not want to do that. Now, though she was free to participate in the worship, she, by her own choice (because she was Christian, unlike the rest of her family), chose to limit her participation to helping her mother prepare the food, "and to eating it!" she added.

Daughters-in-Law and Parents-in-Law

Many daughters-in-law looked to their mothers-in-law for child care for their own children. Mrs. Kim warned that I must be careful in observing mothers-in-law living with their children as a continuation of the traditional pattern. She said that these days the reasons and circumstances were quite different. Today a daughter-in-law wanted the mother-in-law to live with her so that she could have the services of the mother-in-law; "a mother-in-law is much cheaper than a live-in maid." Now the mother-in-law worked for the daughter-in-law instead of the other way around, although this usually would not occur until after the daughter-in-law had her first child.

When Mr. Baek's son first got married, the newlyweds lived with his parents for about four months until their apartment was ready and until his mother returned from a trip to the United States. I was in the apartment one morning, shortly after they returned from their honeymoon, when the daughter-in-law returned from driving her husband to work. She had been wearing a skirt, but then changed into the traditional hanbok, bought by her in-laws as part of the exchange of gifts between families, and put on an apron. She wore this hanbok for a couple of weeks in the house.

The daughter-in-law attended to every need of her father-in-law, who said that although living together was difficult for all, he found his daughter-in-law very obedient and diligent at doing the housework. Even though the phone was right by his elbow, he did not answer it, as I had known him to answer it on other mornings before his daughter-in-law moved in. In tiny steps she circled the table to answer the phone, which was for him. When he indicated he wanted a banana, she got it, partially peeled it, and presented it to him with both hands. Another time, when I was with the mother-in-law, she giggled at watching her daughter-in-law serve her husband (that is, the daughter-in-law's father-in-law), saying it was nice to have someone else tending to him. In an earlier conversation before the wedding, however, she had indicated that she did not want to have her son and daughter-in-law living with them. She remembered how difficult it had been living with her in-laws. Her parents-in-law lived with them until they died in their old age. Her mother-in-law passed away in the 1970s, and her father-in-law lived into the 1980s. I also believe, though she was looking forward to having grandchildren, that Mrs. Baek was enjoying her new-found freedom that came not only with increased wealth but from not having the daily, around-the-clock responsibility of caring for either the elderly or the young.

When we went out to dinner one evening, I asked the newlyweds if they were anxious to move into their own apartment. The son said that because he was the only son he would be responsible for his parents and should continue living with them, but his parents wanted him to move out. He said that perhaps in two or three years they would move back in with his parents, though they did not know that yet. I asked his bride if she wanted to move back in with her in-laws. She left no doubt in my mind that she truly did. The daughter-in-law taught piano at an institute. If she had children and wanted to continue to work, she would have someone to take care of her children if she lived with her in-laws. In the meantime, they moved to their own apartment. Mr. Baek commented to me that the daughter-in-law was told to call her mother-in-law every morning, which Mr. Baek said she did. "They [his son and his son's wife] are very obedient," he added.

Husbands, Wives, and Household Finances

The general perception among Koreans was that the wife controlled the purse strings. Mr. Oh complained to me on more than one occasion that because he married right after he started working, he never had the opportunity to do what he wanted with his pay. For example, when talking with one of his former classmates whom he arranged for me to interview, Mr. Oh would say something to the effect of: "Mr. So-and-So is lucky. He worked for five months before he got married. He had the chance to spend his money as he pleased."

When I first arrived in Korea and was discussing my research with a Korean male professor, he offered his assessment of the situation of housewives: middle-class women were very, very busy, he told me. They participated in such activities as swimming, and it was they who did all the volunteer work. They were also involved in kye. Men brought home the paycheck, he went on to explain, and the women managed everything. Every morning the wives would give their husbands pocket money. During the day, restaurants, from the very poor to the very good, were filled mainly with women having a good time, he added.

Implicitly, this Korean gentleman was telling me that he thought middle-class women had it all: they controlled the money, but at the same time they were the ones out having a good time while their husbands were working for the money. Another man, formerly a professor but now a corporate adviser for a bank, was much more explicit. As a participant on a panel about changes in family relationships, he expressed his male perspective with a sense of humor:

On the surface, the housewife is subservient, deferential; she serves the meal. . . . [However], the change in the relationship of man and wife compared to thirty years ago is disturbing. But it will change into a better relationship in the future; this is not the end result.

Many who were poor in the sixties are well-off today. This has led to a change in the role of the housewife. . . . In the old days, the housewife had to struggle to make ends meet. Nowadays, when we see a housewife complain about incompetence—she is comparing it with those who are [more] successful—she feels she is responsible.

I see so many young men in their thirties hand over their [pay] envelope to their wives. There are very few exceptions. And then he negotiates with her to increase his allowance! I say to them: "Bankers! You are asked to handle billions [of wŏn] for our customers. I trust you! And you are telling me your wife is better to handle your money!?!"

If the husband and wife are equal and share responsibility as well as rights, it's okay. The problem is, once a young wife takes charge, she would allow you an allowance . . . and then pad up her expenses and put the money into savings. . . . She joins kye. . . . She's very good at it. She's the one who shells out the money. And then she says: "I did it!"

Conspicuous consumption is not the issue. There is a large group of people who have had a windfall [from land] or illusions and . . . spend. If [a man is] just salaried, a family can't do this. The problem is, there is no partnership. The man is thrown into a secondary relationship. This poor sop! It is the woman who has friends, money, et cetera. Responsibility and rights are completely flipped. The housewife enjoys enormous power without the responsibilities. She is not responsible for major decisions. A son looks toward his mother for guiding spirit. How can he? . . . I think Korean man will wake up, [though] he hasn't in the last five hundred years. The balances will return where husband and wife are equal.

As might be expected, a woman's perspective on the position of a housewife was often different from that of a man's. Some women said that the men did not want to be bothered with managing the family finances nor did they want their wives working, at least not in the formal sector. Mrs. An did not want to quit working, she said, but her husband and mother-in-law pressured her to quit. Her husband gave her his total earned money. She took care of all the money and admitted that she liked it that way. When she was working, she pooled her and her husband's pay, considering it as one. "My husband doesn't want to bother with it [that is, with the money] and probably doesn't know how much money we have," Mrs. An related to me. Mrs. An and her friend Miss Shim told me that it was typical for the wife to take care of the money in the household.

Moon Okpyo attributes the negative attitudes some men had toward taking care of money matters to attitudes traditionally held among the yangban when Confucian ideology held matters of financial business in low regard:

In some cases, especially in the families of government officials or scholarly pursuits, the ideology seems to direct the division of labour within the household in such a way that the husbands care for more noble business while the wives are supposed to look after the more mundane business of "earning money." This of course does not necessarily mean that men are less interested in raising the family's economic standing, but simply reflects the idea possibly rooted in Confucian heritage that it is unseemly for respectable gentlemen to be engaged in such business. This is why it is always women who are expected to visit real estate agencies or to utilize their own network when the family needs to borrow money from private sources. (Moon Okpyo 1990:36)

Despite the general perception that women controlled the purse strings, this was not true in all cases. We saw earlier that the schoolteacher Mr. Bae, who had his degree in economics and therefore, in his own words, knew more about economic matters, invested in the money market for years without his wife's knowledge. In this way, he financed his trips abroad, trips he took while leaving his wife home to take care of his elderly mother, holding out the promise to his wife that someday he would take her on a foreign trip. He also participated in kye while claiming to ask (order?) his wife to quit her participation in kye because he disapproved of them.

Mr. Baek also controlled his family's income, even calling himself a "tyrant" to describe his manner of control. He explained to me that since he had a master's degree in business administration, he was more qualified to handle the finances. He made good money, but his wife, he told me, had no idea how much he made. On more than one occasion he made the point that although he did not take any money earned by other family members to run the whole household, he kept tight control over the money he earned. I myself witnessed the following instance.

One evening, the evening before his wife was preparing to leave for the United States for a month-long music workshop, Mr. Baek was recommending to her that when she got to the hotel she should put her passport and money into the hotel's safety deposit box. She said that he should give her a credit card to take. He told her there was no way he was going to give her one. She was obviously not happy with the situation, but she was powerless to do anything about it.

Mr. Baek did not always win. One evening after returning from a cultural event, the family talked him into taking us out to an expensive Japanese restaurant. He voiced his objections, explaining to me that his family was always trying to spend money when he thought they needed to be more frugal. But he did concede and we ate well. (I do not know whether my presence made a difference.)

Just because a woman herself earned money didn't mean that she had control over the household finances, or even the money she herself made. Dr. Wang and her husband, for example, were both professors. The husband was the only son, the son of a line of eldest sons eight generations deep. The husband's father died early. The husband's mother, now in her late eighties, became very possessive of her son, who became something of a surrogate husband according to Mrs. Kim, a friend of Professor Wang. The husband and wife were never allowed to go out together and did not always even sleep together. Mrs. Kim tried to get them to go away for a couple of days, to get away from the mother-in-law. Professor Wang refused, saying she did not want to live with the consequences: her mother-in-law would treat her mercilessly.

Dr. Wang never enjoyed any privacy in her own home. Mrs. Kim mentioned that when she went there to visit, the mother-in-law sat right there with them, not allowing them to talk alone. Dr. Wang never saw any of her husband's pay. In fact, up until about five years ago, she herself had given her mother-in-law half of her paycheck. The other half she used to run the household. Professor Wang had never had anything for herself until two years earlier, when she bought her own car. Apparently the mother-in-law could not accept this. Dr. Wang's daughters, now grown, finally convinced their mother to move out. At the time, she was living with a friend. The daughters were taking turns cooking for their grandmother.

Children of middle-class families thus found themselves dependent upon their kin if they wanted to remain middle class. They depended on their families for their education, for their marriage, for setting up households, and perhaps even for capital to set up a business. In turn, the parents maintained considerable control over their children, even if less so and even if manifested in different ways than in the past. For those families who conducted ancestor worship, younger brothers continued to return to their father's house or to their eldest brother's home once the father was deceased. In such a way, the distinction of the elder brother and his wife were preserved. Moreover, younger brothers and sisters might come to depend on their older siblings for financial and other support as well. This would contrast with lower-class families, who were themselves struggling to survive and lacked the resources to help extended kin. Thus just as the yangban had a kinship system that was more complex and ritualized than that of the lower classes, still into the 1990s, the more assets the family had, the more complex its kin relations could be expected to be. With regard to husbands and wives, who had control over the household finances very much depended on the individual household. Nevertheless, it appears that in the majority of cases, the women were very involved in handling the money and even in increasing their families' standing through the manipulation of resources. But the fact that a woman earned money did not automatically translate into power within the household.

4

Lifestyles

For the unlettered gentry Chinese has no charm. They keep a few learned expressions at their finger ends, as a sort of bulwark of defence when hard pressed, but as far as possible they avoid the subject. Their life, since shut off from intellectual pleasure, consists of material pleasure, dress and enjoyment.

—James S. Gale (1975 [1898]:186)

During the Chosŏn dynasty, less tangible qualities such as a good family background, education, occupation, performance of ritual, and adherence to certain family behavioral norms were more important than material considerations in determining status, although one was often linked to the other. These more tangible markers of status, however, took on an added importance in status assertion for those yangban who lacked the educational criteria for high status. As we saw in Chapter 1, this led to more than one style of living among the yangban. In the Korea of today, where status is no longer legally defined or inherited and especially in the urban centers where not everyone knows everyone, conspicuous consumption has become an important means of asserting status regardless of educational level.

It is at the level of the household that consumption practices are most readily observed. Although standards of living change with the times, and such change has accelerated rapidly in South Korea since the 1960s, at any one point in time, household goods, the behavior associated with their use, and the type and even location of residence can all be indicators of class status (see also Bourdieu 1984). As with other means of asserting status, different patterns of consumption or lifestyles are observed among individual urban middle-class households in South Korea today. Differences may result from a wide range of variables, from individual household demographics and economic circumstances to individual household preferences.

A recent but recurring theme in consumer choice is the tension between traditional and modern patterns. Although differences among social strata have always existed, traditional forms of dress, housing, and household furnishings and activities remained the norm as late as the 1960s. Even with the advent of apartments, Western-style houses, and the availability of modern conveniences and foreign goods, traditional dress, houses, furnishings, and certain behavioral patterns, though often adapted to modern requirements, have far from disappeared. Even in the 1990s we find a mixture of traditional and modern elements both among and within individual households. This in itself is not surprising. The dichotomy between tradition and modernity, however, is not just a simple analytic tool used to explain modernization but, as we shall see, a complex construct in the minds of Koreans that was manifested in concrete aspects of everyday life. Depending on the circumstances, the quality of "traditional" or "modern" or "Western" could confer status.

A subtheme underlying the tension between tradition and modernity is the tension between the social and economic status of "being cultured" versus "being conspicuously rich." I found some among South Korea's present-day middle class who would still have preferred to follow the traditional pattern of placing the emphasis on cultural rather than on economic criteria when determining class standing or one's relative status. This preference was commonly found among those who came from former yangban families and especially among those who had not shared in the very recent financial gains made through the highly profitable real estate and money markets of the late 1980s. Many, for example, who had been pursuing graduate studies abroad during those years and who had only recently returned found themselves in this situation.

Many descendants of yangban families whose status in economic terms had been lowered vis-à-vis families with less prestigious backgrounds relied on more traditional symbols of status, such as a good family background, education, and occupation, in asserting their claim to high status. Many were content with achieving or maintaining their middle-class status through these more traditional means and did not get caught up in conspicuous consumption. Others, however, often criticized the ostentatious display of wealth and consumption by certain members of the new middle class even though their own standard of living on an absolute scale had increased immeasurably within the past generation. Of course, there were many Koreans who met both cultural and economic criteria for middle-class status.

Intertwined with this theme of "being cultured" versus "being conspicuously rich" (or social status versus economic status) were themes of practicality, preference, and even nationalistic pride. In some cases, one's status could be enhanced through ownership of certain modern or Western innovations that were still not universal but were highly desirable because they were more convenient than the indigenous alternatives. Other modern or Western-style goods such as certain types of furniture may or may not have been more practical but were nevertheless purchased for display purposes by some Koreans in pursuit of status because the qualities of "modern" and "Western" had themselves been assigned prestige value. At the same time, many other Koreans rejected certain recently introduced products, not on economic grounds, but because they were found to be less practical or less to one's own liking than the traditional. Indeed, some indigenous goods such as high-quality hanbok (traditional Korean-style clothes) have become more expensive than their Western counterparts and thus have themselves become symbols of status. With rising feelings of national pride coinciding with rising incomes in recent years, South Koreans have the choice of asserting their status by displaying such traditional forms over modern or Western ones. The fact that an earlier lack of national pride felt by Koreans was largely attributed to the country's "backwardness" may help account for the fact that the issue of tradition versus modernity has been so relevant in the Korea of the 1990s.

Status, of course, was not derived purely through possession of certain material goods. Associated behavior also played a role. Historically, up until about the 1960s when newer and Western-style housing was introduced into Korea, for example, the larger and more intricate the floor plan of the traditional house, the more able were its occupants to exhibit patterns of behavior that themselves were considered status-enhancing. As discussed in Chapter 1, such patterns of behavior included the physical segregation of the sexes within both the public and the private domains. This physical segregation of the sexes in turn affected the division of household labor between the sexes and thus helped define roles and relationships among various household members. The question then becomes: how have changes in the area of housing and consumption practices in general affected status-seeking strategies and family roles and relationships among the contemporary urban middle class?

Many of the changes in housing, household furnishings, and household activities do coincide with changing concepts of personhood and family roles and relationships. Although it is difficult to determine which is the cause and which is the effect, that the Koreans themselves perceived an association of a traditional physical environment with traditional behavior and a modern one with so-called modern behavior is well illustrated in the popular television soap opera *"Sarang'i mwogillae?"* or "What's Love?" The two contemporary, upper-middle-class fictional households featured in this drama (aired during my tenure in Korea) represent two extremes of a range of possibilities between a traditional, strongly hierarchical, patriarchal family living in a traditional Korean-style house with traditional furnishings and a household where relations between husband and wife and even between generations living in a Western-style house with Western-style furnishings are much more equal, or "modern" as Koreans themselves would call it.

Use of modern or Western-style houses and household goods, however, did not automatically translate to mean adoption of Western-style modes of behavior or family relations, although changes have occurred. Apartments and Western-style houses in South Korea look deceptively like those found in the West from the outside, yet the use of space inside along with relations among household members can be (and often were) quite different not only from Korea's past but also from the West, primarily because of different historical traditions and processes. We will now look at various aspects of housing and household activities in more detail, paying particular attention not only to how they reflected status but also to how they were used to assert status.

Seoul

> The heart of every Korean is in Seoul. Officials have town houses in the capital, and trust their business [in the countryside] to subordinates for much of the year. Landed proprietors draw their rents and "squeeze" the people on their estates, but are absentees living in the capital. Every man who can pay for food and lodging on the road trudges to the capital once or twice a year, and people who live in it, of whatever degree, can hardly be bribed to leave it even for a few weeks. To the Korean it is the place in which alone life is worth living.
>
> —Isabella Bird Bishop (1970 [1898]:60)

When I asked Koreans why they wanted to live in Seoul, their answers did not differ essentially from Moose's words pertaining to the capital city during the Chosŏn dynasty: "Truly Seoul is the soul of Korea. Here is the center of life, social, political, and otherwise" (1911:49). What was once described as "supremely a city of gentlemen" (meaning yangban) (Moose 1911:54) has now become a city of the middle class. Brandt (1983:8) notes: "What is most characteristic about the growing middle class [in South Korea] is the extent to which it is concentrated in Seoul." As of 1991, at least 61.3 percent of the whole population of South Korea and 62.3 percent of the urban residents considered themselves to be middle class (National Statistics Office 1991:307). One-quarter, or about eleven million of South Korea's almost forty-four million people, lived within Seoul's boundaries. Another 25 percent lived in the satellite cities surrounding the capital which have "for all intents and purposes become part of Seoul itself although they are still administratively distinct" (Ryu Choon-soo 1991:46, 47). (The vast majority of those who resided in the vicinity of Seoul commuted to their workplaces in the city [Hong Chan-shik 1991:77]). Thus nearly 50 percent of South Korea's population was concentrated in the greater Seoul metropolitan area, with more than 60 percent claiming middle-class status.

Within this greater Seoul metropolitan area distinctions were made, however between the middle class in Seoul and those outside Seoul. Those living in Seoul proper might claim to be the "real" chungsanch'ŭng or middle class. On the one hand, Kim Eun-shil writes: "Some people commented that the middle-class in Namyang are the people who were pushed out from Seoul; it means *Jungsancheung* [chungsanch'ŭng] in Namyang are not the same class of *Jungsancheung* in Seoul because they cannot afford housing in Seoul and, in general, are less educated than the *Jungsancheung* in Seoul. However, I do not take this kind of Seoul-oriented comment seriously," Kim continues, "because it usually meant the *Jungsancheung* in Seoul considers [itself] to be as a certain exclusive upper and upper-middle class" (1993:36). On the other hand, Kim's informants living in a satellite city of Seoul "described their position as middle-class and [even] as having more social consciousness and responsibility than other middle-class women, for example in Seoul." Some women told Kim that they "bought and ate Korean foods and used environmentally sensitive goods for national and social interests rather than their own economic interests," contrasting their own behavior with that of richer people such as in Seoul who ate foreign foods, "because there were no social sanctions" (1993: 37). Distinctions were also made between different neighborhoods within Seoul itself.

Neighborhoods

Around the North Palace [in Seoul] there are acres of tile-roofed houses which are the homes of the officials. This is where much of the "blue blood" of the city lives and dies. . . . Yonder in the distance inside and outside the great East Gate, we see the brown straw-thatched roofs that shelter the common people. There are also many of these humble houses to be seen in all parts of the city, and they are a sure mark of poverty, as no one cares to have a straw-thatched roof in the city if he can afford one of tile.

—J. Robert Moose (1911:59).

Just as certain residential areas of Seoul during the Chosŏn dynasty were dominated by yangban, certain areas of the modern capital are characterized as middle class. As I noted at the outset, when I first arrived in Seoul in 1991 and told people I was interested in doing research on Korean urban middle-class family life, the advice I received was "go to Kangnam." Initially having little knowledge of Seoul's geography and even less of its contemporary man-made subdivisions, I found *Kangnam-gu* marked on a city map. *Ku (=gu)*, I was to learn, are the largest administrative districts into which the city is divided, Seoul having been divided into twenty-two such districts at the time of my research. The smaller and older ku form the inner core of the capital. Newer and larger ku surround the core. Ku are further segmented into precincts or *tong (=dong)*.

Kangnam-gu was one of the larger and new districts south of the westerly flowing Han River now bisecting Seoul. In fact, the literal translation of "Kangnam" is "south of the river," *kang* meaning "river" and *nam*, "south." It was not until I became more familiar with Seoul that I realized that "Kangnam" had two broader connotations. The broadest encompasses all the districts south of the Han. A slightly more restrictive but more common use of the term referred to multiple, recently developed ku south of the Han, not just Kangnam-gu, which were associated with modern high-rise apartment complexes and the new middle class. It is this latter connotation that was being used when people advised me to go to Kangnam.

The term "Kangnam," I was also to learn, was used in counterpoint with "Kangbuk," the reference name given to the region of Seoul north of the Han, *puk (=buk)* meaning "north." (Koreans I asked who emigrated to the United States in the 1970s or before and who have not returned to Korea since were not aware of this distinction.) Thus the Han River now divides Seoul into the so-called Kangbuk and Kangnam regions. Moreover, "although the only thing truly dividing Kangbuk from Kangnam is the Han River," writes Professor Hwang Keewon of the Department of Landscape Architecture at Seoul National University, "the two areas have come to embody two diametrically opposed urban life styles and cultures" (1991:33), basically the old and the new, or the traditional and the modern. The reasons are historical.

In 1394, shortly after the founding of the Chosŏn dynasty, the capital of Korea was moved to Seoul, and it has been the center of Korean life ever since. At that time a walled city was constructed, encircled by mountains in the north and a great bend of the Han River some four miles to the south. While a few neighborhoods like Mapo, Ich'on-dong, and Yŏngdŭngp'o developed at ferry crossings, until the beginning of the twentieth century the population of the capital, which hovered around 200,000 at that time, remained largely within its ancient walls, above the flood plain of the Han. When the population began to expand, owing to geographical obstacles elsewhere, the principal direction of urban sprawl was to the south.

Within a few years after Korea became a Japanese protectorate (1905), the walls on either side of the South Gate were removed and industries, residential neighborhoods, and a Japanese military compound began to encroach onto the flood plain. In 1917 the first bridge for human and vehicular traffic across the Han River was erected near the ferry town of Yŏngdŭngp'o. Recalling the period of his residence in Seoul between the years 1926 and 1933, Horace Underwood wrote that the population of the city numbered around 300,000, "not even fill[ing] the area within the city walls, except in one or two places" and "spilling out a little ways" beyond the old walled areas "in only a few places" (1991:20).

Upon returning to Seoul in 1939 after a six-year hiatus, Underwood found that "tremendous changes had taken place" in paving of roads, building of bridges and railway lines, and in the appearance of "'modern' buildings" in the form of hotels and department stores. The ferry town of Yŏngdŭngp'o had further developed after the construction of the bridge in 1917 and by 1935 had become the industrial center of Seoul. Han River Bridge No. 1, the first modern road across the river, was constructed in 1939, providing continued access to Yŏngdŭnp'o.

After these initial changes, however, very little followed even in the infrastructure of the city for quite some time. By the end of the Japanese occupation in 1945, the population of Seoul had grown to around 900,000 and over the next five years increased further to 1.6 million as Koreans immigrated from what has become North Korea. What Seoul did have in the way of infrastructure was largely destroyed during the Korean War: "We so easily forget the past that I must mention one more period: Seoul from 1950 to 1955. Few today remember, and probably fewer realize the implications of the fact that Seoul was some 75 percent destroyed during the Korea War. . . . Whole sections of the city were nothing but mounds of ruins where fire and shells had swept through whole districts" (Underwood 1991:26). Han Bridge No. 1 as well as the railroad bridges were destroyed. All but 50,000 of its inhabitants, mainly the elderly and the ill, evacuated Seoul during the second Communist invasion. After the war, many returned, but the population had shrunk to about one million. "It was a gutted darkened city to which they returned, and until 1962 most efforts had to be directed toward reconstruction and recovery, rather than new growth" (Bartz 1972:123). It was not until 1958 that the Han River Bridge No. 1 was rebuilt and not until 1965 that a second road bridge, Han River Bridge No. 2 , was in place, linking Seoul with Kimpo Airport to the southwest.

By the early 1960s, coinciding with the country's rapid economic growth, the population of Seoul had increased threefold from its post–Korean War total to three million people. Although areas south of the Han River had been incorporated into the city by this time, it was not until the early 1970s after the opening of Han River Bridge No. 3 and the completion of the Seoul-Pusan Expressway in 1970 that the development of Kangnam south of the river had began in earnest. Flood control measures were also a precondition for expansion into the original flood plain.

The development of Kangnam was part of a larger government plan aimed at reducing the population pressure in Kangbuk. (Satellite cities surrounding Seoul were also constructed to this end.) Prior to 1970, only 20 percent of Seoul's population of five million lived south of the Han River when Seoul was divided into only nine ku. By 1992, a short twenty-some years later, Seoul consisted of twenty-two ku, nineteen bridges spanned the river, and more than half of the capital's ten million plus citizens lived in the Kangnam area (Ryu Choon-soo 1991:47). (Another nearly ten million resided in the satellite cities.)

Initially people were reluctant to move to Kangnam, which was desolate at the time. The government provided educational and economic incentives. Among Koreans there is a strong-held belief that graduating from a prestigious university will lead to success and that admission to a prestigious university depends upon graduation from a prestigious high school. Capitalizing on that belief the government early in the 1970s moved many of the top high schools (or at least their names) and teachers to Kangnam. In pursuit of status, people took the bait and the popularity of these schools increased. It was not only the already well-off who moved to send their children to these schools. Rather, "informal analysis indicated," according to Hwang Keewon (1991:31), that a significant factor in this growth in popularity of the relocated schools "was the attitudes of parents who were less well educated and therefore wanted their own children to enjoy the fruits of success and status they themselves lacked." Those who bought housing in Kangnam early on were to find that their investment led to financial gains as well.

The government policy to attract people to Kangnam by relocating schools was so successful that a housing shortage soon resulted. Government policies favorable to building contractors and to the middle class led, by the late 1980s, to land speculation that doubled investments overnight. Excess capital was funneled profitably into the stock markets as well. Hwang Keewon's critique of the effect this speculation has had on the Korean people well depicts the stereotypic image held by many Koreans of Kangnam and its inhabitants. Hwang's portrait highlights, with moralistic overtones, the effects land speculation had on lifestyle, family, and consumption practices and at the same time describes what had become new symbols of status, even if what he describes are the extreme cases rather than the average. His disdain for economic status symbols over cultural ones is obvious. The Kangnam lifestyle is perceived as one of a life of leisure:

An unprecedented surge of extravagance and pleasure-seeking has followed hard on the heels of this speculative frenzy, gradually eating away at the social environment of the Kangnam boomtown. Not only can many speculators give up their regular jobs, but many nouveau riche with little culture or education have no idea how to use their new found wealth in a constructive or healthy manner. They loll in bed pondering their account books and then step out for a sauna or a couple buckets of balls at the local golf range before they stop off for a sumptuous feast at their favorite lounge. Their thirst for excitement and novelty isn't easily satisfied, and as a result, Kangnam has become a mecca for luxurious restaurants, extravagant clothes shops and exotic entertainment establishments. (Hwang Keewon 1991:32)

The Kangnam family is perceived as disintegrating as conspicuous consumption becomes rampant:

The male family heads aren't the only ones indulging themselves. The degeneration of wholesome family life in Kangnam has been kindled by nouveau riche housewives who leave the housework and family concerns to their maids and their children who spend their free time partying with their friends. The complete liberalization of government restrictions on travel abroad has also fanned the consumption binge by heightening interest in foreign goods and ways of life. Indeed, the Kangnam core neighborhoods of Apkujong-dong [identified universally by Koreans in the early 1990s as the most extravagant], Shinsa-dong, Panbae-dong and Chongdam[-dong] now rival the glitz and glamour of Hollywood, Piccadilly or Tokyo's Sinjuku [sic]. (Hwang Keewon 1991:33)

Living in Kangnam itself has become a status symbol:

All Seoul's major department stores, restaurants, shoe stores and clothing shops have moved their main branches to the Kangnam area in order to take advantage of the area's vast consumer appetite, and now we are witnessing a similar trend among the capital's educational and sports facilities, galleries, theaters, book stores, and even churches. While government restrictions on the construction of new buildings and facilities that might lure people to the Kangbuk area and administrative guidelines permitting the construction of larger homes south of the river certainly contribute to this mass exodus to Kangnam, a more significant cause is most certainly the fact that there is more money, more power and more educated people to be found in Kangnam. (Hwang Keewon 1991:33)

So stark was the dichotomy perceived between Kangnam and Kangbuk and their contrasting lifestyles that such exaggerated comments as this were elicited among my informants: "A Kangnam woman cannot marry a Kangbuk man, because the woman is used to spending money and the man isn't. It would be disastrous." This informant also added that the amount of spending by those in Kangnam was sometimes sickening, though she herself lived in Kangnam.

Many of my own observations seem to support this image of two different lifestyles separated by the Han River, though not as extremely as Hwang would see it. Dress provides an example. Many of the women I came across in Kangbuk, home to a mixture of classes, dressed in what my American-trained eye would judge to be uncoordinated blouse and skirt or baggy pants outfits, clashing (in my mind) in both color and pattern. Once having moved to Kangnam, where the middle and upper classes are concentrated and form the majority, I was struck by the absence of such combinations except on the few street cleaners, street vendors, and maids I ran into. Most women I came across seemed to be very stylishly dressed.

I attribute this particular difference in style largely to class differences, the lower classes being unable to afford the latest of Western fads, and perhaps to age, as older women may have also dressed this way. However, I also observed differences among the middle class. Except for those living in the most expensive, Western-style homes, those in the north tended to be much more casual in dress than in the south and even less formal in their interaction with me, especially when comparing early stages in the relationship. At the first appointment I had with Mr. Oh, I was surprised when he came to the hotel lobby where we agreed to meet dressed in jeans. He lived in northern Seoul. When he and his wife took me to the first appointment at which he had arranged for me to meet with two other families of coworkers on the outskirts of northern Seoul, they were also casually dressed. Mrs. Mok told me she hadn't started wearing makeup until she moved from Kangbuk to Kangnam; there, because all the women in her complex wore makeup, she felt compelled to do the same.

This very broad generalization that people in Kangbuk tend to be less formal than in Kangnam seemed to hold, although by 1996, those in Kangnam also seemed to have become more casual. In formal situations, however, such as going to work, there were no differences. Among males, a suit, tie, and dress shirt at work were standard indicators of at least middle-class status regardless of residential location, just as uniforms were indicative of those working in blue-collar jobs. Although there was a distinct style of dress associated with the poor, there were no discernible differences in style between the middle and the upper classes.

Differences in dress were not the only things I noted between Kangbuk and Kangnam families. Differences in attitudes and outlook were also apparent. For example, after living in Kangnam for a while and hearing so much about and seeing so much conspicuous consumption, I was beginning to believe that all middle-class Koreans were of that nature. That preliminary conclusion led me to make incorrect assumptions and ask wrong questions on that first interview with the families in the northern outskirts of Seoul. My field notes read:

The Sohs have lived in their present apartment for approximately one-and-a-half years. I made the wrong assumption that they moved because the present apartment was better than the first. So when I asked what was better about the present apartment over the last, the question didn't make much sense to them. So I asked why they moved. Mr. Soh said: "It's hard to explain. We rented, just like we do here. The landlord at the other place wanted to move in." Again I made another wrong assumption, assuming they would like to move to something better when I asked them what things with regard to housing would he like to have that he doesn't have now. I tried to clarify my question by asking about what he would look for in a future move. He just shrugged his shoulders and said: "Why move? I have everything I want."

What I may be running into is the difference between the Kangbuk and Kangnam areas with regard to consumption. I had already noted to myself the casualness of dress I found amongst these three families of the Kangbuk area. When I mentioned the cost of living and inconsistency between salary and spending especially in the Kangnam area [I was not yet aware that such a high percentage of income was non-salary], unlike discussions with others about the high cost of living, I drew blank looks and elicited no [other] response.

Mr. Oh stated that he thought Kangnam was more upper than middle class. Judging by their reactions when I told them I was living in Kangnam, so did many other Koreans living north of the Han River. Even though many Koreans made such generalizations as "the established middle class live in Kangbuk and the nouveaux riches live in Kangnam" or "only older middle-class Koreans can afford to live in Kangnam," in reality the dichotomy between Kangnam and Kangbuk (or the differences with the satellite cities) was not so clear cut. Notwithstanding the differences in lifestyles observed between Kangbuk and Kangnam, on both sides of the river (and in the satellite cities) resided those of all family backgrounds, occupations, educational levels, ages, and attitudes. An individual may have spent part of his or her life moving between the two sides, and stereotypes notwithstanding, there were even marriages between men and women that came from opposite sides of the river.

Even though the Kangnam skyline is dominated by a sea of middle- and upper-class apartment high rises extending as far as the eye can see (contrasting with Bishop's description of late nineteenth-century Seoul as a "sea of low brown roofs" [1970 (1898):60]), a closer look revealed a variety of not only housing structures but also class. Just a few steps outside the perimeter of my high-rise apartment complex I was surprised to find smaller apartment buildings, villas, and even individual homes, a few quite old and now poor looking and some quite modern and exclusive. I was even more surprised to find after living in this area for several months that behind a wall of flower shops that I passed regularly on the way to and from the subway was a community of several hundred people sheltered in shacks. (It took a fire for me to realize what was so well hidden; even though the village was rebuilt, the squatters were shortly afterward forced to vacate the area.)

Just as Kangnam was much more than nouveaux riches living in modern, high-rise apartments, Kangbuk too was more than one-story, single-family residential areas of traditional, mixed, and Western-style houses. Apartment complexes, especially on the outskirts, but also villas and duplexes were part of the complete picture. Moreover, it was not only property owners in Kangnam that benefited financially from land speculation. Prices in Kangbuk also had risen dramatically, as a professor pointed out while showing me around the affluent Yonsei University district north of the Han. As we were walking past an area where there was housing for professors, she mentioned that the housing itself wasn't very good but that now the professors who owned them were very rich because of the drastic increases in land prices.

Although generalizations are useful, South Korea's urban middle class was a diverse and complex group of people. To understand South Korea's urban middle class as a whole, I decided it was important to include in my study families from Kangnam, Kangbuk, and even the satellite cities, where a very significant percentage of South Korea's working population commutes to Seoul on a daily basis.

There were many reasons why a family may have chosen or preferred or even have been "forced" to live on one side or the other of the Han River, or alternatively in a satellite city outside of Seoul proper. Most would have preferred to live in Kangnam because of the schools, the lifestyle, and the status. Kangnam was newer, cleaner, had more amenities (not only with regard to schools and housing but also with regard to modern department stores, health clubs, and so on), and, being more expensive, was more prestigious. A fear of not being able to escape south of the Han River should North Korea invade South Korea again was another reason cited by more than a few for preferring to live in Kangnam.

Preferences aside, a household's economic situation dictated one's choices to a large degree. Comparable housing was generally cheaper in Kangbuk because it lacked many of the modern amenities and facilities that Kangnam offered, and also because of its closer proximity to North Korea (that is, because Kangbuk was on the same side of the Han River as North Korea, North Korea being less than thirty miles away). Satellite cites, though requiring longer commutes to places of employment and to the cultural, educational, and commercial facilities concentrated in Seoul, offered the conveniences of modern apartment living at a considerably reduced cost when compared with Kangnam; they were therefore very popular with the young who would otherwise not have been able to afford housing that was considered suitable for the middle class.

Housing

Home Ownership

Landowning was one of the characteristics of the elite yangban, and for many Koreans home ownership itself, no matter the locality, had become a true test of having attained middle-class status. Professor Pak found this out when he returned to Korea about a year and a half before I met him after having lived several years in the United States. Discussing my research, Dr. Pak asked me how I was defining "middle class." Before I had a chance to answer, he exclaimed, somewhat exasperated: "When I first came back to Korea, all anybody was talking about was how many p'yŏng [square feet of housing] they owned, how many cars they owned, et cetera! By some Koreans' definition, I couldn't be middle class because I don't own a single p'yŏng!"

When I quoted to another professor recent statistics which stated that some 50 to 60 percent of South Korea's population considered themselves to be middle class, her response was: "But how can they be? They don't own their own place!" However, Dr. Lee's next statement revealed that even in her own mind there existed a tension between using social and economic criteria to define one's status: "Today there is much [social] mobility," she continued. "Both upward and downward. Because my husband and I are both Ph.D.s, socially, we are upper class. However, we are not even middle class economically." Until recently, they had been renting a very small apartment until they managed to borrow enough money from family and others to buy. "We own our own now, but we now have all these debts to pay off!" she exclaimed.

Part of the prestige of house ownership in urban South Korea was derived from the fact that housing was so expensive, almost ten times the average income in 1991 according to the Korea Research Institute for Human Settlements (as reported in Park Chang-seok 1992:1). Moreover, the housing generally had to be paid for before a family moved in. As Professor Lee put it, "You have to be rich to own your own place in Korea." But ownership was more than price. "It is different from the U.S.," she continued, "because you have to pay all the money up front. Buying one house here is like buying a hundred in the States, that is, [in the United States] you could buy that many because you have to put only a little down on each one."

Obviously this comparison did not take into account that a buyer in the United States would have to demonstrate an ability to make payments on all those houses. But the comparison did underscore the point that because bank financing for housing of any kind was very limited in South Korea and a buyer had to have considerable resources, including social capital, to pay the total purchase price in advance, home ownership was a very real indicator of at least a certain socioeconomic status. As noted earlier, even leasing a place usually required an initial up-front lump sum payment called chŏnse, or key money, equal to one-third to one-half or more of the purchase price. Although the landlord returned the key money when the lease expired (keeping the high interest earned from investing the key money in the lucrative private money market or elsewhere during the lease), it was no small burden for the renter to come up with such a large lump sum required for housing suitable for the middle class, even if no additional rent was required. Thus many people still considered themselves middle class, especially if they met other educational and occupational criteria, if they could afford even to lease suitable housing. In other words, the type of housing one lived in was also a statement of status. Just what was suitable housing for the middle class?

Types of Housing

The stereotypic image of South Korea's contemporary middle class included not only residence in Kangnam south of the Han River but also life in a high-rise apartment complex. By the late 1980s, high-rise apartment complexes dominated the Kangnam skyline and were also found in the northern outskirts of Kangbuk and in the satellite cities. They first appeared on the scene only in the late 1960s. Lee Hyo-jae's 1967 survey (1971) of three middle-class neighborhoods in Seoul and Bartz's work on the geography of South Korea (1972) are valuable for their descriptions of the housing situation in Seoul at an intermediate point in time. These sources describe the housing situation after Seoul had recovered (physically) from the devastation of the Korean War and had become a modern industrialized city of approximately five million people (an increase of more than 800 percent over its 1945 population), but just before the government push in the 1970s to develop and further expand Seoul south of the Han River.

By the time of Lee's survey, the middle class, according to Lee (1971:12), had become the dominant group in Seoul, making up about two-thirds of the population. The three neighborhoods surveyed exemplify the various types of middle-class neighborhoods of the time: an apartment house community, one of the first in South Korea; a relatively new suburban district with newer, "mixed-style" houses; and a long-established neighborhood in the center of Seoul with traditional Korean houses built during the Japanese occupation to replace older decaying structures. Concrete block and bricked exteriors may have replaced the wood and wattle and daub construction still found in rural and urban poor areas; tile roofs were replacing thatched ones (see also Spencer 1988:44). Moreover, in the 1950s, coal briquettes replaced firewood for cooking and heating fuel. Bartz provides a succinct description of these three types of housing arrangements occupied by the middle class around 1970 and notes the differences among them. Apartments were very new to the scene:

Aspects of Seoul's past are reflected in its present geography. A housing pattern designed to cope with the crowded conditions within the city walls persists over large sections of the city today. Each house has its own wall, wedged into a maze of neighbouring walls, all reaching up to the eaves, with narrow winding alleys between. This style of construction has the advantage of giving, in a minimum space, maximum privacy and living space for individual family dwellings. Only recently has there been a break with this tradition. In modern suburban housing developments, each house has a walled yard, but the front of the house abuts the street, giving a street and block pattern. Problems of water supply and construction in the past kept housing to lower elevations. In the late sixties, the city government began to utilize the hillsides for apartment buildings. (Bartz 1972:119–120)

Many of the upper class of the time lived in modern, two- or three-story brick houses averaging 78.4 p'yŏng (or almost 2,800 square feet). At the opposite extreme, war refugees and rural migrants were living in slums, "the dwelling here [being] the epitome of poverty and disease," offering "only the most minimal shelter" (Lee Hyo-jae 1971:29). Even among the middle class, housing shortage was a major problem. The living space in the traditional-style dwellings of the long-established middle-class neighborhood surveyed by Lee Hyo-jae averaged 16.8 p'yŏng or about 600 square feet. Multiple family occupancy was high (in almost 50 percent of the cases), with as many as six households under one roof. This reduced the average space per household to 10.1 p'yŏng or about 360 square feet (1971:30).

In the new suburban neighborhood surveyed by Lee in 1967, only 1 percent shared housing. The so-called *kungmin chut'aek* or "people's houses" built along well-arranged streets are what Lee terms "mixed-style," because they have a mixture of the advantages of modern and traditional houses. (Lee Hyo-jae [1971] provides floor plans of typical middle-class housing of the time.) These single-family houses ranged in size from about 15 to 18 p'yŏng or about 530 to 640 square feet. Although they had an indoor toilet and a private bathroom, the bathroom and water were unheated. To supplement sponge baths taken at home, most also frequented the public bath house, which offered heated rooms and preheated water, a couple of times a month (Lee Hyo-jae 1971:34–38). These newer-style houses boasted a separate living room in addition to rooms used for sleeping. Bedroom floors were heated by an ondol floor heating system.

The apartment blocks in Lee Hyo-jae's study were built in the early 1960s just north of the Han River. According to Lee (1971:39), when they first appeared, these units held great appeal for the young, small family. The grounds sported a spacious garden, including a fountain, manicured lawns, paved sidewalks, and slides and swings for the children, and the apartments thus presented a very clean and spacious appearance. The living space per household was 13.8 p'yŏng or about 490 square feet, "not crowded by Seoul standards" (1971:41).

Most of these apartment units had an extension telephone. The kitchens were equipped with a sink, garbage chute, and water closets. Housekeeping was considered relatively easy, except that the storage of coal briquettes not only took up space but also dirtied the kitchen. There were actually two types of buildings: "one designed for western living, with individual heating and a hot-water system in the interior of the X-shaped, one corridor building, and another for the traditional Korean life, with an improved *ondol* floor heating system and community stairway which guarantees relative privacy" (1971:39). Lee adds that a central heating system and elevator would have improved the health and comfort of the residents.

Less than 1 percent of Lee's informants liked living in apartments. She attributed this dislike to three factors: apartments were not suited to a traditional lifestyle; Koreans wanted to own real estate which, of course, was not possible with apartments; and "since many households live in the same building, each family is conscious of having its living standards exposed to the scrutiny of immediate neighbors." Roughly 60 percent in the survey stated they would prefer Western-style accommodations, 25 percent the combined kungmin style, and another 14 percent the traditional style (Lee 1971:41).

By the 1990s, high-rise apartments were the type of housing most thought of as characteristically new middle class. In fact, according to statistics (Seoul Metropolitan Government 1993:144–145), at the time of my research 34.9 percent of all households in Seoul lived in so-called *ap'at'ŭ* (apartments) or what Americans would call condominiums because they are individually owned. Because they owned their unit, most owner-occupants of these apartments would likely have considered themselves middle class. There were some high-rise apartments that were called *imdae* apartments and whose occupants were generally not considered middle class. "Imdae" literally means "rent" or "lease," but in this case it is more like a mortgage in the United States, with some differences. The occupants make monthly payments usually for five or ten years if the high-rise is built by a general construction company or twenty if built by the government. After that period of time, they become the unit owners. Only those who did not own other housing were eligible for this arrangement, and they could not sell it before they had paid the full amount due. Those units built by the government were limited to less than 25 p'yŏng. Those built by construction companies had no size limit, but also tended to be smaller. The city government also built high-rise apartments with limited p'yŏng that were not imdae but were sold by lots like middle-class apartments. (See also Han Do Hyun 1997.)

The *tasaedae chut'aek* or *pilla* (villa) housing, occupied by 7.5 percent of Seoul's households, were another type of housing. Villas are characterized as individually owned apartments units, usually with separate entrances, in two- or three-story buildings. There were exclusive villas owned by the upper class. The villas owned or occupied by the middle or lower class, however, were less popular and thus less expensive than living in high-rise apartments. The term "villa" was sometimes also used to refer to tenement houses, technically called *yŏllip chut'aek*. These tenements were home to 8.6 percent of Seoul's households and were generally associated with lower-class living. There were also duplexes among these tenement houses and villas.

Almost half of the total households (48.7 percent) lived in "detached dwellings," including Western-style, mixed, and traditional. Unfortunately, the statistics do not distinguish among these very different forms of housing. As of the early 1990s, traditional-style Korean houses were no longer being built; in fact, they had not been for decades, and were quickly disappearing from Seoul's neighborhoods, largely abandoned by the middle class. Those that were left were occupied primarily by the lower classes and members of the marginal lower-middle class. For example, a Korean-American teenager staying in Korea for the summer with her grandmother, aunt, and aunt's young son related to me that they were living in a traditional house, with no chairs or Western-style beds or running water for a shower, though the toilet had been modernized. Her grandmother, aunt, and cousin just recently moved into this house. Her aunt was divorced, which she noted was rare in Korea. Her aunt was taking care of the grandmother, who was ninety-three, because her grandmother's other children all had their own families.

With no male adult, an elderly woman, and a divorced woman raising a son, this household was unquestionably marginally middle class. Indications that the family was experiencing downward mobility and that at one time it had been at least middle class are that at least one son, the father of my informant, was an engineering graduate of Seoul National University; he had emigrated to the United States where he owned a restaurant. In addition, an older cousin of the girl had been able to buy a house between five and ten years earlier when he first married, but another cousin who had recently married had to rent because the price of housing had gone up so much.

A few larger homes of former yangban families could be found scattered around, maintained and occupied by middle- or upper-class families. Underwood noted that most of the elaborate mansions of the yangban families with their "intricate arrangement of rooms and courtyards and corridors that made up almost palatial homes" had disappeared during the Japanese colonial period, and for the time period between 1926 and 1933 the "bulk of the city houses . . . were those of the poorer classes, usually 'U' or 'O' shape" (Underwood 1991:24; see Figure 1 below). A son-in-law of a prominent scholar related to me that the traditional house of his father-in-law was becoming something of an anachronism in its neighborhood in north Seoul. The rooms that had served as servants' quarters in times past were now rented out. There were also a few neighborhoods where traditional houses were protected by law and preserved and inhabited by middle- and upper-class families.

While it was mainly the lower and lower-middle class who lived in traditional-style houses, at the opposite extreme, many upper-middle- and upper-class households lived in Western-style houses. Characteristically large, two- or three-storied brick or stone structures surrounded by a wall and boasting central heating systems, Western bathrooms and kitchens, and built-in garages, Western-style houses were the best Korea had to offer in the way of housing. Although the statistics do not make a distinction, Western-style houses could be presumed to form a small percentage of the total "detached dwellings." Most Koreans consider these large, Western-style houses beyond their reach. So when I asked, most Koreans, in contrast to what Lee Hyo-jae found in her 1967 survey (1971:41), said they preferred to live in the newer, high-rise apartment complexes.

Apartments built later were very different from the apartments built in the 1960s, offering more creature comforts than the aging mixed-style and traditional houses. Furthermore, by the 1990s apartments were worth so much that ownership had become a symbol of status even without land. Even many of those who could afford Western-style homes opted for a high-rise apartment, which had more appeal than duplexes and the more modestly-priced villas.

Koreans preferred high-rise apartments over other forms of housing for several reasons beyond prestige. Security was one. Theft from homes was a concern, and Koreans liked the idea that they could lock the door to their apartment and walk away without much fear. Although apartments were not immune from crime, the nature of the structure and the presence of security guards greatly reduced the probability.

High-rise apartment buildings in Seoul were built around the concept of the "complex" (*tanji*), defined as "a self-contained compound surrounded by a fence inside which one can find a group of buildings of similar function and design" (Hwang Keewon 1991:29). If not completely fenced off, at the very least the apartment buildings were so arranged as to form a limited-access enclosure (with much of the open area used for parking) that could be readily monitored by security guards. Security guards were generally posted around the clock in guard rooms, one each located at every entrance of an apartment building. This arrangement also allowed close monitoring of who was coming into and going out of the buildings themselves.

Security guards provided other services to apartment residents as well. I myself have witnessed these men help carry groceries, repot plants, babysit latch-key kids, bandage a tot's cut finger, help an older child with his bike, take messages, and provide an ear for complaints and gossip. They also shoveled the snow, sorted the mail into the individual mailboxes, and operated an in-house switchboard and public address system. In short, these men were more than security guards. They were like servants who were grossly underpaid and often taken for granted. In addition to the guards, women were hired to clean the hallway, stairwell, and elevator areas. (Unlike the first apartments built in the 1960s, elevators have become standard; by law, however, elevators in the early 1990s generally did not stop at the second and third floors in the name of energy conservation.)

Garbage collection was another reason often cited for preferring to live in apartment complexes. In the older Kangbuk neighborhoods, the human-drawn garbage cart making its rounds was still a common sight. This scene was a sharp contrast to the large, modern garbage trucks that came to the apartment complex to empty huge dumpsters located in the parking lots. In accordance with a new law, recycling bins for paper, glass, and metal were also placed on the grounds of apartment complexes.

Generally there were playground areas in apartment complexes, but they were very limited in size. More often than not I saw children rollerblading, bicycling, and otherwise playing in the parking lot rather than in the area designated for play. Nevertheless, these apartment complex parking lots were considered by at least one woman safer for play than the very narrow streets found in older Kangbuk neighborhoods.

Mrs. Moon complained about living in a duplex in Kangbuk. One of her complaints centered around the congested streets and lack of playground area for her children. Because of the reckless traffic, the streets were dangerous for the children to play in (though it did not stop them). Mrs. Moon was afraid to buy her daughter a bike, though she was pleading for one, because of the traffic. Mrs. Moon wished she could live in an apartment in Kangnam because she thought the complex parking lots much safer.

When Mr. Ch'oi first brought me home for the weekend to his 32-p'yŏng or 1,140 square-foot apartment in a satellite city of Seoul, the first thing that struck me approaching the apartment was the size of the playground: it stretched from one end of the complex to the other. Moreover, this area was being used much like a park by both children playing and older people sitting on park benches. In one section, boys were actually hitting balls with a bat. The playgrounds I observed around the apartments in the Kangnam area were much too small to think about playing ball in them.

Apartment complexes outside of Seoul proper were often not so constrained by space limitations and land, and thus the apartments were less expensive. Mr. Ch'oi originally bought this apartment because it was close to the medium-sized company he worked for before being hired by the chaebŏl in Seoul. At the time I met him he could not afford to buy a big enough apartment in Seoul proper. However, as mentioned earlier, he had recently contracted for a smaller apartment in Seoul to be used as a rental. His plans were to be able to sell both apartments and buy a suitable one in Seoul in time for his daughter to attend elementary school in Seoul. He admitted, though, that he may have been a year or so behind in meeting that goal. (By 1997 living on the outskirts of Seoul or in satellite cities had become more popular as these areas developed and more amenities became available. For four consecutive years beginning in 1993, the population of Seoul even declined [Korea Times, April 3, 1997, p. 3] as more people opted to move out to the suburbs.)

Women often stated, as yet another reason for preferring apartments, that the apartments themselves were much easier to keep clean than houses. The modern apartments were not heated by coal briquettes and thus did not have the storage and dust problems Lee Hyo-jae's informants complained of in the 1960s (1971). Except in the poorest neighborhoods, most housing in Seoul originally built with under-the-floor flues has also been converted to use with other types of fuel such as oil. Nevertheless, the older, mixed-style houses, duplexes, and the smaller villas appeared somewhat dark and dingy in contrast to the brightness and cleanliness of the middle-class apartments. Cleanliness itself had become associated with modernity, much as the high-rise apartments themselves had.

Apartments and newer houses utilized, in place of flues, under-the-floor pipes through which hot water flowed. The first high-rise apartments built in Kangnam in the 1970s, still used in the 1990s, might not have had hot water pipes running under all of the rooms. Usually, one bedroom was an ondol room. Because of consumer demand, however, newer apartments did have such pipes under all the rooms. Furthermore, the temperature in individual rooms could be controlled by regulating the flow of heated water to each room through valves located in the individual apartment unit. In 1997 I observed thermostats in each room in an apartment built in 1993.

The size of the average middle- and upper-middle-class apartment units ranged generally from 22 to 55 p'yŏng or roughly 780 to 1,960 square feet. Even the smallest exceeded the 6.8 p'yŏng or 600 square feet of the average traditional-style house Lee Hyo-jae's middle-class informants occupied in the 1960s. Moreover, the mixed-style houses and apartments in her sample were even smaller than the traditional-style houses (1971:30).

The additional living space in the modern apartment unit was made more significant by the fact that the frequency of multiple-family occupancy per unit had been greatly reduced since Lee Hyo-jae's 1967 survey (1971:30), being nonexistent among my middle-class informants. If we also take into account the reduction in the number of children per family, more than two being rare in the youngest generation, it is difficult to accept the argument based on size alone that apartment-style living was less conducive to extended families than traditional-style housing. Yong-soo's family is one example. Yong-soo, a six-year-old boy whom I tutored in English, lived with his maternal grandparents, his mother, and his maternal uncle, uncle's wife, and their infant son in a four-bedroom, 55–p'yŏng apartment in Kangnam.

Even taking differences in the use of space between traditional houses and apartments into consideration, I would argue that other factors such as changes in concepts of personhood and privacy were more responsible for the increased incidence of residentially nuclear families than changes in architecture. The Baek family provides a good example. The newly married son and daughter-in-law expressed a wish to live with his parents. The daughter-in-law especially would benefit from her mother-in-law's help with housework and child care. The mother-in-law, however, while looking forward to having grandchildren, was also undoubtedly looking forward to enjoying life without the burdens co-residence would place on her. Thus, even though the structure of the apartment itself allowed for an extended family and the younger couple wanted to live with the parents, the parents thought it better that they each have their own place.

Household Activities and Use of Living Space

As already noted, it was not until the 1960s that newer styles of housing began to appear in Korea. Thus a significant percentage of the adult population in the early 1990s in the greater Seoul metropolitan area were born and had spent a portion of their life in the countryside or in traditional-style housing in the city. It is useful to look at what they experienced at an earlier stage of their life, because these patterns continued to influence their lives into the 1990s. As we shall see, although the face of Seoul and the standard of living changed rapidly and radically from the 1970s on, many patterns of the traditional house and household activities were carried into the modern-day, high-rise apartment.

Rutt (1964 [1957–58]) provides a description of the L-shaped home characteristic of central Korea and most common among Seoul's urban middle class up to even the late 1970s and early 1980s. (See Figure 1.) Although the structure of the house hadn't changed much, incipient changes within the traditional house itself and in the behavior of its inhabitants were under way by the time Rutt wrote in the late 1950s. The urban households by definition would not be involved in the agricultural tasks, of course, but the lifestyle in the home was quite similar in both the city and the countryside. In his description, Rutt imposes over the traditional style the modern elements beginning to creep into the Korean home in the years following World War II and the Korean War:

The plan of the typical house is L-shaped. In the angle of the L is the largest room, the living room [anpang] of the family. It has the famous *ondol* or hot floor, built by making flues under a floor of stone and mud. The floor is finished with several layers of oiled yellow paper, which darkens with age and the heat of the flues, sometimes to a warm russet color.

The furniture is generally only a chest or two and a few cushions, with a tiny writing table. The main cupboards are [set] into the wall, a large one for bedding and a smaller one for medicines, tobacco, food dainties, and the like. The walls are generally covered with cheap wallpaper, sometimes with newspaper or other scrap, really intended as an undercoat. . . .

The fireplace, over which the floor is too hot to sit on but is the proper place for a guest, is seen and fed in the kitchen, which is next to the living room in one arm of the L. It has an earth floor, much lower than the other rooms of the house. (Rutt 1964 [1957–58]:21)

Rutt continues with details of the kitchen:

There is a chopping board and a cupboard or two for crocks; little meal-tables hang from the walls or ceiling; there are one or two cauldrons built into the fireplace, so that the fuel that cooks the food also heats the living-room floor. Beyond the kitchen, at the end of this arm of the L, is the fuel store, and possibly the cowhouse. (Rutt 1964 [1957–58]:22).

Rutt also provides us with a description of the verandah and its uses:

On the other side of the living room is a space which is open on the courtyard. This has a wooden floor and is call the *maru* in Korean, the ceremonial meeting-place of the household, which for want of a better word I call verandah in English. Shoes are kicked off before one steps on to it. Here are the big rice-chests and here, generally, are the shrines for the tablets of the recently dead, and on the rafter the inscription about the date of building the house. Photographs may be displayed there. It is a fine place to sit—under the shade of its roof—in the hot summer days. (Rutt 1964 [1957–58]:22)

More details about the courtyard (madang) and its uses are also given:

Larger houses have two L-shaped blocks, almost enclosing a square. Behind the living room [anpang] is the garden where the pickle jars and vats are kept, with the well and a few fruit-trees and plants. This is the women's preserve, and here the spirits of the site have their home. There is a thick earth wall around the property, but the great gate, with its double doors, opens on to an unwalled yard of beaten earth in front of the house, where the threshing is done and grain is spread to dry in the autumn. The men's parlour [sarangbang] is always in the front block and its outside door gives on to this yard. (Rutt 1964 [1957–58]:23)

Up to this point, we see that the early post–Korean War lifestyle did not differ all that much from that of the late Chosŏn dynasty. However, Rutt's contrasting descriptions of the furnishings of the sarangbang or traditional male quarters, which continued to be much as it was in the past, with the room a married son in this early post–Korean War period might share with his bride hint at an increased preoccupation with both modern and foreign furnishings as well as closer conjugal ties among the younger generation. (The room directly on the opposite side of the maru from the anpang is technically known as the *kŏnnŏnbang* or literally "the room across" the maru from the anpang):

Beyond it [the maru], finishing the second arm of the L, is another hot-floored room. Sometimes this is the men's parlour or study. [That is, if there is not a second, usually either rectangular or L-shaped wing.] It has another door on the outside, and is the place for receiving male guests, but very often in these days it is the room for the married son and is called the "bride's room" [*sinbang*]. If it is so used, you can be sure to find in it a miniature dressing-table with a mirror and many cosmetics; some ugly cheap modern chests and wardrobes; and the bridegroom's suits hanging on the wall under white linen covers with bright satin-switch embroidery which often proclaims:

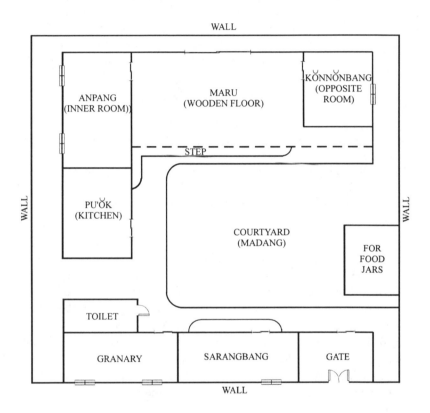

Figure 1   Layout of a traditional-style house (adapted from Lee Hyo-jae 1971)

"Home Sweet Home" in florid English lettering. And of course, a photo of a poker-faced wedding group. But if it is the men's parlour, then there will be one door to the outside world (nearby is an elemental urinal) and one door to the yard, to which the womenfolk bring the wine and food; inside it will be very bare, but there may be a few books and cushions and probably a straw mat on the floor. (Rutt 1964 [1957–58]:22).

The changes described attest to a weakening in the rigidity of segregation of the sexes but not an abandonment of traditional practice, as underscored in Rutt's next statement about sleeping and eating arrangements:

The sexes are still very much segregated, even for sleeping, when the quilts and mat-tresses are simply taken from the cupboards and unrolled across the floor of the day-rooms. At mealtimes the men are fed at little tables on the verandah or hot floor. The women eat afterwards in the living room [anpang] or kitchen. Children often eat separately from adults, or at least at different tables. (Rutt 1964 [1957–58]:22–23).

For the same time period, Ha Tae Hung (1958:75) observed not only that cooking was still time consuming but that husbands continued to eat sepa-rately from their wives and children: "A Korean family meal generally con-sists of hot rice, hot soup (fish, meat or vegetable), *kimch'i* (pickle), boiled or stewed meat and fried or broiled fish with vegetables, and pepper paste with soy. These are laid out all together on low tables at which the children may sit (on the floor) together, but separated from the father, while the mother and elder daughters do the serving."

One of the most fundamental changes we observe during this period is that women were beginning to appear in public, both in the countryside and in the city. With regard to the former, Sorensen (1983:71) attributes this in part to the gradual commercialization of the rural economy since the end of World War II: "Until only recently, women needed little money to manage the household from day to day. Most households were almost entirely self-sufficient in foodstuffs. With the gradual commercialization of the rural economy, more and more ordinary items—noodles, canned fish, ramen, candy—are purchased at the periodic markets scattered around rural Korea, and consequently, markets are now patronized by women rather than men."

Another possible explanation for women's greater visibility in the coun-tryside is related to the land reform around 1950 that undermined the eco-nomic base of the former yangban estate. No longer able to rely on rent from hereditary lands, many more descendants of yangban were required to work the land themselves and no longer had the means to employ servants to carry out household chores. Nevertheless, some of these women tried to maintain as much segregation and seclusion as the circumstances allowed. At least as late as the late 1960s, Brandt (1971) observed differences in behavior between a yangban neighborhood and a commoner neighborhood in his village study. In the "upper-class" yangban neighborhood, Brandt (1971:46) noted, "Women remain mostly inside their own homes, or if they go outside on errands to the well, the fields, or to other houses, they rarely loiter along the paths to gossip. One almost never sees them in conversation with men." In the neighborhood of commoner origin, "Women and girls are more in evidence than they are among the Yi households. . . . Extremely crude language is used without restraint, and women join in some of the discussions, talking back to men in a way that is seldom heard" in the yangban neighborhood (Brandt 1971:47–48).

In Seoul, changes were occurring much more quickly. According to Ha Tae Hung (1958:64–65), although "an old-fashioned woman [still] feels ashamed to be seen by any strange man and she seldom talks with a man, even a very close friend of her husband," the younger generation was not so constrained. Undoubtedly the increased opportunity for public education enjoyed by the girls of the younger generation contributed to their more liberal outlook. Ha reports that when schools for girls were first established in Seoul and in the country, students wore a *chang ot* or veil. "Later they discarded the 'jang-ot' and carried parasols to hide their faces from the sight of men. More recently [1958] the parasol has gone and now most younger women wear short skirts, stockings and high-heeled shoes as well as make-up and beauty-shop hairdos" (Ha 1958:65). Ten years later, among Lee Hyo-jae's middle-class apartment-dwellers, husbands and wives not only slept together with their young children, but may or may not have eaten together depending on their schedules.

What is the situation with today's urban middle class? In earlier sections of this chapter I have already described traditional and mixed-style housing. Here I will focus primarily on apartment life.

The typical middle-class apartment of the 1990s had two to four bedrooms (and sometimes a room the size of a walk-in closet for a live-in maid, as in the apartment where I lived); one or two bathrooms; a living room; dining room; kitchen; two enclosed balconies (called *peranda* or verandah and even sometimes *madang* or courtyard), one in the front adjacent to the living room and one in back near the kitchen; and a vestibule (*hyŏn'gwan*) at the entrance of the apartment. Deceptively Western in plan, the space was nevertheless often used in typically non-Western ways.

To begin with, upon entering a Korean apartment, or any Korean home for that matter, shoes were removed and left in the vestibule. To make the best use of the radiant heat of the modernized ondol heating system, most floors remained uncarpeted. Living room, dining room, and kitchen areas in the high-rise apartments were usually covered with white-colored linoleum. Although I am told more recently that linoleum is beginning to appear in bedrooms as well, bedroom floors still tended to be covered with the brownish-yellow oiled paper also found in traditional and mixed-style houses. Bathrooms were tiled.

In contrast with the traditional Korean house, the modern apartment had an indoor bathroom and separate areas designated for sleeping, eating, and entertaining. Nevertheless, Western modes of behavior in using these spaces have not necessarily followed.

Bathrooms and Bathing

Shower shoes were placed so that one could slip into them as one entered the bathroom. Korean bathrooms in general tended to be wet. Tubs, shower heads (with running hot water), and shower curtains were rather new features and were not universal. Even the most modern and exclusive apartments may not use curtains or have fixed shower heads. Some of the older apartments and even Western-style houses had shower heads but no shower stall or tub. In those cases, the runoff was not prevented from spilling and splashing into the toilet and sink area. Even with modern facilities habits were not automatically changed. Plastic wash bowls were found in the modern bathrooms for sponge bathing and water still seems to be splashed all over. Occasional trips to public baths or health clubs were also enjoyed by some.

On my return to Korea in the fall of 1996, I did find something in the bathroom of the five-bedroom, nine-year-old apartment in which I stayed that I found particularly innovative: connected to the ondol system of heating the floor were pipes on the wall arranged so as to form five towel racks, one above the other, thus serving to dry and warm the towels as well as warming the room.

With regard to toilets, the traditional Korean commode is a hole in the ground that is straddled over. A modernized version of this, a hole lined with a porcelain bowl and a flushing water system, was used in public buildings, including some office buildings, universities, subways, and rest stops along the freeway. Many Koreans still considered this style more sanitary than the Western-style commode upon which one sat but which was now standard in Korean urban middle-class homes.

Bedrooms and Sleeping

Although there were some variations, the floor plans of most South Korean urban middle-class apartments were remarkably uniform. Typically, in a two-bedroom apartment, the two bedrooms would be on the opposite side from where the front door was located, one room each in the left- and right-hand corner, with a bathroom in between. In a three bedroom, the third room would be to the left or right of the vestibule, that is, on the same side of the apartment as the front door; and if four, there would be a room to either side of the entranceway with a second bathroom adjacent to one of these rooms. (See Figures 2 and 3.) The general living space then was between these two sets of bedrooms.

Among household members, these bedrooms were often designated by their use, such as "grandmother's room," "children's room," "guest room," "study," "music room," and so on. However, one of the two rooms farthest from the front door was also commonly known as the anpang, the term traditionally used to refer to the inside room or house mistress's room, which was also the room farthest from the gate leading to the outside.

Today, with conjugal couples generally sleeping together, "anpang" was used most often to indicate what Americans would call the master bedroom rather than the house mistress's room. But the modern-day anpang was more than the place where the male head of the household and his wife slept. Not only was it common for children to sleep with their parents until their first or second year of school, but depending on how the room was furnished, the anpang may also have been used as a day room, to entertain, and to conduct rituals such as ancestor worship or formal bowing to elders. This situation was similar in the mixed-style houses as well (and in at least one Western-style house I visited in the countryside). For example, Mr. Oh and his family lived in a mixed-style house in northern Seoul. On my first visit to Mr. Oh's house, after being introduced to his family, I was invited into what Mr. Oh identified as the anpang to converse with him as his preschool-aged daughter sat with us on the heated floor watching television and his wife and sister-in-law finished preparing dinner in the kitchen. The anpang was where Mr. Oh, his wife, and his daughter slept.

The principle of senior male as household head was recognized and upheld not only legally but in the living arrangements within the mixed-style houses and apartment dwellings. In Mr. Oh's case, when I first met him, as mentioned above, his newlywed brother and sister-in-law lived with them. As eldest male, Mr. Oh occupied the anpang with his wife and child while his younger brother and his wife slept in another room. Shortly before leaving Korea I went to the Ohs' house to join them on a trip to the mountain gravesite of his mother outside of Seoul for graveside ancestor worship services traditionally held at Ch'usŏk (Fall Harvest Moon Holiday). At that time, the anpang was closed off. Mr. Oh's brother and sister-in-law had moved out (although his brother came to the house as was expected of younger brothers and joined his brother's family for the ancestor worship of their mother). Subsequently, even though his mother was deceased and his wife was de facto the house mistress, Mr. Oh, his wife, and daughter vacated the anpang and moved into the room his brother had been using. Mr. Oh explained that he was trying to talk his father into moving back in (that is, into the house his father in fact owned and had lived in for the last twenty or so years). According to Mr. Oh, if the anpang was being used, his father, as senior male and actively working as a government bureaucrat, would say that there was no room for him in the house. Thus the anpang was thought of not as the house mistress's but rather as the household head's room.

While in Mr. Oh's case the father was still living and the mother deceased, in Mr. Ch'oi's case it was the opposite. Mr. Ch'oi, who was an only son, lived with his wife, daughter, and widowed mother in a three-bedroom apartment. Giving me a tour of his apartment, Mr. Ch'oi pointed to the room adjacent to the vestibule. This, Mr. Ch'oi explained, was his daughter's playroom. It would become her bedroom when she was a little older. She would cry, Mr. Ch'oi claimed, if she were put alone in that room right now. For now, the three-year-old slept in her parents' room, one of the rooms opposite the front door.

Continuing the tour, Mr. Ch'oi identified the third bedroom, the one on the other side of the bathroom from his, as his mother's. I asked Mr. Ch'oi whether this room was the anpang. The answer was a definite "No!" The room he and his wife occupied was considered the anpang, again upholding the principle of senior male as household head in the use of space. While in the past "anpang" was designated as the house mistress's room, since younger conjugal couples tended to sleep in the same room, the anpang more often now referred to where the head of the household and his wife slept.

In other cases, whether or not the eldest male occupied the anpang may have depended on his actual power within the household and on other circumstances. Lee Kwang Kyu noted that a shift in residence within the home marked de facto (rather than legal) transfer of household headship. The couple who actually managed the household occupied the anpang; the members of the succeeding generation occupied the room across from the anpang; and members of the retired generation resided in the sarangbang (Lee Kwang Kyu 1984, 1975:81–82 as cited in Janelli and Janelli 1982:44). In the case of Mr. Oh, his father had not only built and owned the house, but was also still working and was economically independent of his son.

Sometimes grandparents let the younger couple use the anpang, which was usually but not always bigger than other rooms, if the younger couple themselves had young children and needed more room. I have been told,

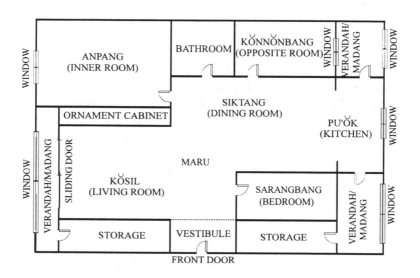

Figure 2   Layout of a 32-p'yŏng three-bedroom modern apartment

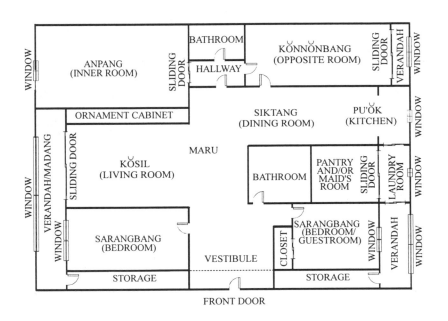

Figure 3   Layout of a 55-p'yŏng four-bedroom modern apartment

though, that in some cases the mother-in-law did not occupy the anpang but would later complain to others that her daughter-in-law and not she was in the anpang.

Sometimes an elderly couple slept in separate rooms, as did Miss Young's parents. When I asked her if she thought that was a vestige of the traditional custom of men and women sleeping in different quarters, she replied that it was the opposite. In the past, she explained, the seclusion of women in the anpang or inner areas of the household compound was a reflection of their docility. "Today," she continued, "if a woman sleeps separate from her husband, it is symbolic of her power. If a woman sleeps in the same room, she ends up serving him as he asks her for this or that. If she sleeps in a different room, it is saying that she doesn't have to serve him."

This woman's parents, now in their sixties, though having slept together earlier in their marriage, had been sleeping in separate rooms for the past ten years or so, each in one of the two rooms opposite the front door. I asked who slept in the anpang, her father or her mother? She replied that her father did, but that in fact the sizes of the two rooms were not much different. After thinking more about it, she noted that her mother's room was slightly bigger and "more luxurious." The reason for this, she explained, was that her mother stored more things in her room and needed the extra space. Furthermore, her mother used her room for daytime activities as well, such as sewing and praying, whereas her father was either at work or spent his waking hours at home in the living room. In the process of explaining this to me, she began to wonder whether her father's room really should be called the anpang, although apparently up to this time it had been thought of as such.

Yong-soo's grandparents also slept in separate rooms in their four-bedroom apartment. It was the grandmother, a domineering woman who was indisputably in charge of the household, who slept in the anpang. Yong-soo's mother, who had no husband, occupied the room on the other side of the bathroom from the anpang. These two rooms were connected through a small hallway, off of which was the bathroom (see Figure 3), making it easy for Yong-soo to sleep with either his grandmother (his primary care-giver) or his mother.

A second bathroom was located near the two rooms adjacent to the front door where Yong-soo's uncle and grandfather slept. The uncle, who was his parents' youngest son, slept with his wife and infant son in the larger of the two rooms to either side of the vestibule. The grandfather occupied the other room nearest the apartment entrance. If the grandparents were to sleep separately, this arrangement was the most practical based on the demographics of the household and the layout of the apartment. The arrangement carried another meaning as well, however.

Although the term "sarangbang" is not used as frequently as "anpang," it nevertheless had meaning in the context of the modern apartment. Basically, it referred to one of the rooms nearest the front door, just as it referred to the living space found nearest to the outside gate in the traditional house. The male head of the household may or may not have slept in it. In the case of Yong-soo's grandparents, the senior male member did occupy the sarangbang.

In Miss Young's parents' three-bedroom apartment, there currently were only two household members, her father and her mother. Each occupied one of the two rooms opposite the front door. One parent slept in the room commonly called the anpang. The other slept in the room across from the anpang, on the other side of the bathroom. This room, while it may not have been referred to as such among household members, nevertheless was recognized as the kŏnnŏnbang or "the room across" from the anpang. This was the same term used to identify the room across from the anpang in the traditional house, though now it was the bathroom or hallway rather than the maru or verandah that separated the two rooms.

Thus while the terms sarangbang and kŏnnŏnbang were not usually used among household members, if they were asked which room was the sarangbang or kŏnnŏnbang, there would be no question. For example, one day Miss Young's mother said to her son-in-law, "Why don't you put the baby in the sarangbang?" Without questioning, he knew exactly where she meant and put the infant in the room nearest the front door in the three-bedroom apartment. As Miss Young pointed out, her parents' as well as her own first experience with apartment life only began in 1984. It was natural, she said, that there was some carryover in the way they thought about space in the home. This observation would apply to the vast majority of adults living in Korea today. In 1985, only 14 percent of the homes in South Korea were apartment units (Korea Annual 1992:352). For that same year, the Housing Administration Bureau reported that 23 percent of Seoul's whole population and about 45 percent of those who may be designated as "middle class" were living in high-rise apartments (Housing Administration Bureau, Korea National Housing Corporation 1987:3, as reported in Moon Okpyo 1990:32).

At some level of consciousness, then, perceptions about the traditional layout of the house and use of space were being imposed on the modern apartment. Essentially, the two bedrooms opposite the front door were the equivalent of the inner wing, while the bedrooms on either side of the front door were equivalent to the outer wing of the traditional house, with the counterpart of the front gate being the front door. Furthermore, as we shall see, the living room (*kŏsil*) and dining room (*siktang*), enclosed as they were on either side by the inner and outer rooms, assumed the combined functions of both indoor courtyard and especially *maru*. Indeed, this open space, including both the living and the dining room areas, could also be referred to as maru, originally the covered, but open to the outside, wooden-floor area between the anpang and kŏnnŏnbang that was often used for eating, relaxing, or even sleeping, especially in the summertime. At least one person told me this space could also be called madang, originally meaning courtyard, but most others I asked vehemently denied this usage existed. Many applied the term madang to what were also referred to as *peranda* or verandahs, or what Americans might call enclosed balconies placed on either side of the apartment. (See Figures 2 and 3.) The balcony, entered from the living room through a sliding glass door, usually contained potted plants, including trees. *Hang'ari*, or jars used to store condiments such as soy sauce and bean paste, typically kept in the madang of single-house dwellings with land, may also be found on either balcony of the modern apartment unit.

With regard to the furnishings of the bedrooms and the use of space within, though Western-style beds were not uncommon, there were still more Koreans who continued to sleep on the floor, using the traditional thin mattress (*yo*), quilt (*ibul*), and tubular-shaped pillow (*pegae*). (A flat but hard pillow, also called pegae, had also come into use.) Traditional bedding was not only more economical. Many Koreans found it to be more practical and even more comfortable than Western-style beds, not only for its firmness but for the heat radiating up from the ondol floor. Sometimes beds were bought for their display value only, while members of the household continued to sleep on the floor. A few chose to sleep on beds in the summer and, in order to enjoy the radiant heat from the floor, on yo in the winter. In some cases, people had owned beds but had gotten rid of them.

Western beds take up a great deal of room and rigidly fix the sleeping arrangements. Yo, in contrast, are spread out every evening and arranged according to need, easily accommodating guests, children, and changes in household composition. Picked up and stored in a wardrobe during the day (built-in closets were rare), yo were then out of the way, leaving room for other activities such as entertaining, playing, and studying. Thus a traditionally furnished bedroom was very open and empty looking. When there was Western furniture in the bedroom, the bedroom was mainly that, a room for sleeping, though a table and chairs might be included to create a conversation area. A few examples illustrate the variety of uses that existed among South Korean urban middle-class households.

When I first met them, Mr. Oh, his wife, and his daughter slept together on a yo. Mr. Oh's younger brother, who lived in the same house, had recently begun sleeping on a bed; his bride brought the new item into the house as part of her dowry. Mr. Oh explained to me that his daughter had been pestering him about getting a bed for her. She had first seen them on television. But he told her there was not enough room for one, and it would have to wait until sometime in the future. But she kept on asking. The fact that a Western-style bed came with the little girl's new aunt probably increased her interest.

When Mr. Oh's younger brother moved out, Mr. Oh, his wife, and his daughter acquired the bed of his brother and sister-in-law, as there was not enough room in their new place for the bed. A short time later, when Mr. Oh's son was born, his wife reverted to sleeping on a yo on the floor with the new infant while Mr. Oh and his daughter slept in the bed. Mr. Oh commented that he liked the bed because it did not have to be picked up and put away each morning.

There were other combinations in sleeping arrangements. Mrs. Baek and her husband as well as their adult children all used Western-style beds, the adult children of course having rooms separate from their parents. Mrs. Moon and her husband slept on a yo. Her daughters, however, slept on beds they had bought while they were overseas. The situation was reversed between generations in the Ch'oi household. Mr. Ch'oi's three-year-old slept on a yo in her parents' room, while her parents slept on a Western-style bed. Mr. Ch'oi explained that when the time came for his daughter to move into her own room, they would buy her a bed, too. Meanwhile, his mother's room, though small, had plenty of room for a small table, a television set, and the wardrobe in which the traditional bedding she used was stored. Except for a portrait of the extended family, with the women dressed in hanbok, commemorating Mr. Ch'oi's mother's *hwan'gap* or sixtieth birthday, the room was quite sparsely furnished. Thus in the same household both traditional and Western-style bedrooms were in use.

Yong-soo's uncle and aunt provide an example of those who bought Western items for the sake of their prestige value but in the end decided that not everything Western fit their lifestyle. This couple had many of the trappings young American parents might have for their infant, including a stroller, a swing, a walker, and a crib, items still rare in Korea in the early 1990s but readily available a few years later. One day I noticed the baby's crib disassembled on the living room floor. It had been in his parents' room, next to their Western-style bed, which, combined with the enormous wardrobe, filled the room. The baby was only five months old or so at the time, and it seemed a bit early for him to have outgrown the crib. So I asked about it. Apparently the baby had been hitting his head too much on the crib's bars. The crib was replaced by a yo upon which both the mother and her infant son then slept, as in the case of the Ohs.

Even Western-style houses could accommodate traditional as well as Western patterns, such as the Western-style house Mrs. Kim's elderly parents occupied with their eldest son in Kangnam. The first floor of this two-story home was divided into a Western-style furnished living room on the left of the front door, a Western-style furnished dining room down the center, and a traditionally furnished anpang to the right. This last room, which included a large wardrobe, a traditional-style, that is, low-to-the-floor, scholar's desk, pillows for sitting on the floor, a television set, and books, was where Mrs. Kim's parents slept, entertained guests, and otherwise spent most of their day. Meanwhile, the bedrooms of the eldest son and his family were upstairs.

Living Rooms, Dining Rooms, Eating, and Entertaining

In traditional houses, Koreans ate and entertained either in the sarangbang for men or the anpang for women and children. Sometimes the family would eat out on the verandah (maru) or, for the women, in the kitchen. Mixed-style houses without sarangbang did have a separate living room. The floor of the living room in the older mixed-style house was not heated, however, and much of the activity of the family, such as watching television, eating, and entertaining family and friends in addition to sleeping was done in the anpang. The living room was often left for the more formal reception of visitors.

As already mentioned, when I first visited Mr. Oh, we conversed in the anpang while his daughter sat alongside us on the floor watching television. After a while we were called out to the living room, where a low table (*sang*) had just been set up to serve the evening meal. Mr. Oh related to me that his sister-in-law had brought in a Western-style dining room table and chairs, though I never did see them. Although the living room contained a couch and a vertical knickknack cabinet, it was otherwise sparsely furnished and reminded me more of a large vestibule that the family passed through more than lived in. Several years earlier, the mother had run a cottage industry in lace, and this room would have been an ideal place for the hired women to work. The second time I had dinner at the Ohs, we ate on the floor in the anpang.

The anpang was obviously where the Ohs spent the greater part of their time together while in the house. In addition to the television, there was an accompanying videocassette recorder (known as VTRs in Korea), videocassettes, and books on a stand stretching along one wall. I was told that in the evenings it was not unusual to watch television or a video in bed, that is, on their yo, even as their daughter slept beside them. Along the opposite wall of the television was a large wardrobe of the type used to store traditional Korean bedding as well as clothes. It was just in front of this wardrobe where they slept or watched television. At the far end of the anpang (which was not too far away) was a small table used to conduct household ancestor worship for Mr. Oh's recently deceased mother. English-word posters with pictures decorated the wall at the end near the door. Although most apartments had a space for a dining room or kitchen table and chairs, not every middle-class Korean household owned such items. Even when present, they were not always used. Instead sang, the traditional low tables, were simply pulled out of storage and set up, usually in the living room, or even in the kitchen if adult male members were not present. Sometimes floor cushions called *pangsŏk* were used, sometimes not. Many Koreans found this arrangement more comfortable and convenient. One was not constrained by the availability of seats and table space as could easily happen with Western-style tables and chairs.

There were many middle-class Koreans who did regularly use a dining room table and chairs. Being at ease with this Western furniture, however, does not translate into being at ease with Western cuisine or table etiquette. When I invited the Ohs over to my apartment for a steak dinner, Mr. Oh's wife was constantly looking to her husband for clues to make sure she was not violating any rules. The same occurred with some of my Korean informants when I took them to a restaurant on the American military installation in Seoul. Many Koreans did not look comfortable with knife and fork in hand. Chopsticks and spoons remained the norm, even if Western silverware was found in many homes. I observed, though, that some parents gave their preschoolers a fork to use before they learned to use chopsticks. Apparently the children initially found the forks easier to use. But then Mr. Oh's young daughter was chided because she continued to use a fork instead of chopsticks. Back in the United States, a five-year-old boy who had emigrated from South Korea a few years back with his family said "I'm not a baby!" when my husband asked him if he wanted a fork instead of chopsticks.

Whether a family ate together or not depended on the individual family circumstances. Men, women, and children as a rule no longer ate separately just for the sake of observing differences in status between gender and age. If all members of the household happened to be home at the time of a meal, they would eat as a family. The busy schedule of each household member, however, often made arranging a family meal difficult. During the week many men stayed out until late in the evening socializing with their colleagues or clients, eating out at restaurants. Or they might have eaten something when they eventually found their way home. There was always warm rice in the electric rice cooker, and the nature of Korean cuisine allowed wives to quickly pull out from the refrigerator kimch'i and side dishes (*panch'an*) prepared earlier.

The peer pressure among salary men to socialize with co-workers after work was notorious. This socializing involved heavy drinking as evidenced by the intoxicated men in suits filling the subway cars in the later evening hours. Many men expressed their displeasure with the need to participate in this daily ritual and were increasingly beginning to resist it. Mr. Byŏng, a middle-aged civil servant, was praised by his colleagues as a good husband and father for never going out drinking after work but rather going home to his family every evening and tutoring his two daughters in English. Mr. Oh told me just after receiving a promotion that he was glad that he now had an excuse for not going out after work hours: he had to be available for work earlier in the morning. Some men would sign up for evening classes, such as language classes or art classes, to enrich their lives and avoid drinking. (Mr. Oh had taken a pottery class one evening a week while I was in Korea.) Mr. Ch'oi was able to avoid much of after-work socializing because, as a salesman for one of the large business conglomerates, he was often out of his office in the afternoon and not around when the workday ended. A university student told me her father was home much more often now that he had resigned from his salaried position and had started his own business. The percentage of salary men not coming home for dinner nevertheless remained significant.

Older children, especially high school students preparing for the university entrance exam, would be out late at private reading rooms studying. Mothers would pack one or sometimes two lunches for their children to take. Sometimes mothers would bring their children a meal or alternatively the children would eat out at nearby noodle shops or the like. In general, it was expected that should her children or husband be home at a meal time, the woman of the house would be there to serve them.

With regard to receiving guests in apartments, if there were no Western bed consuming space, women were more likely than men to entertain friends, and only very close ones at that, in the anpang. Women were also likely to do daytime activities such as ironing in a traditionally furnished anpang. If household demographics and apartment size allowed, some used one of the bedrooms, usually one near the front door, as a reception and recreation room. In the Baek household, for example, all three rooms used as bedrooms had beds. However, because Mrs. Baek and her daughters were musicians, the fourth room to the right of the front door was converted for use as a music room, with sound-absorbing padding on the walls and carpet on the floor, complete with a string bass set in a stand on the floor, a piano along one wall, and a bookcase unit along another. Besides serving as a place to practice music, this room, which contained a couple of couch sectionals, also served as a reception room for the mother. This is where I conversed and had tea with Mrs. Baek and where I tutored her daughter in English. In fact, this room reminded me of what I would imagine a drawing room to be. However, I was also reminded that this was a Korean family when I was directed to stay in there with the other women at a private reception after the son's wedding, segregated from the men as they gathered in the living room.

Whenever my interaction also involved Mrs. Baek's husband or son, it occurred in the living or dining room. In fact, whether yo or beds were used, the apartment living room in general had taken over the reception area function of the anpang and especially the sarangbang. Moreover, with increased wealth had come an increase in leisure, and the apartment living room had become for household members themselves the center of leisure activity. The living room, for example, was where most apartment dwellers watched television and may have had a stereo. (Additional televisions were also occasionally found in the bedrooms, especially in the anpang or bedrooms of adult members of the household.) The living room also served as a play area for young children, allowing the mothers to closely supervise their children as they carried out household tasks nearby.

It is in this sense that the combined living room (kŏsil) and dining room (siktang) area, enclosed by the inner bedrooms on one long side and the outer bedrooms and front door on the other, a kitchen at one short end, and a sliding door leading out to a balcony on the other end, has assumed many of the functions of the courtyard and the maru of a traditional housing compound. As noted, the open space excluding the bedrooms may even have been referred to as the madang, the term traditionally used for courtyard, but much more likely as maru.

Despite the imposition of certain spatial traits and uses of the traditional dwelling onto the modern dwelling, there were some changes in the meaning and use of those spaces. The anthropologist Lee Kwang Kyu (1989:176) notes that in urban dwellings in general, whether single-family or apartment, the "authority space" found in traditional dwellings was no longer observed:

In traditional houses, the house mistress and her children occupy the Inner Room [anpang] while the house head occupies the *sarangbang*, usually the room facing the street. Within rooms, moreover, the lower portion [*araenmok*] is reserved for the higher status persons than the upper portion [*winmok*] [*sic*]. Thus the distribution of space in traditional houses expresses and maintains traditional authority relations. In urban dwellings, parents and children watch television together, laugh together, and joke together in the same room of their confined urban quarters. Under these circumstances it is impossible for parents to maintain the distance necessary for their traditional authority. (Lee Kwang Kyu 1989:176)

Whether or not the disappearance of "authority space" is actually a result of the architecture, the fact that it was no longer observed is a reflection of the changing relations between the household head and other household members; the household head still maintained much authority but was also weaker than traditionally.

I believe the typical middle- and upper-middle-class apartments I observed had enough room for "authority space." However, it has only been very recently that urban, middle-class housing has been so roomy. It seems likely that this recognition of "authority space" disappeared during the phase of extreme housing shortage that virtually all families now living in these apartments went through, especially if these apartments were not their first residence in the city.

Most urban middle-class apartment living rooms boasted "reception room furniture," that is, a couch. Some had coffee tables, but it was more typical to bring out a traditional-style, low table (sang) when the occasion warranted. Whether there was a couch or not, many Koreans still found sitting on the floor, with or without pangsŏk (cushions), more comfortable.

One piece of furniture that did appear to be almost universal in the modern middle-class high-rise apartment living room was the *changsikchang* or, literally, "ornament cabinet." This wall-length, roughly waist-high, built-in piece of furniture was the centerpiece in and on which a household could showcase decorative and sometimes practical objects of conspicuous consumption. It was here that the television was most likely to be placed. Beyond that, the cabinet's use and decoration reflected the character of the particular household.

Although the front door was as effective as the wall and gate of the traditional housing compound at screening the household from public view, some housewives seemed to thrive on opportunities to show off their home. After all, how can one assert one's status if nobody can see what one has? In their work on ancestor worship in the countryside, Janelli and Janelli (1982:134) remark that "lineage rituals confer prestige by giving a lineage an occasion to display publicly opulence, erudition, and other trappings of Korean gentry." Housewives in the urban apartment also had opportunities to display their "opulence." It was not uncommon for housewives to exchange visits with their neighbors. Minimally, housewives visited their immediate neighbors at the *pansanghoe*, or monthly, government-mandated neighborhood meetings, the location of which rotated among the ten to twenty-five or so homes of member households. (In contrast to the village meetings, where land issues were addressed [see also Sorensen 1983], it was generally the women who represented their households at these urban meetings, where housing issues were addressed.) Additionally, neighbors and other friends may have visited for tea or the like to chat or so that their young children could play with one another. The women could use these occasions to discuss consumer products and to either show off or check out the newest in household furnishings, fads in interior decoration, and consumer goods in general. In this way a type of competition ensued, leading to increased consumer spending either as a result of acts of "keeping up with the Joneses" (or Kims, as the case may be) or by "one-upmanship."

Korean middle-class apartments were quite uniform in structure. This was especially true, of course, for the apartment units in the same building. Thus home furnishings and decorations in general were used by housewives to acquire a distinctive status, and such matters as coordination of color, paintings, furniture, and other interior design issues were concerns of many housewives. How the home, and especially the living room where most visitors were received, was furnished could say much about the household's economic status and attitude toward conspicuous consumption. Some were more caught up in the competition associated with conspicuous consumption than others. The following cases illustrate different lifestyles based on different ways status was asserted according to one's assets in the form of economic, cultural, and social capital.

Case: The Ch'ois' apartment. When I first arrived at Mr. Ch'oi's apartment outside of Seoul, where apartment prices are cheaper, Mr. Ch'oi said: "As you can see, we live very simply." I commented that it seemed very comfortable. He disagreed, saying: "Comfortable, no. Simple." Indeed, for its size, 32 p'yŏng or about 1,140 square feet, this three-bedroom apartment with its minimal living room furniture or clutter of any sort looked spacious, very clean, airy, and modern. A couch stretched along one wall of the living room and faced the ornament cabinet along the length of the opposite wall, with nothing but whitish linoleum floor in between. A television, videocassette recorder, and stereo sat atop the cabinet, and a Korean-made cuckoo-clock was mounted above. Otherwise, the cabinet lacked any notable objects, appearing uncluttered and neat, as did the whole apartment. I do remember, though, that inside the cabinet was a multivolume, hard-bound set of his family's published genealogy. Mr. Ch'oi brought it out to show me where he was listed.

A small kitchen table, which we used during meals, occupied the space between the living room and kitchen, abutting the wall on one side. The kitchen itself was modern, equipped with microwave and dish dryer. Besides the two bedrooms previously described, the third room, which Mr. Ch'oi identified as his daughter's playroom, was filled with both toys and books organized in wall-length bookshelves. A Korean alphabet chart carefully drawn by his wife was hanging on the opposite wall. On the wall opposite the door hung a photo of his daughter in hanbok, taken to commemorate her first birthday. A child's swing was hanging in the doorway.

The Ch'ois' apartment contained all the essential comforts but was otherwise unpretentious, much like its occupants. Mr. Ch'oi, young, college-educated, and a white-collar worker, wanted the best for his family, but he was not overly ambitious. Gradually and methodically they were acquiring the articles expected in a middle-class home, and although the home was comfortable, functional, and well kept, there was nothing there just for the sake of impressing others. Mr. Ch'oi possessed enough economic capital to live a middle-class lifestyle, but it was modest by middle-class standards. Mr. Choi's status was derived not from wealth but from his ancestry, his English-language abilities, and his scholarship. Rather than assert status through conspicuous consumption, Mr. Ch'oi asserted status by displaying his chokpo or genealogy and photos of family members dressed in hanbok, speaking fluent English, possessing a library, and trying to engage me in philosophical discussions, even offering to introduce me to a Korean philosopher of scholarly reputation with whom he was acquainted.

Case: Yong-soo's apartment. If the Ch'ois' apartment reflected the possession of more cultural and social capital than economic capital, Yong-soo's family's 55-p'yŏng apartment in the affluent Kangnam region of Seoul provided a study in contrast. Though larger than the Ch'ois' apartment, the living room of Yong-soo's family actually looked smaller for all its clutter. Besides an over-stuffed couch, there were two ornament cabinets, the surface of both covered with various articles. The one opposite the couch contained a large television, videocassette recorder, videocassettes, and various knick-knacks. An air-conditioning unit was off to one side near the enclosed balcony. The second cabinet, located directly behind the couch, had bookshelves extending toward the ceiling and displayed, among other things, a complete set of English-language tapes, although no one in the household spoke English fluently.

The room was also filled with knickknack cabinets displaying delicate porcelain pieces, Yong-soo's toys, his baby cousin's walker and swing, collapsible clothes-drying racks, Western paintings with gaudy frames on the wall, kids' stickers of animals, cars, and so on, stuck on the sliding glass door to the balcony, and more. A low, formica table used by Yong-soo for drawing and painting and to study English was squeezed, when in use, into the middle of the living room floor between the couch and the opposite-facing ornament cabinet.

I could not know what this family's background really was ("These days everyone claims to have yangban heritage" was a common sentiment expressed to me), but the grandparents were artists, one a dancer, the other a painter, traditionally low-status occupations. Yong-soo's uncle handled the Korean side of an apparently successful import/export business. The uncle's older brother managed the overseas side of the business in New York. The collection and display of material goods, and especially those that were foreign, even if of cheap quality, were being used by this household to assert their newfound wealth and status. At the same time, they were investing their economic capital in cultural capital by hiring a private tutor for Yong-soo so that he might acquire the education associated with middle-class status.

Household Chores: Who Does Them

In a conversation with Professor Lee, the topic of family relations came up. She started off by explaining that changes in the residential structure have caused changes in the family:

Before, the kitchen was separate from everything else. The woman did all the kitchen work away from everyone else and no one really saw what she did. Kitchen work was considered labor, low work. It was considered work for a maid. But with the changes that came with apartment complexes, the kitchen is not separate and the children can see what the mother is doing and learn from her. It is no longer considered labor. They can even have fun doing it. My youngest daughter likes to bake. Her favorite is carrot cake. She also just recently made a chocolate cake.

Continuing, Dr. Lee, who was in her forties, explained that younger men (*not* men of her generation) helped out more at home, not just with the cooking but with other housekeeping chores and with child care, including changing diapers, which the fathers would never do before: "It [keeping house in general] has become more of a family affair."

With regard to her own husband, when she did not feel like cooking and suggested that they go out to eat, he, also a professor, went along with it, but he never volunteered to cook. "He does do dishes once in a while though. He does it to relieve tension. You know [she motions washing dishes with her hands], the running water is relaxing. So whenever he has writer's block, he'll go wash dishes. Actually, I told him that [washing dishes relieves tension]. I brain-washed him!" she laughs.

The division of household labor was a subject of negotiation in many households. One evening while I was eating dinner with the Ch'ois, Mr. Ch'oi asked me: "Who does the dishes in America?" Jokingly, but with a straight face, I told him, "The husbands always do the dishes." "Husbands!?!" he reacted with genuine surprise. I did then explain to him that that wasn't really the case, and inquired why he asked. He got a silly grin on his face, somewhat of a guilty look, and glanced sideways at his wife, explaining that his wife thought he should help.

It appears that Mr. Ch'oi was able to escape doing dishes, but there were other household chores he could not totally get away from, though they appeared almost token. When we were talking about Korean cuisine, Mr. Ch'oi and his wife both said that making kimch'i was very difficult. I asked Mr. Ch'oi whether he helped. He said, "Of course!" I pressed and asked him what he did. He said that he carried the ingredients and then laughed, saying that is all he did. I did see him making their Western-style bed in the morning, though. And on Sundays he was responsible for taking care of their pre-school-aged daughter, a job, he said, that was tougher than his regular office job. Even then, however, his wife had ultimate responsibility. One Sunday morning after breakfast, Mr. Ch'oi and I were talking in the living room. His wife was cleaning up in the kitchen. The daughter, who was in the bathroom, started yelling for help. Mr. Ch'oi ignored his daughter's cry. His wife looked our way, gave her husband more time to respond, and finally, without saying a word but giving a meaningful look at her husband from across the room, ended up going to help her daughter.

In many households, the father could be seen watching the children on weekends and carrying them in public. Some told me they were also responsible for such things as cleaning the floor in the anpang (that is, in their bedroom), for doing some of the shopping, and in the fall kimch'i-making season, for carrying vegetables and helping cut vegetables up. I noticed a newlywed husband helping clear the coffee table. Though in its incipient stages, a movement in such media as advertising appeared to project an image of the "modern" father as one who helps out at home. Many men, though, including as yet unmarried college students, thought that if their wives did not work outside the home, they should be responsible for all the housework.

In most households the inside work remained largely if not solely the domain of the wife. The contribution on the part of the husbands to domestic labor did not seem to me much more substantial than what Lee Hyo-jae (1971:55) had found twenty-five years before. Husbands still referred to their wives as *uri chip saram*, literally meaning "our house person." One woman told me that she would be insulted if her husband referred to her in any other way. Housework was still considered to be the responsibility of women even if a woman also worked outside the home. Mrs. Im, a young, recently married schoolteacher, for example, was told by her husband, a white-collar, salaried employee, that because she worked fewer hours as a teacher than he did as a company man, she should be responsible for the housework. However, she attributed most of his attitude to the fact that he was an eldest son and accustomed to being waited on. For that reason she advised an unmarried colleague not to marry an eldest son. Whether she worked the same or even more hours than her husband at her outside job would not have made a difference, she thought.

I knew of no Korean men who had anything to do with laundry. (Apparently they exist; Clark Sorensen reports of knowing some unmarried men who washed their clothes by hand [pers. comm.].) Even though there were a few closet cooks, the vast majority of males "would starve," I was told by not a few Korean women, if they had to rely on their own cooking. One woman told me her brothers wouldn't know the difference between the meat from a cow and that from a pig. If their wives were out of town or not otherwise available to cook, most men would go out and eat if they did not have a daughter old enough to cook (that is, usually at least of college age). Many male university students, however, were proud that they were able to make instant ramen (which amounts to boiling water).

Among the university-aged women I interviewed, those who came from the countryside were more likely to have claimed to have helped their mothers with housework before moving to Seoul to attend the university, but not by a very large margin. Before my return to Korea in 1996, I would have said that children in the city in general, girls as well as boys, were not forced to do any household chores and that mothers usually discouraged their children from doing housework because such chores took away from their schoolwork. In the past only the yangban elite could afford to have their children devote their time to cultivating their minds rather than the fields. Thus being able to study rather than work was a sign of status. That continues to be the case today. My experience in 1996 of living with a family with three girls for a month, however, makes me question whether girls actually were freed from doing chores or whether they just claimed to be. In particular, I found the eldest of the three girls I was staying with, a middle-school student, doing dishes, setting out food, making tea, doing some laundry when her parents were out of town, and in general looking after her two younger siblings. To a much lesser degree, the middle girl, a fourth grader, was seen occasionally doing the dishes and taking care of the youngest sister. I commented to the eldest that I thought she did a lot of work around the house. She replied that it was actually very little. When I asked her about her friends, she said that all of them did some work around the house, but again, very little.

Whatever the reality, the ideal was for children to be freed from household chores in order to devote their time to study to attain the educational credentials that would allow them to acquire or maintain status, just as it was for their yangban counterparts of yesteryear. And as I discuss below, undoubtedly many children in fact did not do any chores. For some of those girls, once they entered college they might have begun to do a few things around the house. It was at this point that some university women began to perceive a noticeable difference in the way their parents treated their brothers. For example, a young woman may have been expected to make dinner for her father and brothers if the mother was not there, though the expectations for the quality of the meal may have been low. Many young women, however, did continue to refrain from doing anything in the way of housework, even picking up after themselves, until they got married in their mid-twenties or so. My own personal experience with women at this stage of life provided the one major area of friction with the woman I lived with, Seung-hyo. Seung-hyo had employed a live-in maid until I arrived. (My research budget did not allow for continuing to keep her on.) An actual aunt or *ajumŏni* of the woman I lived with, an elderly, but very spry and intelligent woman who had lost her husband and son and now lived with her daughter-in-law, took the full-time maid's place, coming three times a week to clean and prepare food.

At one point, Seung-hyo's niece and two daughters, all college graduates in their twenties and as yet unmarried, were staying with us. An incident that occurred the day Seung-hyo picked her eldest daughter up from the airport illustrates that even Seung-hyo could become very upset with these young women. Although she didn't expect help from her daughter who had just arrived, Seung-hyo, who had prepared dinner, was very irritated that her younger daughter and niece did not lift a finger to help with the dishes. Seung-hyo expressed her irritation, telling me they were "spoiled brats," as she and I cleaned up. Seung-hyo must have said something to her daughter about my helping and their not, because a little later while I was in my room the daughter came in and asked if I wanted some cherries prepared in a special way by Ajumŏni. When I replied in the affirmative, she said she would bring them. When she brought them, she thanked me for doing the dishes.

In my field notes written that evening I noted that the daughter knew that Ajumŏni did not come every day, and yet the daughter left her dishes in the sink. I wondered, "Who does she expect to do them?" I also wrote that although I thought the niece was beginning to get the picture, the niece too had been doing the same thing. Seung-hyo had been regularly cleaning up after both her daughter and niece when Ajumŏni was not there. I made the following entry at the time:

In line with what Pierre Bourdieu writes in *Distinctions*, I can't totally become comfortable with personal maid service, as I was not brought up with it, but it's obvious these Korean kids have. Even the niece, whose family is supposed to be in economic straits as the father has been switching jobs, had had the same Ajumŏni working for them in the past. When the niece moved in [with us], she had no trouble picking up where she left off. For example, Ajumŏni showed me a note the niece wrote to Ajumŏni requesting her to do some laundry. [The fact that Ajumŏni showed it to me indicated that she did not totally approve of the situation, though she did do the laundry.] The niece does not do her own laundry or clean her own room or even clean our now shared bathroom, which she must have noticed (maybe not?) that Ajumŏni does not clean. . . . (Sueng-hyo has her own bathroom which Ajumŏni cleans.)

This phenomenon [this sense of entitlement] is not unique to these three women. If a family doesn't have a maid, or even when they do, the mother serves as one. Koreans themselves tell me (such as Miss Shim and Mrs. Im yesterday) that it starts when mothers tell their kids to let the dishes be, or whatever, and go and study. "Only study." It must really be a shock for a woman when she has to start doing all those things when she becomes wife and mother.

Once a young woman married and became responsible for others, her life was turned upside down, changing from a life of leisure (with regard to housework) to one that included a great deal of hard work. In the process, a woman becomes less self-centered. As one man put it, "Before a woman is married, she is treated like a queen. After she marries, she is treated like a slave." I looked at his wife for her reaction; she sadly agreed. (In contrast to women, Korean men in general, if not universally, never lost their sense of entitlement to being served.)

As most young women had little or no experience with cooking or other housework before they got married, or at least until after they graduated from college, I was curious as to how they learned. A few women in a university home economics program were required to go through a "boot camp" lasting a couple of weeks where they lived together and learned domestic skills such as cooking. Mr. Ch'oi's wife went to cooking school instead of college for a year after graduating from high school. (This showed in the quality of her cooking.) When I asked most women how they learned, though, most would answer: "Naturally."

One day while I was having a conversation with Mrs. Baek, her daughter, a recent university graduate, brought in on a tray, as is proper, a pot of one of Korea's many special teas with tea cups for her mother and me. After her daughter left the room, her mother expressed to me her surprise that her daughter even knew how to prepare the tea, because she had never known her daughter to have done so before. Obviously, she must have picked it up "naturally" by observing her mother. In an earlier discussion about this subject, Mrs. Baek had joked that she was going to buy her daughters cookbooks for wedding presents. At a later time, after Mrs. Baek's new daughter-in-law moved in, we overheard the daughter-in-law in the kitchen busily asking the part-time maid various questions about cooking. I did observe the girls with whom I was staying on my visit in 1996 occasionally watch their mother or grandmother prepare something and even participate in the process. They seemed to enjoy this, as long as they were not forced.

Many daughters-in-law of middle-class families, whether married to the eldest son or not, would spend some time at the beginning of their marriage living with their in-laws, during which they learned to cook like the groom's mother. Several university students indicated that they would like to live with their in-laws for a while upon first being married for this very purpose. If a newly married woman and her husband lived on their own, she was also likely to be without the aid of a maid, at least in the early years, and trial-and-error would be the primary method of learning housekeeping. Alternatively, I was told of one daughter-in-law who, though living separately from her in-laws, went to her in-laws' home on a daily basis for the first few months after marriage to learn how to cook from her mother-in-law.

In her 1967 survey, Lee Hyo-jae found that more middle-class families were able to afford a maid than in the past. About half of Lee Hyo-jae's households employed a live-in maid. These maids took over the duties of housecleaning, food preparation, and care of clothes, formally the responsibility of the wife. However, "housewives," according to Lee, "say that maids used to be obedient and faithful to their jobs, but nowadays they tend to be selfish and prefer to work in the better-equipped homes that own labor-saving devices and television" (1971:54). Wives themselves would have preferred to have these labor-saving devices over maids, but maids continued to be more affordable and necessary: "Though middle-class homes are beginning to be able to afford the luxury of mechanical aids, they continue to employ a maid. Salaries are low and the extra person is needed to help with the complicated and time-consuming task of preparing and serving Korean food. The presence of a maid also ensures against theft, because someone is always present in the house" (Lee Hyo-jae 1971:55).

The number of live-in maids had declined by the 1990s, but the use of part-time maids among the middle-class was quite common. Even if a maid was not employed on a regular basis, maids might be hired as temporary help, especially for food preparation for special occasions. The increasing cost of retaining a maid as fewer women were available to do that work was somewhat offset by the increased availability of modern conveniences. Although electricity had been made generally available in the previous twenty-five years, the use of many electric appliances and other modern conveniences was still relatively new or not present in some households. Many Korean women had the impression that American housewives had an easier time because of all the appliances available to them.

I showed Ajumŏni how to use the washing machine and vacuum cleaner and introduced her to furniture polish and to a mop (which I bought at the U.S. military exchange) so that we didn't have to get down on our hands and knees to wipe the floors with a rag. (I kept my own room clean.) The woman I lived with complained that the live-in maid she previously employed was from the country and could not adjust to urban lifestyles. She was always shrinking expensive clothes, breaking things, and even took the rubber gaskets out of the jars used to store kimch'i and sauces—rubber gaskets being an adaptation to having to keep the jars inside apartments rather than outside in courtyards.

Even with maids, some help from husbands, and the increased use of labor-saving devices, the burden of housework still by far, even in the most "modern" of households, fell heavily upon the women. If there was a mother-in-law living in the house, she was now more likely to help out the daughter-in-law than the other way around.

Clothes and Laundry

One afternoon I found Ajumŏni sitting crossed-legged on the floor of the anpang, stitching back together, by hand, a freshly washed *ibul* or blanket. Although the ibul I used in 1996 had a zipper, traditional-style ibul, far from having disappeared (Ajumŏni showed me five other ibul, each of a different thickness for different seasons, each with a different name, stored in the wall-length, almost ceiling-high anpang wardrobe), required, like padded winter clothing of times past, that they be ripped apart and have their stuffing removed before washing, and then be restuffed afterward. Watching this laborious process, I made the comment that Korean women had a lot of work. She agreed, but added that things today were not nearly as bad as when people wore hanbok, the traditional Korean dress, on a daily basis.

In 1958 Ha Tae Hyung wrote: "Korean women have to cook three meals a day, wash, starch, iron and sew the white clothes, and therefore have little time to leave their homes" (Ha 1958:65). The sewing machine was beginning to lighten the load somewhat in some households, but "young mothers and shy maidens [continued to] sit opposite each other at the calendering stones, beating the washed clothes with flattened wood clubs (*pangmang'i*) to a smooth and shiny ironed finish" (Ha 1958:72). By 1967 electric irons were "considered to be [one of the] indispensable daily necessities," but sewing machines were "among the luxuries every household" wanted (Lee Hyo-jae 1971: 46).

In the 1990s, it was still not that unusual to see people of the eldest generation wear hanbok. For the younger generations, however, the wearing of traditional attire was limited to official occasions, holidays, and special family gatherings such as weddings. Being custom-made and now patterned after those worn by the elite class of yangban of times past, hanbok could be quite expensive. Owning and wearing these expensive garments on special occasions had become a way of asserting status. In some families it could also be a matter of propriety, and a woman might be chided for not dressing in hanbok when expected. I often saw people, especially women and children, wearing hanbok in large hotels where special events were being held or out on the streets and palace grounds (now public parks) on holidays. In 1996 one day a month was designated as Hanbok Day, but I am not sure that was widely known. In any case, men were much less likely to wear hanbok than women, generally wearing Western suits even on those occasions when their wives would wear hanbok.

At the time of Lee Hyo-jae's 1967 (1971) survey, only children's clothes were generally found ready-made. There was a trend toward employing a professional dressmaker, however, and younger women were losing traditional skills, though they expressed an interest in learning how to make Western clothing. By the early 1990s, ready-made clothes in all the latest styles in all price ranges were available in all sizes. It was now the brand name of the Western-style clothes worn on a daily basis that had become the symbol of wealth and status. But even in the 1990s, it was not uncommon among the middle class for certain everyday clothes such as Western-style suits and dresses to be custom made. But rather than the female members of the households pulling out sewing machines, tailors or seamstresses, who would come to the home, were more likely to be employed.

Doing laundry, though not as time consuming as in the past, still required more effort than what I was accustomed to. Owning a washing machine was no longer unusual, but was nevertheless far from universal among South Korea's urban middle class. If there were two balconies, a washing machine, if owned, would be placed in the enclosed balcony in the back, that is, on the balcony opposite the living room and near the kitchen. If there was only one balcony, the bathroom was often the only place a washing machine could be placed, even in many of the larger Western-style houses. In the early 1990s Korean washers tended to be smaller and much less sturdy than the ones typically found in American homes. By 1996 larger and sturdier models were readily available. Still, even when there was a washing machine in the house, some hand-washing, done in large plastic bowls, was usually carried out. It was thought that washing machines did not get clothes very clean. Thus some clothes, especially underwear, were hand scrubbed, often with the use of boiled water and a great deal of detergent. To address the consumer concern of sanitizing clothes, one company advertised a washing machine that boiled water.

Clothes dryers were not manufactured in Korea and were only beginning to make their appearance in Korean homes. I personally knew of only one upper-middle-class family who had one installed in their apartment, the Baeks. Mrs. Baek, however, complained that it took so long to dry the clothes (she asked me how long the ones in the United States took to dry a pair of jeans to make a comparison) and that it required so much electricity that she rarely used it. Clothes were hung out to dry on metal, tubular racks usually left permanently set up on either balcony. Additional smaller, collapsible racks could be placed in any available spot throughout the house when more rack space was required.

Electric irons were one of the first appliances quickly adopted in the 1960s once electricity became available. Ironing boards like those used in the United States were available but not common (though I noticed they were readily available in the markets by 1997). Rather, thick mattress-like pads without legs were used. Ironing on them was difficult, but Korean women excelled at getting wrinkles out. Ironing a few blouses occasionally was the one thing I did ask Ajumŏni to do, and I compensated her well for her trouble. The woman who owned the dryer told me her husband went through ten dress shirts a week, and she was only too happy to give them to the young maid that came to her apartment twice a week to iron and do other chores.

Until I moved into a lower- (but not low-)class neighborhood in 1987, I was unaware of any laundromats in Korea. Dry cleaners were ubiquitous. Three competing businesses daily chanted up and down the twelve-story stairwell of our middle-class highrise apartment, picking up and delivering clothes. Business suits, the daily work attire and mark of the middle-class man, and dresses were usually sent out to the cleaners.

Cleaning and Cleanliness

As already noted, many appliances such as vacuum cleaners were by no means universal and were often relatively new in South Korean urban middle-class homes. Even if they were owned, moreover, they may have been used more for display value than for lightening the household workload. The reason for this, according to one informant, was that many Korean housewives believed that these electric appliances did not clean as well as doing chores by hand.

The belief that washing machines did not use water hot enough to sanitize clothes is one example of this perspective. Because vacuum cleaners kick up dust on the bare floors, many women continued to get down on their hands and knees with damp rags once if not twice a day. Others did eventually come around to using vacuum cleaners, as was the case of the mother of the informant cited above, but might still wipe the floors with a damp floor rag (kŏlle) after vacuuming.

Spending a great deal of time on the uncarpeted floor even in my own room, I became aware of how quickly a floor becomes in need of cleaning, and this was without shoes being worn in the house. For several months after returning to my carpeted home in the United States, I thought how filthy the floor must be, being vacuumed at most once a week and cleaned (shampooed) so infrequently. Add to this the fact that shoes were then worn inside the house, and it took me a while before I lost my paranoia about cleanliness.

In Korea cleanliness was often associated with modernity. Recall that the traditional houses, with their dirt floors in the kitchen, and ash and dust from firewood, and coal briquettes for heating, were thought of as being dirty and difficult to keep clean. The modern apartments, in contrast, were much easier to keep up. Their newness alone exuded cleanliness, and for this reason also they appeared cleaner than even the early mixed-style houses and duplexes.

The one other major electric appliance that would aid Koreans in keeping house is a dishwasher. The only dishwasher I saw was small enough to be placed on the counter but bulky enough to be difficult for one person to move. The woman I lived with was given a dishwasher by one of her brothers who no longer wanted it. It proved quite inconvenient. The only place to hook up the water intake hose was to the sink. And of course there was the matter of the water discharge. There was also insufficient space on the kitchen counter near the sink for the dishwasher to be left there permanently. Thus every time the dishwasher was to be used, it had to be moved. Even when it was placed on a cart, the cart had to be wheeled close enough to the sink for the hoses to reach. Moreover, there was insufficient room in the dishwasher itself to load dishes from even a small dinner party. The woman I lived with ended up calling the dishwasher a "white elephant" and understood why her brother (or rather his wife) had wanted to dispose of it.

Food and Cooking

In 1967, maids or not, Lee Hyo-jae (1971) reported that women were invariably busy in the fall making kimch'i to last the family through the winter. Many followed with the making of soy sauce, though some were beginning to buy it in the market. In all three of Lee Hyo-jae's neighborhoods, most staples were bought in neighboring markets. The markets in the suburban and apartment-dwelling neighborhoods, however, were small and did not stock many of the foods needed to make side dishes. Thus the women in this area usually also shopped at the large wholesale markets at South and East Gates. By the 1990s, if not before, it was the areas around the apartment complexes that were better stocked.

Food preparation in the Korean household, though still time consuming, had been greatly facilitated over the last couple of decades by such developments as improved marketing and the increased availability of a wide range of food products and modern appliances. Even with regard to rice and kimch'i, the two basic staples many Koreans considered a meal to be incomplete without, innovations were apparent. Ready-to-cook rice, for example, was delivered in large sacks directly to the home, and an electric rice cooker, constantly in use, had become standard in every household. *Pinil hausu*, vinyl greenhouses on the outskirts of Seoul, meanwhile, provided the capital's population with fresh vegetables all year long, obviating the need to pickle enough vegetables in the fall to sustain a household through the winter.

Kimch'i, along with every conceivable Korean side dish, soup, and more, could even be found ready-made in grocery stores. Bountiful supplies of such prepared dishes were elaborately displayed fresh daily in the expansive but crowded grocery departments of the modern, high-rise department stores found especially in Kangnam. Judging by the amount on display and by the crowded conditions in the stores, I would conclude that many households consumed food not made from scratch. Nevertheless, most Koreans did not think store-bought kimch'i was as good as home-made, not only because of the taste but because of possibly added chemicals such as preservatives.

Even though the amount of vegetables a household pickles in the fall season may have been reduced by as much as 75 percent from the past (according to rough estimates by middle-aged women I consulted), the fall ritual of kimch'i making was still observed in most households, and fall was not the only season it was prepared. The making of kimch'i was considered to require skill and experience. All of the university-aged women whom I asked whether they could make kimch'i exclaimed, "Oh, no! It's too difficult!" or something to that effect. It was not uncommon for a mother-in-law or some other senior female relative, whether living with younger relatives or not, to provide a young bride with kimch'i. This way the groom would have the type of kimch'i he grew up with. I know of more than one case where a woman had been married ten years or more and was still receiving her kimch'i from her mother-in-law. One newly married woman who had no mother-in-law and whose natal family was living on Cheju Island received a supply of these spicy, pickled vegetables from a maternal aunt who lived in Seoul. (After returning from Korea and living in Washington State, I was provided with a regular supply of kimch'i from the wife of my taekwondo master; they were recent immigrants to the United States.) Often, whether living together or not, the mother-in-law and daughter-in-law would make kimch'i together. Whether a woman could make kimch'i or not, if she had relatives in the countryside, she might occasionally receive kimch'i from them either when a relative came to Seoul or when someone from her household went to the countryside.

There have been some adaptations, especially in apartment dwellings, with regard to the storage of kimch'i and other food products such as soy sauce and red pepper paste traditionally stored in *hang'ari* or earthenware jars, also known as *tok*. The jars not only have rubber gaskets, but, as mentioned above, are kept on the balcony (which was sometimes called a madang or courtyard) or even hung out the balcony window in a wire container shaped much like a flower planter. Earthenware jars could be seen on the roofs of tenement houses and villas. Smaller amounts of kimch'i as well as all kinds of perishable foods were stored in the refrigerator, now also universal in middle-class homes. Some people complained that even this home-made kimch'i was not as good as that which was allowed to ferment in jars partially buried in the ground, as was traditionally done in courtyards.

Many dried vegetables such as mushrooms and red peppers are used in Korean cuisine. However, these were usually bought by urbanites predried. Once I did see a young woman, who happened to be from my apartment building, spread out red peppers to dry on a piece of cloth on the lawn directly in front of the apartment. It was possible that a family who lived in the city but also owned land in the countryside or had relatives there might dry their own vegetables on a trip to the country.

Electric or gas ranges and sometimes even microwave ovens were improvements over the oil burners and stoves owned by more than 70 percent of South Korean households reported in Lee Hyo-jae's survey (1971:46). Other smaller electric appliances such as can openers and mixers had also become common in urban middle-class households by the 1990s.

Hot running water was standard. Tap water in Seoul, however, was not considered potable. At the same time, although Ajumŏni boiled water to make *porich'a* or barley tea used as drinking water, she, or the woman I lived with, was not concerned about rinsing off fruits and vegetables with tap water. Some people installed water filters. One was operating, noisily, when I first moved into the Kangnam apartment; the woman I lived with had had it installed upon the urging of her daughter. It eventually burnt out. Although buying bottled water was illegal at the time of my residence in Seoul, because it was thought to discriminate against the poor who could not afford it, many did so anyway. Legally, bottled water could be bought only by foreigners. This issue was controversial during my tenure in 1991–92, and the law was largely ignored. Many had bottled water delivered to their home by companies who blatantly drove their trucks with no effort made to conceal the cargo. As of 1994, however, bottled water had been made legal (Laurel Kendall, pers. comm.). In the fall of 1996 I observed that even many of the smallest restaurants served water from a five-gallon jug rather than barley water. An apartment dweller, however, asked if I was sure the jug wasn't just filled with tap water. She thought bottled water was too expensive for these restaurants to be able to afford to use it.

Other items besides bottled water and rice could be delivered directly to the home, including milk, yogurt, orange juice, Chinese dinners, and even pizza. Itinerant merchants selling all kinds of articles from furniture to rice cakes periodically set up their wares under a typically blue-and-white vinyl tarp tent on the compound parking-lot area or drove their trucks through the complex, either broadcasting their products through a hand-held loudspeaker or going up to each guard room and asking the guard to make an announcement over the public address system piped into each apartment unit.

Until recently customers were able to have their groceries delivered upon request to their front door. However, this service was discontinued by the larger stores during my residence in Seoul. An increase in personal cars was partially compensating for this loss of service. Also, most residential areas are surrounded by business districts that provided a wide range of consumer products and services within a short walking distance. When I first moved into my apartment, I felt the complex, which I initially entered by foot off a main road, was quite an isolated residential area. When I took my first walk around the neighborhood, it was as if a whole new world had suddenly opened up.

Right outside the vehicular entrance to this complex was quite a community of small businesses, including banks, tailors, dry cleaners, car repair centers, tire centers, beauty shops, a pharmacy, private extracurricular schools (hagwŏn), video stores, churches, hotels, and a furniture store. The purveyors of food included a fruit stand, butcher's shop, bakery, restaurants, and grocery stores (called "supermarkets" or "super" for short, but actually not much bigger than a U.S. convenience store; one of the grocery stores was underground). There was also a store that sold blackmarket items, such as American beer, presumably from the U.S. military installation, and even a newly opened, twenty-four-hour, Western-style convenience store (a relatively new phenomenon in Seoul at the time).

Although the older neighborhoods in Kangbuk boasted these small businesses as well, residents of Kangnam also had relatively easy access to the chaebŏl-owned, high-rise department stores spread around Kangnam's apartment complexes. Clean, modern, and offering quality merchandise, these department stores, like the Western-style convenience stores, have become popular at the expense of the "mom-and-pop" businesses, which in contrast often appeared cluttered and dirty (see also Kwak Young-sup 1992:30). Of course, many Koreans opted to go to the large traditional markets, especially at East and South Gate (Tongdaemun and Namdaemun, respectively), and, for example, to the large fish market, for special items and bargains not necessarily available elsewhere. As I discovered in 1996, there were also several newer and smaller but still considered traditional-style markets scattered around Seoul. Prices were often lower than in the department stores, and thus these markets were also frequented by women whose apartment complexes were conveniently located closeby.

Finally, with regard to food, going to restaurants has become a favorite labor-saving strategy for housewives, though not necessarily an economical one. The restaurants run the gamut from small, inexpensive Korean restaurants, to medium-priced foreign fast food restaurants, including McDonald's, Burger King, Kentucky (Fried) Chicken, and TGI Fridays, to very fine and expensive restaurants, Korean and otherwise.

Consumption and Standard of Living

In the early days of my residence in Seoul, I recall being struck by the absence of old cars on the road, although there certainly was no lack of shiny, new vehicles. In fact, I was struck by how modern the city in general appeared. Seoul, with its high-rise buildings, glitzy shopping districts, clean, state-of-the-art subway system, and evidence of new construction seemingly everywhere, exuded a sense of prosperity that surprised me. I was not blind to the dirty, hole-in-the-wall businesses, dilapidated neighborhoods, or the existence of an underprivileged class, but it was the sense that South Korea as a whole was no longer a poor but a wealthy nation that stood out.

This sense of prosperity was only heightened as I began to meet and learn more about South Korea's urban middle-class families. The amount of money spent on children's education, housing, televisions, videocassette recorders, cars, clothes, maids, occasionally chauffeurs, pricey health and golf club memberships, travel within the country and abroad, and much more impressed me. A significant segment of the middle class seemed almost obsessed with conspicuous consumption, as if they were in a feeding frenzy. What was difficult for me to realize at first, and even now, is how very recent this affluence was.

There was a reason why all the cars were new, although it did not initially occur to me. Until just a few years earlier, most private citizens could not afford cars. Lee Hyo-jae reported in the early 1970s that automobiles were too expensive for the middle class (1971:46). As recently as a decade before my research, Brandt noted that "a family in which both parents are university graduates with reasonably good jobs and a little extra money on the side . . . [could] even possibly drive a small car," but "in most cases, there is no car" (1983:8).

In just the previous three years leading up to my research, between 1988 and 1991, the numbers of private passenger vehicles more than doubled, almost tripled, from 975,000 to more than 2.5 million (Korea Annual 1992:301). While I was in Korea, the media reported an additional 500 cars being added to Seoul's already congested roads every day. A *Business Korea* journal article illustrated the increase in privately owned cars by noting that in 1987 there was only one car for every sixty people in South Korea; five years later, in 1992, that ratio was one for every nineteen people (Chang 1992:42). The author of the article at the same time took note of the fact that the GNP had more than doubled between 1987 and 1990. In 1997 the ratio was 1:4.

In general, in the early 1990s members of the lower classes did not own private vehicles. My middle-class informants were just as likely to have a car as not. Many of those who did not were considering purchasing one. When Mr. Oh's second child was on the way, he thought his wife should have a car because her hands were going to be full enough taking care of the children. Mr. Ch'oi lived in a satellite city outside Seoul and commuted by bus every day. He too was considering buying a car. In fact, after I returned to the United States he let me know that next time I went to Korea, to be sure to let him know because he would come to the airport and pick me up. Some households owned more than one car. In my apartment building someone during the monthly neighborhood meeting complained that one family was taking up too many parking spaces with its five vehicles. Two families I knew who owned successful businesses and were considered upper-middle class had chauffeurs as well. These cars were well cared for. Walking around the neighborhood surrounding the university campus in Kangbuk near where I lived my first summer in Seoul, I was struck by how many cars were being washed and polished outside of their private garages. In the apartment complex in Kangnam, an enterprising individual or individuals came and offered daily car-washing service. By 1996, even factory workers, I was told, could own a car.

Travel by private vehicle was not all that had seen a recent rise. The drastic increase in travel abroad also illustrates a seemingly compulsive consumer behavior, caused by a sudden ability to afford and obtain things that had been beyond one's reach for so long. Prior to 1987 Korean citizens were strictly limited by the government from going abroad. (Even now, Koreans are required to obtain an exit visa.) In 1983 Brandt noted that, for the average middle-class family, travel abroad was a "cherished goal" and "usually possible only if related to professional activities." "This kind of professional family, while not rare, is, of course, much more affluent than most," Brandt added (1983:9).

The 1987 liberalization of overseas trips led in the following year to a 67.3 percent increase in the number of such trips, a 28.7 percent increase in 1990 over 1989, and an 18.9 percent increase in 1991 over 1990, with 1,856,000 people traveling abroad in 1991 (Korea Annual 1992:175). Notwithstanding the decrease in the growth rate in the few years following the initial year of liberalization (attributed to the Gulf War and an austerity campaign by the government [Korea Annual 1992:179]), in one year alone, in 1991, the equivalent of more than 4 percent of the total population of South Korea made a trip overseas. No longer was Cheju-do, a resort island off the southern tip of the Korean peninsula, the place to go on one's honeymoon. Hawaii had taken that honor. (Of course, honeymoons themselves were a relatively recent phenomenon.) Money was invested in kye and monthly savings plans (offering high interest) with the specific purpose of financing trips abroad. Television game shows with themes of geography, travel, and exotic places reflected the people's hunger and interest in international travel.

The domestic leisure industry was also a high-growth industry in South Korea. When asked what she thought differentiated the middle class from the lower classes, one university student in 1992 replied "leisure." Many members of the lower classes could afford neither the time nor the money to participate in these activities. Ten years before, Brandt noted that while most middle class could not afford a car, "they will still probably be able to join a modest tennis club and take vacation sightseeing trips" (1983:9). By the 1990s, full-sized clubs in Seoul with Olympic-size pools, full-sized bowling alleys, provision of work-out attire, along with other standard amenities such as sauna and weight rooms, made the American middle-class counterpart appear as miniature golf does next to an eighteen-hole golf course. But then the membership fees gave the health clubs in South Korea much more capital to work with. Health club as well as golf course memberships were artificially high, as they were in Japan, in order to claim a certain exclusivity and thus status. Leisure activity was by no means limited to health clubs and golf.

Owning time-share resorts, going skiing and so-called mountain climbing, frequenting amusement parks, and traveling within the country in general were all status markers and popular leisure activities among South Korea's middle class.

A look at the rate of acquisition of certain household goods reveals the rapidity of the increase in the standard of living. If we consider that most of the population of Seoul did not have electricity as late as 1960, the rise in less than a decade in the standard of living among Seoul's urban middle class, reflected by electrical appliances and other modern household goods, is impressive. Lee Hyo-jae (1971:46) reports:

The present-day [1967] living standards of the middle class are indicated by their household goods. Clocks or watches, radios, electric irons, and coffee sets are considered to be indispensable daily necessities and are owned by every household. A sewing machine, electric fan, television set, telephone, and refrigerator are among the luxuries every household wants. More than two-thirds of the residents have a camera, television set, oil burner, record player, or a telephone; only one-third have an electric mixer, an oil stove, reception room furniture, or a refrigerator. Pianos and automobiles are too expensive for the middle class, especially since maintenance and taxes on a private car would require almost the entire monthly expenditure of a middle-class family. Accordingly, only members of Korea's upper class can afford to own automobiles.

Pianos were owned by any middle-class household that wanted one, apparently since at least the early 1980s. Brandt noted: "At least one of the children (more if they are talented) will be taking intensive classical music lessons" (1983:9). As reported by the National Statistics Office (1991: 315), television sets, owned by only 14.5 percent of the total urban population in 1970, were one of the first items to become universal, that occurring by 1985. In 1970, less than 10 percent of urban households had phones and even by 1985 almost 50 percent remained without. Today, phones are universal among the middle class. In 1970, less than 5 percent of urban households had refrigerators, a proportion that jumped to roughly 50 percent by 1980 and almost 80 percent by 1985; they are universal in middle-class homes today. Statistically, there were no washing machines in 1970, less than 2 percent owned them in 1975, and by 1985 about 33 percent of the households owned washing machines. By the 1990s, a middle-class household was as likely to have a washing machine as not. Because most residential units, including large, Western-style, single-residence houses, were not built until very recently with washing machines in mind, prospective buyers may have been limited by space to put the machine as much as by cost. Finally, the latest major household good people were clamoring to acquire was an air-conditioning unit. The woman I lived with bought one during my stay. No statistics on this acquisition were yet available. In 1996, what struck me was the number of hand-held phones visible on the streets.

People born before 1960 have witnessed if not experienced the whole spectrum of remarkable changes in lifestyle and standard of living. Most have themselves experienced severe economic and other hardships and now, for those who have managed to obtain middle- or upper-class status, the good life. In the 1990s, many in the youngest generation seemed totally oblivious to how poor their country and their own parents had been in the not too distant past. The Baek family illustrates these generational differences, as well as differences in attitudes found within a segment of the older generation regarding how to use their newfound wealth.

On a visit I made to the zoo with Mr. Baek and his wife, Mr. Baek exclaimed: "The animals [living at the zoo] live in better shelter than we had!" referring to earlier times. Though the Baeks now owned rentals and they themselves lived in an apartment in Kangnam worth close to a quarter-million dollars, their living conditions had not always been so comfortable, as was the case with most Koreans (except for the youngest generation) who now lived a middle- or upper-class lifestyle.

Recall that Mr. Baek, whose father had been a rich landlord in what is now North Korea, lost everything. However, Mr. Baek went on to graduate from one of the South Korean military academies. During his twenty-some years in the service, he and his wife lived rather simply on fairly low pay. When they first married, for example, where they were living had no running water. His wife would get up early in the morning and use a hose to get water from a neighbor.

It was not until after Mr. Baek retired from the service and started working for a company and investing in stocks and rentals that the family's standard of living increased drastically. Now he made good money but kept tight control over it. Mr. Baek went on to explain to me that because of hard times, he knew the value of money and was very strict about controlling the spending. The rest of the family, his wife and three now grown children, did not understand, he said. They did not think he should be so tight with his money. He gave the following example. He rented out several apartments. When a tenant moved out and there was a bill remaining for something like electricity, he tried to get the tenant to pay. His family told him he should "be a good Christian and just let it go," that is, absorb the cost. Although his family may have considered him tight with his money, "a tyrant" in his own words, Mr. Baek did spend a great deal of money so that his family was now living a very comfortable upper-middle-class lifestyle.

On more than one occasion Mr. Baek told me he was worried about his children's generation [born after 1960] "because they do not know hardship; they do not know the value of money." Although Mr. Baek paid for his own marriage and housing, this was not the case for his own children. His son was surprised when I told him that most children in the United States either move out after they graduate from school or pay their parents rent. As described earlier, after the father gave this son upon his marriage an apartment probably equivalent to ten or fifteen years of the son's salary, the son had asked his father to pay for the remodeling as well; the father agreed to pay half. The father's concern was typical, as members of the younger generation seemed to expect that their parents would continue to foot the bill. Nevertheless, the parents did continue to foot the bill. It was a matter of status.

Finally, the high standard of living South Korean urban middle-class families enjoyed may be compared with a description of the living conditions of the working-class neighborhood on the outskirts of Seoul studied by Kim Eun-shil (1993). The contrast is stark:

My informants who had one or two children lived in a room with a tiny attached kitchen, whose rent was around 70,000 won (about $100). A deposit was required of 500,000 won ($700). Several families in this area shared houses that were built to contain several households. The inside of the house in this area was usually dark and cool, so even in summer they used the Korean style of heating, in which the underfloor was heated with a briquette to make the floor of their rooms dry and warm at night. They took out the briquettes in the day time because they made their small space steam. When people were in their houses, they opened the door, so that outsiders could see the inside. This open-space living style, in which their everyday life was visible and audible to outsiders, was different from the closed space of middle-class apartment houses which were guarded by janitors. The front door was always locked in middle-class apartment houses. The open and interpenetrating housing in working-class districts did not guarantee safety from thieves. . . . The women in 1991 said that even soy bean paste and hot pepper paste or clothes that had been washed were stolen and some women had almost been raped and tied up by thieves.

Yaksan was an area not well served by the urban infrastructure, which was apparent in the unpaved muddy alleys. . . . Recently, to accommodate the increasing population in Seoul's metropolitan area, the central government decided to redevelop the *Yaksan* area into a residential district for middle-class people. However, no action had yet been taken during my [that is, Kim Eun-shil's] fieldwork in 1991. Thus, when I did my fieldwork in the *Yaksan* district, poor people's housing and small factories were crowded together and the housing in the *Yaksan* area was considered cheap, bad and dirty. Korean society had been successfully industrialized as the result of workers' hard labor, but workers were looked down upon as the poor, ignorant masses or as angry, violent protesters, as the television news sometimes showed. Thus, the image of the "muddy," "dirty," road of *Yaksan* encapsulated the image of the worker's poor living conditions, low social status, and oil, dust-stained body, and it signified the exclusion of workers from the urban neatness and conveniences brought about by Korean development and modernization. (Kim Eun-shil 1993:176–178)

Kim Eun-shil's description reminds us that the high-rise apartments we have explored, with their attendant lifestyle, are not the only kind of dwelling in urban South Korea. In the 1990s a life of luxury and leisure truly does set South Korea's middle class apart from the lower classes, much as a lifestyle characterized by relative luxury and leisure might have distinguished some members of Chosŏn society's yangban stratum from commoners and lowborn.

5

Education

If our boy belongs to the higher class, he will not be expected to work, but to study as soon as he is old enough to take up that duty. If he belongs to the middle or lower class, he will be compelled at an early age to take part in the struggle for rice.

—J. Robert Moose (1911:91)

A college or university education has become one of the most important markers of middle-class status in South Korea. Although in the 1990s there was a strong correlation between education and occupation, the guarantee of a good job was not the primary motivation behind most Koreans' pursuit of higher education. Rather, the Korean people's pursuit of education was more than anything else a pursuit of status. Just as with their yangban predecessors, that pursuit started at a very early age.

The earliest years of childhood were spent quite happy and carefree. Young children were allowed to run about and shout to their hearts' content without seeming to disturb their elders. Moose's words, "From the very first our village boy is petted, spoiled, and allowed to have his own way in nearly everything" (1911:89), held as true in the 1990s as in times past as contemporary toddlers, girls and boys alike, were indulged and pampered.

This carefree period, however, was short-lived and often came to an abrupt if not traumatic end about the time a child started school. Leniency was replaced with high expectations. Etiquette and education being among if not the most important indicators of status in Korea, children were expected to display the best behavior and manners as well as develop disciplined study habits.

Education, including learning proper behavior, becomes an all-consuming process for the young Korean middle-class child just as it did for the children of the yangban estate in yesterday's Confucian world order. Confucian doctrine places heavy emphasis on the importance of education. In the 1990s education, moral worth, and status were still linked in the minds of Koreans. Preparation for the state-administered university entrance exam and mastery of the English language served as the functional equivalents of the civil service exams and literacy in Chinese of times past. A university education and English had become characteristic features of South Korea's modern-day middle class. Furthermore, because education was so important to the status of the family, whether yangban or contemporary middle class, it is and always has been the family rather than the government that has carried the primary financial burden for the education of their young.

Through all the change and adversity experienced by the Koreans during the first half of the twentieth century and since, the value of and family responsibility for education have remained unwavering constants. The curriculum may have been adapted to meet modern requirements, but, as Brandt explains, education for its own sake and for the sake of the prestige it bestows on the individual and the individual's family leads families to endure great sacrifice. A modern education beyond elementary school often involved leaving home for those who lived in the countryside. Brandt writes:

If asked what contributes most to high prestige and social rank, most villagers without hesitation will cite education. At this ideational level education has almost ritual efficacy. It really does not matter whether the person in question has studied the Chinese classics or has attended the regular public schools; his moral worth has been augmented. Only men with an education are qualified to direct others. This traditional ethical principle is not restricted to old people, since informants in their twenties also tended to rank people by degree of schooling. . . .

A child who goes to middle school and high school is irrevocably separated from his village and age mates by years of different experience and training and by his changed status when he comes home. He has been transformed into something too precious to waste on ordinary manual labor. Somehow he has been exempted from the bitter struggle for subsistence and reserved for finer things more suitable to his superior talent and virtue. Such a person often becomes a costly ornament decorating a hard-pressed family. The fact that his family takes great pride in having a son wander idly through the village, perhaps graciously lending a hand at harvest time, is undeniable. (Brandt 1971:95, 96)

Brandt was writing of the mid-1960s, when enrollment, though almost universal at the primary level (91.6 percent in 1965), was still a luxury many families could not afford at the higher levels. Enrollment at all levels steadily increased along with the general and significant increase in the economic wealth of the country and of the people.

Today almost all children attend primary and secondary school, and dropout rates are low. As of 1990, 99 percent of boys and girls attended primary school and 97 percent middle school. The high-school enrollment ratios for the same year were 90.0 percent for boys and 85.0 percent for girls. In colleges and universities, the enrollment ratios were 50.4 percent for males and 23.8 percent for females. Except at the tertiary level, there seems to be no significant disproportion in enrollment by sex (KWDI 1991:17).

The percentage of members of the middle and upper classes attending an institute of higher learning was much higher, of course, with the vast majority of middle- and upper-class males pursuing a college education. The total enrollment in colleges and universities in South Korea would be even higher if not limited by a government-imposed cap. An estimated additional 15,000 to 20,000 Koreans leave South Korea every year to go abroad in pursuit of higher education.

Higher Education

According to a recent poll, more than 93 percent of *all* South Korean parents expected their children to enter a university or college (Kwak Byong-sun 1991:45; Bae Chong-keun 1991:56). Although the expectation that their children would receive higher education was almost universal, the reality is that there were only 300,000 positions available in South Korea for the more than 800,000 who applied annually for admission to an institute of higher learning (many of those being repeat applicants). Kwak Byong-sun of the Korean Educational Development Institute comments, "These figures indicate the extent of the people's excessive aspiration for higher education and . . . the inevitable competitive nature of the admission race to colleges or universities" (1991:45).

According to a survey on "The Purpose for Educating Children" published by the National Statistics Office (1991:197), approximately 60 percent of parents surveyed cited "character and culture" or "improvement of nature" as the most important reason for educating both their sons and their daughters. The more educated the parents, the higher this percentage. For example, this figure rose to 75 percent among parents who were college graduates themselves. Associating "improvement of nature" and "character and culture" with education is consistent with traditional Confucian ethics that equate education with moral worth and ultimately with prestige and social rank.

According to this same survey, "job" considerations accounted for 29.9 percent of the total respondents' purpose for educating sons and this dropped to 18.4 percent for parents who themselves had attended college. Only 8.3 percent (6.0 percent of those with tertiary education) considered "job" a reason for educating daughters. Yet all the university women I interviewed who had brothers indicated that they felt their parents treated sons and daughters equally with regard to providing an education, at least through undergraduate school. (One university student, though, who wanted to continue her education in graduate school was very hurt when her father told her she should think about marriage instead. She felt particularly hurt because her father did not say the same thing to her older brother.)

The higher value placed on "job" considerations for sons over daughters is consistent with the reality that most university-educated women did not work, at least not in the formal sector. Although the majority of women I interviewed who were currently enrolled in university studies responded that they expected to work even after getting married and having children, as of 1990 only 8.3 percent of the female work force were women holding college or university degrees (KWDI 1991:38). Between 1965 and 1990, more than half of all female graduates did not work (at least in the formal sector) after graduation (Yoon In-Jin 1993:17). Except for those with professional occupations or those who owned their own business, most of those that did work later resigned.

What reason, then, besides "culture" did parents give for educating their daughters if not for jobs? More than 25 percent cited "advantage for marriage" for daughters and only 7.8 percent did so for sons, an inverse of the ratio for "job" between the sexes. The common sentiment expressed to me was that Korean men get a good education in order to get a good job, while Korean women get a good education to get a good husband. One mother of a middle-school girl explained to me that a university education was necessary for her daughter so that that particular qualification could be listed with the matchmaker when it came time to seek a husband for her daughter. This again was a matter of status, and this statement represented a common attitude among parents.

During the Chosŏn dynasty, education of women was also a matter of status. Even at the time, "the relative degree of education enjoyed by Korean women as compared with men is not thoroughly understood by foreigners, judging by what we find in print," Hulbert wrote (1969 [1906]:361). "It is commonly believed that education here is almost wholly confined to the men, but this estimate must be considerably modified." It is true that girls were taught "within the walls of their own homes" (Hulbert 1969 [1906]:362). Nevertheless, they did receive an education either from their female kin or from hired female tutors. Li Mirok described his sister's education:

Like my other sisters, Setze did not go to our school which was for only boys. Daughters were to be taught the female accomplishments by their mothers and the older women. Setze was still too young. She did not yet know how to sew or embroider, nor how to cook, and spent her days prattling and playing. . . . At other times I found her lying in a corner engrossed in reading a fat book. She loved reading stories and romances.

The books she read were written not in the difficult Chinese, but in the easy Korean script which consists of some twenty letters. As Setze explained to me by and by, the individual characters were not called, say, "heaven" or "earth," "sun" or "moon," but A or O, E or K or N. Setze had learned them very early from her foster mother, and since then she was able to read all tales and romances, which were printed in these characters, so that there should be something to read even for the women who did not usually go to school at all. (Li Mirok 1986:18)

According to Hulbert (1969 [1906]:361) the native Korean writing system, *han'gul*, was "well known and extensively used by all Korean ladies. [Moreover] if one of them [was] lacking in this accomplishment, she [was] looked down upon." Some women of the upper strata also learned selected Chinese characters: "Among the women of the upper class, perhaps two in five study a little Chinese, but not more than one percent of these ladies ever learn to read it," Hulbert estimated (1969 [1906]:361). "The so-called mixed script in which the daily papers are printed can be read by very many ladies, for it requires no knowledge of the Chinese idiom, but only the meaning of some eighteen hundred characters," Hulbert adds.

Regardless, there were certain Confucian works women of the upper class were expected to master. "The Three Principles of Conduct," referring to the treatment of parents, the rearing of family, and housekeeping, is one such work. "Many women who cannot read learn this book by proxy," Hulbert explains (1969 [1906]:362). "It is written in Chinese and Korean on alternate pages, so that no one may have an excuse for not reading it." There was also other required reading for women of the upper classes. Those who were not knowledgeable about their contents were held in less regard:

Next comes "The Five Rules of Conduct," relating to the relations between parent and child, king and subject, husband and wife, old and young, friend and friend. Then there is a book on "Interesting and Proper Things," a mass of anecdotes illustrative of the virtues, and the "Female Physician's Remedy Book," a sort of domestic medical work dealing with prenatal conditions, parturition and the care of infants. Such are the most important books studied by women, and ignorance of their contents is looked upon with great contempt among the upper classes and to a less extent among the middle classes [i.e. commoners]. (Hulbert 1969 [1906]:362)

Thus during the Chosŏn dynasty, an education was valued for women as well as for men, not for employment purposes, but for cultural reasons. In the 1990s, education was also pursued for reasons other than enhancing one's employment opportunities. In fact, the media was full of reports on the difficulty male and female college graduates alike were facing in finding suitable employment; at the same time, there was a shortage of manual labor. Between 1965 and 1990, the average unemployment rate for male college graduates was 30 percent and would have been higher if there were no three-year compulsory military service for males (Yoon In-Jin 1993:24). Yoon In-Jin (1993:17) reports:

Not only the immediate economic rewards of a college education, but also the contemptuous attitude of college graduates toward noncollege graduates in a face-saving culture motivate people to seek higher education with little specific reference to economic returns on education. Particularly for women, college education is a means to enhance one's position in the marriage market. Graduates from prestigious women's universities in Seoul have a better chance than their less fortunate peers of marrying men of high social and economic status. For this reason, women's education and labor force participation are inversely related to each other in South Korea.

Yoon goes on to say that "college-educated women are not strongly inclined to work because their high-status husbands earn enough income to support the family, whereas less-educated women are more likely to work to supplement their husbands' meager earning." For reasons discussed in Chapter 2, I do not completely agree with this latter statement. Basically, a husband's income alone, especially if he was a salary man, *was* generally insufficient, but there were multiple other ways his income was supplemented, including the involvement of the wife in the informal sector.

Regardless, the guarantee of a good job was not the primary motive for seeking a tertiary education for most men or women. Status was. Because a married woman's status was largely derived from her husband's status, it was not as essential that she receive a college education. A man's status was also influenced by his wife's education level, however, and a woman without a college education would have less value in the marriage market. It was unlikely that a woman with a college education would marry a man without at least equivalent educational credentials. During the Chosŏn dynasty, passing of the civil service exams and thereby earning a degree was the surest way to acquire status. In 1990, acquisition of a university degree was the surest way for a man, or woman, to acquire status. However, now higher education was not limited to a small group of elite but was also characteristic of South Korea's middle class as a whole.

English and Other Foreign Languages

During the Chosŏn dynasty, literacy in Chinese was a requisite skill of the cultivated man. Since then, English has replaced Chinese as a marker of status. The study of English by Koreans goes back more than a century, when missionaries first set up schools in Korea. However, English has re-

cently experienced an explosive upsurge in its use in South Korea, coinciding with the marked growth of the middle class and its wealth, as my own
experience indicates.

Seeing me off at the airport on my way to Korea, my Korean language tutor asked me where I initially intended to stay. When I told her I had made
reservations for the first few nights at the moderately priced New Naija Hotel, she, wanting to ease my transition into her native country, took my notebook and jotted down in the Korean script (han'gŭl), "Sae Naija," translating
the English word "new" into Korean. Perhaps this woman, a Korean immigrant to the United States, would be as surprised as I was to find out how pervasive the English language has become in South Korean society.

It was not just that this particular hotel's logo read, in English script,
"New Naija" instead of "Sae Naija." But as I immersed myself into South
Korean urban middle-class life, English seemed to surface everywhere, from
the countless university students, salary men, and middle-class housewives
who approached me to practice their English to the bilingual street signs and
restaurant menus, to advertisements, newspaper headlines, and storefront
signs that contained words that, though written in han'gŭl, when spoken
came out as "bargain sale," "sports news," "supermarket" (or "super" for
short), and the like. Just as Chinese was very much a part of the yangban culture of yesteryear, English was becoming part of South Korean middle-class
culture today.

Even as far back as the Japanese colonial period, English was already being
viewed by some as a mark of culture much as Chinese was during the Chosŏn
dynasty. Li Mirok, having trouble learning the language while studying for
the entrance exam for the Medical Institute of Seoul, which he entered in
1917, recalls: "I was discouraged, for was not English the most important language to learn if one wished to approach true European civilization?" (1986:
126; the manuscript is circa the 1920s).

Li Mirok was not alone among Koreans in assigning value to the English
language at that time or since. This value is reflected in many subtle ways. One
Korean family I know provided several examples extending from the Japanese
period through the present. Mr. Kim, an elderly Korean gentleman with yangban ancestry, had no problem holding a conversation with me in English and
in fact seemed to take great pride in his ability to do so. He explained to me that
he had been required to learn English during the Japanese occupation as a student in what has become Seoul National University's business school. His eldest daughter, now a professor in her mid-fifties, showed me a picture of herself
at the age of one. What struck me was that "one year" was lettered in English at
the bottom of the picture, put there by her father in the 1930s.

In the years following liberation from the Japanese, the daughter herself studied English in school. She had vivid memories of the first time she had occasion to put her knowledge to use. During the Korean War, her family vacated Seoul and went to the Pusan area in the southern part of the Korean peninsula, away from the fighting. Her grandmother, however, remained behind in the Seoul area. Because of the destruction of the bridges during the war, access to Seoul over the Han River was limited and controlled largely by the United States military. When conditions allowed, her parents sent this then young girl to visit her grandmother on the other side of the river. She needed to cross the river but did not have the proper documentation. When the American soldier approached her, she recalls standing up and explaining, in English, her predicament. She was allowed to proceed.

Professor Kim also related to me how delighted her father was when he received from her a letter written in English during the 1950s while she was a student in America. Having received her degrees in the United States, she continued to fill her conversation with English words and phrases, even when talking to other Koreans. Her own children were attending universities in the United States. On one of their occasional visits to Korea, they sat around the table with their mother and one of their maternal uncles, fondly discussing, in English, their grandfather and some comical aspects of his relationship with his wife, their grandmother. One quote they attributed to the family patriarch when commenting on his wife, namely, "She doesn't even know English," was reflective of the view generally held by educated Koreans.

The prestige that English brought was in part a reaction to historical circumstances, to national feelings of backwardness and a need to "catch up" following centuries of isolation and delayed development in terms of industrialization and involvement in a capitalist economic system. Learning foreign languages, especially English, the language of both scholarship and international commerce, was associated with modernization and was viewed by the government and the Korean people alike as necessary for both national and personal development.

Study of other foreign languages besides English was encouraged as well. In 1992 the Education Ministry ordered high schools to begin offering two secondary foreign languages (that is, besides English), saying, "Multiple foreign language education is necessary to cultivate the capable workforce which is much needed in the process of internationalization of Korean society" (*Korea Times*, April 4, 1992:3). Japanese, Chinese, French, German, and Spanish were taught as selective subjects at high schools.

Testing of English was a requirement for all university entrance exam takers. A university could also require an aspirant to select a second foreign language as well in which to be tested. In a move upheld by the courts, Seoul National University (SNU) and other major universities in Seoul decided to exclude Japanese as a selective foreign language on the university entrance exams beginning in 1994. According to one press report, "SNU and other school officials argued for the exclusion of Japanese, citing that it is still not a proper language necessary in general academic fields. However, the actual reason for the exclusion of Japanese is in part tied to the fact that the language is relatively easy to learn for Koreans" (*Korea Times*, May 1, 1991:3). At the same time the Education Ministry announced that more government scholarships would be available for overseas studies in non-English-speaking countries.

The people themselves were motivated to learn foreign languages. When South Korea established formal diplomatic ties with China in the summer of 1992, for example, an increasing number of students and company employees were knocking on the doors of language institutes specializing in teaching Mandarin. Knowledge of Chinese characters became more important once again as South Korean businesses expanded into Chinese-speaking countries. Samsung, one of the large business conglomerates, recently announced that it would begin testing knowledge of Chinese characters along with English proficiency when recruiting new workers (*Korea Newsreview*, February 19, 1994:13).

Although the Korean language can be written solely in the native Korean alphabet, a mixed script employing both Chinese characters and the native Korean alphabet is commonly used in newspapers, scholarly works, and documents. Beginning in 1994, Chinese characters, previously only an extracurricular activity for primary school students, began to receive more emphasis at an earlier age: "From now on, teachers will drill students on Chinese characters every day before the regular classes start," stated a spokesman from Seoul District Office of Education (*Korea Newsreview*, February 19, 1994:13).

Thus there was a push by the government and a desire by the people to learn other languages in addition to English. Unlike other foreign languages, however, English was a required subject throughout middle and high school and was also one of the core subjects tested on the university entrance exams. Knowledge of English has a special place in South Korean society, and the majority of South Koreans, especially those born after liberation from Japan in 1945, have had exposure to the language.

This is not to say that all Koreans, or even all middle-class South Koreans, spoke English fluently. They did not. Nor were all yangban literate in Chinese: though "among Korean gentlemen there [were] very few indeed who have not studie[d] at least a few Chinese characters, . . . not one in six can pick up a book written in pure Chinese and read it with any degree of fluency.

Most of them have the merest smattering of it" (Hulbert 1969 [1906]:360). For those yangban that did master Chinese, however, the rewards were great. "Not all the gentry by any means are scholars," wrote the missionary James Gale (1975 [1898]:185), "though they [ought] to be if they came up to the standard of Confucian requirement. Those who have attained this are marked and honored men." The situation was not unlike the situation today with English.

In the contemporary context, there was much criticism that the emphasis in schools was too much on grammar and not enough on composition or conversation. Even though South Koreans studied English for a minimum of six years in middle and high school, many Koreans were unable to hold a conversation in English. (The same is true of many Americans in foreign language programs in the United States.) To partially remedy this, beginning with the university entrance exam administered in 1994, aural comprehension of English was also tested.

Even without such changes on the part of the government, many Koreans went to extreme efforts to find help beyond what was offered in the school system to acquire a working knowledge of the language. They were motivated not only by the prestige English fluency brought but for other more concrete benefits as well. For example, government bureaucracies and many companies tested English competency when recruiting and again when promoting white-collar employees. Owners of businesses involved in import-export were also highly motivated to learn English. Koreans were embarrassed and often apologized to me (unnecessarily, from my perspective) if they did not know English or even a particular English word. It was a matter of family prestige and pride that even housewives conversed in English.

Many salary men attended language classes before or after work at universities, private language academies (hagwŏn), or at work in company-sponsored classes. Housewives also filled hagwŏn during the day, and many formed conversation groups among themselves. Many of the contacts I made in Korea were initiated or at least facilitated by the desire of Koreans to improve their English language skills with a native speaker. Mr. Oh, for example, was preparing for a competitive exam that would allow him to go overseas to further his studies and his career in civil service at government expense. Mr. Ch'oi was a salary man for one of the large business conglomerates and was planning to start his own export business within the next couple of years. The elementary school teacher Mr. Bae, who learned much of his English from a radio program, just enjoyed associating with foreigners. (He volunteered to act as a translator during the 1988 Summer Olympics held in Seoul and frequently made trips abroad during the school breaks, putting to use his knowledge of

English and gaining prestige by escorting non-English-speaking friends.) Mrs. Moon, who tutored middle-school students in her home, wanted to improve her English skills so that she could one day open her own hagwŏn. Mrs. Yu's husband owned his own export business and often entertained foreigners; thus, as she explained to me, it was also important to the status of her family that she too know English. Her three children were studying in universities in the United States.

Mrs. Baek subscribed to an English-language correspondence course. Her husband and her children, in their twenties, spoke English. One daughter was studying in Australia, and the family had relatives in the United States. Mrs. Baek herself had traveled to these two English-speaking countries. In her fifties and having risen from the poverty of the Korean War to upper-middle-class status, she felt it incumbent upon herself to learn English as well. Her husband and children in a good-natured way laughed at her attempts, but she was determined and welcomed the opportunity to study with me. Her husband was also interested in my tutoring her, and asked the apartment guard to approach me about the possibility. In a negotiating maneuver, the husband expressed his concern about the cost of tutoring. When I told him I was not interested in money but just in the opportunity to conduct participant-observation for my research, he told me I was welcome to spend as much time with his wife as I wanted. He consciously included me in family activities, saying, "This will be good for your research," and at the same time encouraged his daughter and wife to practice English with me as much as possible.

Among university students, English clubs were very popular. One English conversation club's statement of purpose read as follows: "The purpose of this club is to improve member's [sic] conversational ability in English, and to help foreigners to understand the image of Korea through intimate friendship. It is hoped that experiences in this club will help prepare our members to be good Korean citizen [sic] and leaders of tomorrow." The whole club met weekly to discuss, in English, various issues, the topic announced the week before. In addition to these gatherings, the club's officers met on another day of the week to put out a weekly newsletter. I was invited to and attended several of these so that I could interview their members and so they could have an opportunity to converse with a native English speaker. Subsequently I was invited to be the chief judge at their annual speech contest, quite an impressive affair.

The membership of this particular circle included both male and female students and represented a wide range of disciplines, not just English majors, though there were those too. The diversity of the students and of my other informants who wanted to improve their English indicates that, while not all Koreans spoke English fluently, English proficiency was nevertheless pervasive among the middle class and was associated with middle-class culture just as Chinese was associated with yangban culture in times past.

Sihŏm chiok: "Examination Hell"

Interest in obtaining English proficiency and a university education coincided at a critical point in the life of a young middle-class South Korean: passing the university entrance examination. Preparation for the state-administered college entrance exam, including studying English, constituted the main focus of a Korean child's life. The process was referred to as *sihŏm chiok*, or examination hell. That the process started at an early age was very much in evidence. More than once I overheard a preschooler singing the ABCs on the subway, and alphabet and English word charts could be found prominently posted on a child's bedroom or playroom wall. English-language books and even videos for children (as well as adults) were not an unusual sight in homes. One salary man told me that he had already bought a couple of Sesame Street English-language videos for his three-year-old daughter, although he admitted that she was not very interested in them yet.

Almost without exception, every time I was introduced to a young child, the child was required to demonstrate his or her extensive English vocabulary, if not also some basic phrases. While Americans may be proud when their children first learn to count, many Korean preschoolers could count not only in the two number systems used in Korean but in English as well.

Among the middle and upper classes, these very first lessons in English were often taught by family members, even if they themselves could not hold a fluent conversation in English. The next step often involved hiring a tutor, even before the children formally entered school or shortly thereafter. My own experience tutoring a six-year-old boy demonstrates a typical situation, though the tutor would more likely have been a Korean university student or graduate. A scene from the childhood of Li Mirok (1986) presents striking parallels.

Li Mirok was born into a wealthy landowning family in 1899 during the twilight years of the Chosŏn dynasty. As noted earlier, in those days, "If our boy belongs to the higher class, he will not be expected to work, but to study as soon as he is old enough to take up that duty" (Moose 1911:91). At that time, of course, to be educated meant to be literate in Chinese, and as Moose explains, "The mastery of these characters is nothing short of the work of a lifetime . . . so our village gentleman begins in early childhood to study Chinese." And so it was with Li Mirok.

At the tender age of five or six, Mirok received his first lessons at the feet of his father. One of Mirok's earliest memories was of watching his cousin Suam, a half year his senior, struggle as his father "kept pointing with a little stick at a difficult character in [the] primer [which] Suam was to explain." "My Father, who was an ambitious man," Mirok explained, "had determined to start Suam's Chinese lessons as early as possible because the language was so difficult." It was not long afterward that Mirok joined his cousin in study (1986:1–2, 7–8).

After these two young scholars had completed *A Thousand Characters*, Mirok's father, being of a wealthy family, hired a teacher for them and opened up a domestic school to which the children of other elite families were invited. There were no public schools and education was a family responsibility. As Mirok remembers, this marked a great change in his life: "From now on both of us were to go every morning to the strange teacher, writing and reading the whole day long under his supervision. We didn't care for this new life at all, because we had to sit still and learn until the evening" (1986:14). At all times a few bamboo sticks the thickness of a finger were within the teacher's reach.

Kim Yong-soo was a six-year-old boy who lived in the same upper-middle-class high-rise apartment complex in Kangnam as I did. One day while the apartment guard and I were conversing in front of the apartment building, Yong-soo's grandmother approached us to ask if I would be interested in teaching her grandson English, preferably three times a week. During the week, the grandmother explained, the boy was busy in the mornings and he attended kindergarten until three o'clock in the afternoon. Viewing this a good opportunity for participant-observation, I agreed to tutor a couple of evenings during the week and first thing on Saturday mornings for an hour each session. The scene was reminiscent of the one related by Mirok.

The following day at the hour when I had arranged to meet the boy for the first time in their apartment, it was obvious that he had received no prior warning and was very nervous. The grandmother, who could not hold a conversation in English, grilled her grandson on English vocabulary to demonstrate to me the extent of his knowledge. He already knew how to count and knew several other words, such as those for the colors and days of the week. The second time I went to their apartment, an English ABC picture book with accompanying English words was brought out by the boy's mother. The boy dutifully identified the pictures by their English names as the mother pointed to them. Later I found out that they also had videos of children's songs for the boy to watch and listen to.

The earliest lessons provided by the family might be made more of a game. But once a tutor was hired or a child formally began school, seriousness of purpose and proper study habits were emphasized, though it may have taken some time before these were instilled. The boy I tutored was admonished to show his teacher due respect, to sit properly, and to give his undivided attention for an hour at a stretch. This is not to say that there was not considerable resistance on the part of this particular young scholar, and in fact he often did not meet these rather high expectations. He more than once remarked to his grandmother how tedious it was, no matter how interesting and gamelike I tried to make it. The grandmother often sat down with us on the floor at the low table, prodding the boy through the lesson. More than once the grandmother slapped the boy or hit him with a large wooden spoon when he became too unruly. However, the boy did put on some air of importance over the fact that he was taking private English lessons when two neighborhood children were at the apartment during a lesson; he told them not to disturb him until his lesson had ended. One university student explained to me that Korean children learned to sit at their desks for hours. Presumably this boy too would be molded into that pattern.

One-on-one tutoring was not the only arrangement available. Mothers often got together and arranged to have their children taught in groups of usually anywhere from two to six, either rotating among the homes of the students or meeting in the home of the private instructor. Again we see the antecedents for these practices among the yangban families of the past. Moose explains how the well-off families in a village might typically organize a village school (*sŏdang*) for their sons. He underscored the fact that it was the family, not the government, who bore the responsibility of educating its children:

Our village school is wholly a voluntary arrangement entered into by a number of men in the village who want to educate at least a part of their boys. The government formerly took very little notice of education except to hold examinations for those who were striving for political preferment. . . .

It is not the hope of any village that a school shall be established to accommodate all the boys in the community, but only the favored few whose parents can afford to let them go to school. So when a number of men get together and decide that they will open a school, the first step is to see how much money can be raised. . . . When a sufficient amount has been subscribed to justify the calling of a teacher, he is secured and the school started. . . . The teacher being secured . . . the room where the school is to meet is next selected and the work begins. The room may change with the coming of every moon, since the teacher will most likely board among the pupils, staying only a month at each place, until he has made the entire round of the patrons. (Moose 1911:121–122)

One American Korean-language student supported herself in Korea by teaching groups of children in their apartments. She "inherited" the jobs from another American who was returning to the States. One of my regular informants, Mrs. Moon, taught up to three groups of middle-school students daily after regular school hours in her own house. Hundreds if not thousands of Korean children were going to the U.S. army post at Yongsan in Seoul, where at least one Korean had made it his job to match students with U.S. army personnel or their dependents. Sometimes parents who were fluent in English would assume the responsibility of teaching their own children. One government official whom I interviewed regularly gave his two daughters lessons in English. There were also the private academies or institutions (hagwŏn) that offered English as well as other extracurricular classes. Finally, though English instruction was not formally a part of the curriculum until middle school, many parents were demanding that elementary schools and even kindergartens provide it. Early in 1994 the government announced that beginning with fourth grade, English conversation would be offered as an extracurricular activity. With the school year that began in March 1997 two hours of English per week became part of the regular curriculum from the third grade on. This policy, though, was not without controversy.

English, while among the most popular, was not the sole extracurricular class children were enrolled in. Extracurricular classes could be divided into two types: those that prepared students for the university entrance exam and those that were culture- and character-building. Among the former group, of course, was English. But math and especially something called *soksem*, or speed counting, were also very popular. Again these private lessons could begin before a child formally began school. For example, Mr. Ch'oi's preschool daughter learned math, English, and Korean along with songs and games with three other children every morning. The mothers of these children had gotten together and hired a teacher. Agencies were available to match teachers with students. The location of these classes rotated among the homes of the participants on a weekly or monthly basis, much as a teacher of Chinese and Confucian classics did in times past.

Most children of middle- and upper-class families also participated in music, art, dance, swimming, taekwondo, and other after-school lessons. This was especially true at the elementary school level, before children become bogged down with studying first for the high school entrance exam (the exam for middle school had been eliminated) and then for the university entrance exam. Parents wanted to give their child every advantage and opportunity they could provide and used especially the earlier years to help develop well-rounded children. According to one newspaper article, a recent nationwide survey of 1,700 children from third to sixth grade revealed that 99.7 percent of the children of those polled took at least one course after school. Of the 381 polled in Seoul, only one student did not go to an after-school session. In another survey by the Korea Consumer Protection Board, 67 percent of the surveyed parents in Seoul were sending their preschool children to at least one hagwŏn (Kang Yeoun-sun 1992).

It was mainly mothers who took the responsibility of seeing to their children's education in general and arranging these extracurricular activities. Mr. Oh explained to me that mothers and fathers often had different agendas. Mr. Oh's preschool daughter, for example, was enrolled in a drawing class. The enrollment in the class had increased to ten. His wife wanted to take their daughter out of that class and hire a private instructor for her, because she thought the daughter was not getting enough individual attention. Mr. Oh said that he would not permit it. He would rather enroll in a night class and learn drawing himself and then teach his daughter. He said mothers were always competing with regard to their children's education and extracurricular activities. He thought a child should be exposed to a variety of different activities and if the child showed real interest or promise in something, then more intensive instruction could be pursued.

One university male student explained the different agendas between mothers and fathers in this way: "Fathers have their own careers to worry about. Mothers only have their children's. Therefore it is they who get very involved in their children's education and push them to study." Mothers also assumed the responsibility if their children did not do well. One day an elementary school girl did not do well on a math test. While the mother was telling me about this, the girl was hitting the mother, blaming her, while the mother agreed that it was her fault for not making sure her daughter was prepared for the test.

Attendance at hagwŏn or extracurricular classes also served other functions. Parents benefited as these classes effectively served as day care for after-school hours in a country where day care was almost nonexistent. For children, it was where they socialized with their peers. There was a great deal of controversy, however, over the amount of time and money spent on extra lessons. Even when a child was a good student, there was pressure on the parents to provide extra help for fear that if they did not, their child would not be successful in the university entrance exams. The following case illustrates this point.

When I first arrived in Korea, Professor Lee told me that she hated the competitiveness of the school system in Korea. "It's hell," she said, "not only for the children but for the parents, and especially the mother, as well." The system demanded the support of the parents, but she said she refused to participate. She refused to pressure her children in the "normal" way. She said "no" to piano lessons and to extra tutoring in English, math, and to prepare for the exams. She noted that high school students even committed suicide because they could not handle the pressure. She instead encouraged her children to read newspapers, books, and other material not required for school or exams and told them to go and play. But, she said, her two daughters, one each in elementary and middle school, told her they had no one to play with because all the other children were studying.

About six months later in a subsequent conversation, this professor said she had been very busy not only with her own job but with driving her elder daughter after regular school hours to additional lessons at a hagwŏn to help prepare her for the entrance exams to a special high school for foreign languages. She said her daughter had to study very hard, as the entrance exam was very tough. She was successful, however, and was admitted into the program. I asked, now that the daughter was accepted and enrolled, whether she was finished with extra lessons. The mother answered in the negative. She said it was necessary for her daughter to continue going to the hagwŏn to help her get through the school. "Everybody is doing it. So my daughter must also." These words came from a mother who only a short time before was adamantly against putting her daughters in extra classes. Statements like these indicate that surveys reporting that private tutoring is anything less than almost universal among the middle class were very conservative; they probably reflected the fact that for about a decade beginning in the early 1980s until September of 1992 such tutoring was illegal and therefore underreported.

These extra classes did not come cheaply. Early in the 1980s, private tutoring for subjects which were part of the regular school curriculum, such as English, Korean, and math, was made illegal in a bid to ease the trend toward excessive out-of-school study, both because it was responsible for unreasonably high education costs to parents and because it put those who could not afford such lessons at a disadvantage. The government was not successful, however, in discouraging private tutoring. According to a Korea Educational Development Institute estimate, with increased affluence generally, in the five-year period between 1985 and 1990, tutorial expenses, including the hiring of private tutors, tuition for private prep schools, and buying study guides and reference books, rose twofold and equaled 40 percent of the Korean government's annual spending budget for 1990 (*Korea Herald*, April 26, 1992). Effective September of 1992, the Seoul City Board of Education, citing the escalating cost to parents as families turned to expensive private tutors to focus on college entrance exams, lifted the ban on attending classes at private institutes for middle and high school students.

Mrs. Kim, who had spent a great deal of time in the United States, was surprised one day to find out how much her brothers were spending on private lessons for their children: about US$2,000 per month ($250 to $400 per child, I found out, was not uncommon). Mrs. Kim thought this was ludicrous. She did not realize the problem was so bad even in her own family. One of her nieces had just begun her senior year of high school. Mrs. Kim did not think this girl was going to make it into the university. It may or may not have been a matter of intelligence, Mrs. Kim commented. Rather, her niece might just be tired of having private tutors. Mrs. Kim considered it a waste of money. Her brother thought so too, but he, according to Mrs. Kim, was not strong enough to fight the wishes of his wife. Her brothers' wives would rather spend money on private tutoring for their children than on a maid. "So what can the husbands do?" she asked. Mrs. Kim called her sisters-in-law child centered.

The above account is an example of *ch'imat param*. Literally meaning "skirt wind," ch'imat param in its broadest sense refers to the influence of a woman's power. Miss Shim, a middle school teacher, brought up the practice of ch'imat param, using it in reference to the frequent appearance of mothers on campus where their sons and daughters were attending school. These visits usually involved offering their children's teachers money or other gifts, called *ch'onji*. "Parents are not buying grades, though," James Robinson (1994:518) concluded. "Instead, they are buying a chance for their child to be a student leader, buying more opportunities for their child to be called on, and buying more chances for them to receive extra attention in overcrowded classrooms. This attention is purchased to improve the child's future and the family's claim to modern *yangban* status."

Miss Shim explained that because her school was in a poor area where both parents needed to work, parents only infrequently showed up at her school and orange juice was the most frequent gift. However, she did have a female student who had no mother. This student's father owned a clothing store and on more than one occasion provided Miss Shim with nice outfits.

In wealthier areas, including middle-class neighborhoods, most mothers delivered *pongt'u*, or envelopes containing money, amounting to several hundred dollars per student, several times a year to teachers lest their child be treated unfairly. When Mrs. Kim returned to Korea after an extended stay overseas, she did not realize at first how important this custom had become. Her daughter, who was in elementary school at the time, was not treated as well as the other children by the teacher until Mrs. Kim too started to give pongt'u.

Teachers' Day, which was observed in May, was one special occasion when mothers were supposed to express their gratitude to the teachers of their children. It often caused great anxiety, not to mention a financial burden, for parents. They had to decide how much to give, afraid that if they gave less than others, their child would be disadvantaged. Many teachers had come to depend on this extra income, sometimes amounting to several thousands or even tens of thousands of dollars per year. Although the practice of pongt'u was the subject of much criticism in the media and considered bribing by many, it had become ingrained. It was believed the practice would continue as long as competition to get into the best universities continued to be stiff. Of course, there were some teachers who refused money, I am told.

It was not just extra lessons and gifts to teachers that were costing families. As was true for the yangban of the past, because of the lack of government spending, even the brunt of regular school expenses, public as well as private, was borne by parents. The average public expenditure for each student in South Korea was only a fraction of that spent in advanced countries. State financial support lagged far behind need. Parents made up the difference. Only primary education, which was compulsory, was nominally tuition free. Even elementary schools, though, along with middle and high schools, required what were called school support fees. Parents were also compelled to pay fees to the Parent-Teacher Association and make other solicited donations to fill the gaps in school budgets (see also Bae Chong-keun 1991).

Bae Chong-keun, president of the Korean Society of Finance and Economics of Education and a member of the national Council of Education, believed families were spending up to 30 percent of their household expenditure for education to cover expenses related to regular schooling as well as various private tutoring. In 1991 Bae concluded, "Parents are shouldering as much as 87 percent of the total education expenses needed in and out of school. In this regard, it may be said that education in Korea is carried out on the strength of enthusiasm of parents for education rather than on public funds" (Bae Chong-keun 1991:57–58).

As a rule, and as mentioned earlier, contemporary urban middle-class Korean children were not required to do any household chores or relatively few. Rather, in the tradition of their yangban predecessors, they were expected to devote their energies to study. One anecdote related to me by an American woman who taught English to groups of middle school students in their homes illustrates how children were even discouraged from helping themselves at the expense of study.

Jane taught a small group of middle school boys in the apartment of one of the students. One day the boy in whose apartment they were studying called out to his mother, "Ma! Juice!" or the equivalent thereof. This was not the first time Jane had observed this type of behavior, and she was determined to teach the boys something of what she considered good manners and respect for one's mother. She said to the boy: "You have two legs, don't you! Why don't you get the juice yourself?" The next time the boy wanted juice, he got up and went into the kitchen to get it. Jane then heard the mother chastising her son: "What are you doing in here? If you want juice, just yell for it!"

My own experience with the ajumŏni who came to do the housework gave me a feeling for this. When I was home during lunch time, for example, she would fix and serve me something to eat. Whenever I tried to clear the table afterward, she would always shoo me away, telling me to leave the table as it was and to go and study, that is, go and do my work.

What was lacking in demands to help around the house was more than made up by the demands of both parents and teachers to study. Basically, it was the child's filial duty to pass the exams. The parents, however, did not leave it all to chance and were very active in providing the motivation and a conducive environment to study as well as any discipline necessary. Although mothers saw to the daily needs of the children, including their schooling, both mothers and fathers could be very demanding and administered discipline, including physical punishment. Most university students said their parents were strict, but they thought they were raised well.

Being strict was viewed as a parent's responsibility and a way of showing love. For this reason, at least one middle-aged Korean man could not understand Americans' negative attitude toward corporal punishment. When I asked up to what age a child might be hit, he just threw up his hands and said, "Well, until they get married [of course]!" underscoring not only that a child was not socially accepted as a full adult until married but also that Korean parents maintained significant control over their children.

While mothers could be very demanding, the relationship between fathers and their children was more formal than that between mothers and their children. The authority of the father as head of the household was upheld. This authority was reflected in the language. While children may have used more casual language with their mother, by the time they were in middle school, children always used the more respectful language with their father.

Discipline in the Korean schools themselves was also rigidly enforced. The following speech given by a university freshman in the English speech contest that I judged illustrates this point well. The speech was entitled "Unforgettable Teacher" and describes an experience she had with her teacher of Chinese characters in middle school:

I'm going to introduce my teacher of Chinese letter [characters] to you. He was a typical strict teacher of Korea. With short stature, suntanned face, he always carried a lot
of books with him. Especially, Whenever he spoke to us, he sounded through his
nose. Before we took exams, he gave us a lot of homework as well as frequent punishment. He forced us to be perfect in everything. Finally, we got to encounter with an
awful problem. He gave us homework that we should write the Thousand-Character
Text fifty times during summer vacation [about six weeks' duration]. All of the students were surprised at the fact and disliked him very much. I gave it up after I started
to do it. At last, the second term began. Most students failed to finish the detestable
homework. At that time, he got very angry and said to us, "You could do anything.
Why did you give it up without constant efforts. Make a steady, patient effort!" In the
end, I was forced to complete the homework by being hitted [sic] and punished every
day. I was proud of the fact that I completed the homework. In those days, it was hard
for me to understand him. But, now, I'm sure I owe what I am to him: I heard he was
studying very hard in Canada. I sincerely like to meet him. . . . [He] showed me the
way of study.

As the time of the university entrance exam approached, aspirants were
under increased pressure but also received increased pampering from other
family members, especially from the mother. Students were rarely at home,
typically leaving early in the morning and not returning until after 10:00 P.M.
or later. Regular school was five and a half days a week. After school hours,
when not attending cram schools or otherwise being tutored, high school
juniors and seniors often went to a private reading room, called a *toksŏsil*,
rather than studying at home. Inadequate space at home was not the problem. Most children these days had their own room or shared it with just one
other sibling. It was the distractions at home, I am told, such as the television,
which led students to these study halls. Mothers typically packed dinners,
some even delivering them personally at an appointed hour. One university
student who had a brother preparing for the exams told me that her mother
made sure her brother had meat in his meals. The mother had done the same
thing for her when she was going through that most demanding stage of life.
    Social life and leisure time were almost nonexistent during these years.
From my own observations of the students at the toksŏsil adjacent to my
apartment, however, I know that not every moment there was spent deep in
study. Students were often seen socializing outside, sitting on the steps or
playing frisbee. For the individual student, though, these moments were
relatively rare. One woman, now a university graduate, had unpleasant
memories of those times, memories that appear to be shared by the majority: "High school was a bad time," she recalled. "It was not good. Most of
the learning is just rote memory. Some schools make you attend extra

classes in the summer to prepare for the exams. We have a saying: We only see the stars. We go to school in the morning when it is still dark and it is already dark when we return home." This statement reminded me of Moose's observation of young yangban scholars during the Chosŏn dynasty: "The school hours would be considered long by people whose children are nervous, since they are from early morn till dewy eve, seven days in the week and twelve months in the year, with only an occasional holiday thrown in now and then. The boy who expects to make proper progress must study every night as long as he can keep his eyes open" (1911:125).

We might wonder what happened to those who did not pass the university entrance exams. There were several possibilities. Most would attempt it a second time the following year. Some would even attempt it a third time. There is even special terminology for these second- and third-time repeaters, namely, *chaesusaeng* and *samsusaeng*. One university woman explained to me that a second attempt was almost mandatory as far as the Koreans were concerned; a third attempt was optional.

Failing the examinations does not necessarily mean one has performed more poorly on the exam than everyone else who passed. It would be more accurate to say a person has not been accepted by a particular department in a particular university. Universities in South Korea were classified as being in either the "first group" or the "second group," those in the first group being more prestigious. Although the process has changed over time and major reform was under consideration at the time of my research, a student was allowed to apply to only one department in one university of each of the two groups per year. Each department had only so many openings. Even if a particular student scored higher on the exam than another who applied to a different department, the second student may have been accepted while the first would not be if there was not enough room in that department. Especially in those cases, many students, when notified that they had not been accepted, scrambled to find a university overseas to attend.

If individuals still failed to get into a college, the family often tried to set them up in a business. We may recall that, although most salaried positions by the 1990s required a university degree, a salary-man position was not the only suitable position for a person of middle-class status. Even many of those with a college education preferred to go into business for themselves, and many business owners were college graduates.

Finally, in order to emphasize the effect social origins and family support had on an individual's education and life chances in general, I again cite from Kim Eun-shil (1993) an excerpt about a working-class woman, who, though offered help not typically available to women in her situation, still found it impossible to overcome the effects of her earlier socioeconomic conditions:

Hyunsuk's mother's family was poor; hence, she could not pay the tuition fee for high school. She worked in a small furniture factory . . . after she finished middle school. One day she got off a bus in front of a university in Seoul and entered. . . . Since that day, she had gone to the library of that university with a math text for middle-school students and some novels. She said, "I was not doing anything but enjoying the atmosphere, which seemed to be lofty and foreign. When I was there, I felt I was one of the college students." She met a college man. . . . When he realized she was a factory worker who just spent time there, he bought her dinner several times and recommended that she study to get a high school certificate. She did not know how to do it and was worried about quitting her job. One day he brought her a certificate which he had paid for so that she could enroll in a high school course. When she told her parents that she would quit factory work to study for a high school diploma, her parents opposed her decision, wanting her to make money for her family. However, she quit the factory and began to study. Finally, she passed the exam and entered a college. Her friend—this college student—paid the first semester of college tuition. She said, "Even though I entered the college, I had a lot of problems, including financial difficulties. I did not know what other students had learned from their regular high school and I did not know any cultural or literary work. Students got together according to their high school networks. I did not have networks. I was very lonely and I was quite scared of being left out." She dropped out of college after one year of attendance because she could not pay for tuition and began to work in a garment factory as a cutter. (Kim Eun-shil 1993:190–193)

As a result of the pressures endured leading up to acceptance into a university, once one entered the university, social life often became more important than study for many Korean students. One of the most important aspects of that social life was association with the opposite sex. Most had minimal experience in this area prior to this time. Even most high schools were segregated by sex. The following chapter looks at how Korean boys met Korean girls as well as how one's family status was preserved through class endogamy.

6

Marriage Strategies

From the day one is born the chief concern of the parents and near relatives will be that of a suitable marriage. Hence the negotiations for such marriages are often begun at a very early age and carried on to completion without any consent on the part of those whom it most affects. Let it be clearly understood that the business of every Korean is to get married and the sooner this business is completed the better satisfied those will be whom it develops to see that it is carried out.

—J. Robert Moose (1911:158)

In Korea a suitable marriage implied marrying someone with the proper status. Class endogamy, or marriage within the same class, was another strategy employed by South Korea's status-conscious middle class as a means of maintaining a family's status. This strategy was patterned after that traditionally employed by the elite yangban: "Although never explicitly stated in the law codes, the strong status consciousness of the yangban prohibited intermarriage with lower social groups so that group endogamy was a major factor in the marriage strategy" (Deuchler 1977b:9–10; see also Deuchler 1992:239).

Traditionally, "marriage strategy was . . . an intricate game that could be played well only under certain conditions" (Deuchler 1977b:10). Those of lower status often did not have the economic means to play this "game" and needed to resort to less ideal means of recruiting a spouse (Kim Choong Soon 1974). In this regard I found the continuity between modern and traditional marriages to be strong. Although the specific mechanisms of ensuring class endogamy had been modified to meet modern requirements, such mechanisms were nevertheless operative among South Korea's contemporary middle class. Moreover, different socioeconomic classes followed different marriage patterns.

Traditionally, as discussed in Chapter 1, young boys and girls were separated physically and socially beginning at an early age, usually through seclusion of girls in the female quarters of the family compound. With such barriers to social intercourse between the sexes imposed from a young age, the responsibility for finding a mate suitable for marriage fell on the parents without any involvement whatsoever on the part of the children. Marriages were arranged through matchmakers who may or may not have been professionals. Kin often served as go-betweens.

Child-bride (*minmyŏnŭri*), adopted son-in-law (*terilsawi*), concubine (*ch'ŏp*), and junior wife (*chagŭn manura*) marriage arrangements were not considered the ideal but out of necessity were often made among commoners (Yoon Hyungsook 1989). "High class and well-to-do people," in contrast, had "little trouble in making matches" (Moose 1911:161) and did not have to resort to such arrangements. Moose reports that sometimes engagements of "well-to-do" families were "made on the plan of reciprocity, an exchange of sons and daughters often taking place between families of equal social standing" (Moose 1911:109).

Moose's reference to arranged marriages based on a principle of reciprocity appears to be an example of *yŏnjulhon*, marriage through connections or what Kim Choong Soon (1974) calls the "chain-string" form of marriage arrangement. The yŏnjulhon, according to Kim, was especially important in maintaining class endogamy among those with yangban ancestry in villages composed of only a single patrilineal clan. Traditionally, rules of clan exogamy and class endogamy necessarily led to village exogamy in villages composed of a single predominant clan. Patrilocal residence was the rule. A woman who married into a clan could act as go-between to arrange a marriage between a relative of the clan in which she was a member before her marriage in a different village and a relative of her present clan (Kim Choong Soon 1974:577). In such a way, class endogamy was achieved: "They do not need to manifest class endogamy in the system. Instead, they utilize the *yon'jul-hon* to manipulate the system of class endogamy. This allows nobles to marry amongst themselves. Therefore, class endogamy can be practiced through this *yon'jul-hon* instead of having an institutionalized class endogamy system" (Kim Choong Soon 1974:579).

Kim Choong Soon (1974) observed the yŏnjulhon or chain-string form of marriage arrangements between rural villages as late as 1964 and believed it to be still practiced at least as late as a decade later in the countryside among families with yangban heritage. In his mid-1960s village study Brandt also found many traditional patterns with regard to early segregation of the sexes, marriage arrangements, and class endogamy and village exogamy (1971:133–134, 121–122). However, he also detected the beginnings of an easing of strict segregation of the sexes, much of it brought on by the determination and imaginative scheming of the young people themselves to the point of institutionalizing premarital meetings between the sexes:

Parents insist that sexual morality was more strictly upheld in their youth and men in their late twenties and early thirties agreed somewhat enviously that behavior has changed greatly in the last ten years. Cousins living in different neighborhoods were often able to serve one another as go-betweens in the pursuit of illicit pre-marital love affairs. . . .

The young people find various ways to escape the scrutiny of adults. Girls go off oystering on deserted stretches of the coastline, sometimes by prearrangement but often just on the chance that boys, who know by the tides when the rocks are bare, will find them. Separate groups of boys and girls often sing outdoors at night, and when they eventually break up, a certain amount of merging into smaller groups takes place.

In the last few years an institutionalized form of meeting has developed in which girls of one neighborhood meet the boys of another by appointment on the beach at night. Again there is only innocent fun and games until the end of the evening when the group gradually dissolves, and pairs wander off. (Brandt 1971:135–136)

Kim Choong Soon noted that for those that went to the city for a university education, "the college campus may provide a place where an individual can choose his or her own spouse instead of relying upon the *yonʾjul-hon*" (1974:579). What I found on the campuses in Seoul was the same ingenuity on the part of young people in developing an institutionalized form of meeting between the sexes, perhaps having its roots in the institutionalized form of meeting observed by Brandt in the village.

Over the past few decades, South Korean university students have developed a mechanism (sometimes also used by high school students) called *mitʾing*, or "meeting," that serves as an "ice breaker" and pairs off students for a Korean form of a "blind date." This word and others in this context are taken directly from English and are used by Koreans without translating them into any native Korean word equivalent. The use of English words even when Korean equivalents were available, I believe, is both a status statement from the use of English as discussed in Chapter 5 and a reflection of the recognition that this practice is based more on Western ideals of mate selection and equality of the sexes (though whether these ideals are in fact realized is another matter). Moreover, participation in mitʾing serves to maintain class endogamy, should any marriage result, since only those in college, and therefore presumably at least of middle-class status, participate.

I found several types of mitʾing. Specific types often had names that ended with "*tʾing*" or "-ting," from the ending of the word "meeting." Mitʾing for the benefit of university freshmen and sophomores were often arranged by upperclassmen, one male, one female, called *chusŏnja* or intermediaries.

These organizers arranged to have an equal number of boys and girls meet at a particular place, such as a coffee or tea shop or disco. Typically there would be four or five boys and girls each, but there may have been as many as ten or so each. Once the young people had gathered, the intermediaries chose one of a number of different mechanisms to pair off their charges.

The mechanism to pair off the participants might be as simple as asking each man to provide some personal object such as a lighter or pen. Each woman then picked out one of the objects, not knowing which belonged to whom, and was thus paired with the owner of the object picked. There were also more creative ways of pairing. Although each of these types may or may not have been widespread in practice, they were well recognized among the university crowd. Such imaginative types of mit'ing were known by such names as *elevator-t'ing*, *car-t'ing*, and *stop/go-t'ing*.

In elevator-t'ing, a man stood on each floor just outside of the elevator of an office building or some other high-rise. A woman rode the elevator, stopping at each floor, looking at the man. If she liked what she saw, she got off. If not, she continued on to the next floor. I happened to catch a daytime television drama that included a scene of just such a type of mit'ing. (The employees of a restaurant where I was eating lunch with a university student informant were watching the show on a television set up in the restaurant.)

In car-t'ing each male participant provided a car. The cars were parked together with the drivers stepping aside so as not to reveal who owned which car. Each female participant selected one of the cars and thus was paired with its respective owner.

I have heard two versions of stop/go-t'ing. In the first, a boy paraded himself up and down a hallway with several doors. Just inside each open door was a girl. As the boy passed by each doorway, the respective girl said "stop" or "go" depending on whether or not she wanted to get together with that particular boy. In the second version, all the young men put their names in a pile. The young women then picked out a name: if the woman liked the person whose name she picked, she said "stop" and his name was permanently removed from the pile. If she did not like him, she said "go" and put the name back in the pile. Conversely, the women's names could go in the pile and the men picked.

One university woman commented that once when she was discussing mit'ing with her friend, her friend had counted nine types, though she herself thought there must be more, adding: "New kinds are being invented all the time."

The name of a specific type of mit'ing may refer to other attributes of the mit'ing besides the pairing mechanism, such as location or a commonality shared by the participants. *Kyŏngbok kung-t'ing*, for example, refers to mit'ing that were held at Kyŏngbok Palace. *Hangnyŏk kosa-t'ing*, translated by one informant for me to roughly mean "S.A.T.-t'ing," involved groups of students who intended to sit together for the national university entrance examination. More specifically, they were often young people who had graduated from high school but who were not successful the first time in gaining admission to a university and thus were studying at hagwŏn or private cram schools. Mit'ing then were arranged between groups of students from these different cram schools.

Variations on the basic pattern also occurred. *James Bond-t'ing*, also know as *007–t'ing*, for example, involved only one woman and one man. The man, provided with the phone number by an intermediary, called the woman and arranged to meet her at a certain place. Not knowing what the other looked like, he told the woman some distinguishing mark she would be able to recognize, such as that he would be wearing a certain type of glasses or holding a rose. When the woman showed up and identified the man (he would not be able to identify her), she decided on the spot whether she wanted to go out with him or not. If she decided not to, she left without identifying herself to him. One female university student told me that many men did not like this type of meeting, presumably because they could end up without a date.

Phone-t'ing, as described to me, did not employ an intermediary but rather occurred at special restaurants or coffee shops established only recently, especially in the entertainment centers of upper-middle-class sections of Seoul, and set up specifically for this purpose. At these places, eligible young men and women went and sat at tables equipped with in-house phones. They then looked around the room. If they saw someone who had potential, they called that table and tried to arrange a mit'ing. The August 20, 1994, issue of the Sunday magazine of the *Hankuk Ilbo* newspaper reported that 9.8 percent of young people have participated in phone-t'ing (Clark Sorensen, pers. comm.).

I gained some insight into the historical development of mit'ing in the course of a conversation with two women, Miss Han and Miss Ko. After Miss Han, who graduated from college in the mid-1980s, listed a few types of mit'ing such as phone-t'ing, Miss Ko, who attended the university in the late 1970s, commented: "We never had such [pause] strange meetings when I was in college. We did it the more traditional way." When I inquired as to what that traditional way was, she replied: "Friends would arrange meetings in a *tabang* [teahouse], for example, between students in departments from different colleges. Certain universities usually only did it with certain other universities. Many women would turn down mit'ing if they weren't [with men] from a prestigious university. For men, though, they were more interested that the women were pretty than in the prestige of the university."

What Miss Ko described was a type of conventional mit'ing that still took place. Once the young people had gathered, a randomizing game such as picking a personal object from a pile would be used for pairing. The more recently invented forms such as elevator-t'ing, car-t'ing, and phone-t'ing, involved less random and more direct means of selection than the elaborate randomizing games used in the more original forms. The newer forms also required special devices and circumstances, such as elevators, cars, and phones in special facilities, that were not necessarily available in the past, reflecting not only modernization but also increased wealth among the population.

There was also a special kind of mit'ing arranged between universities that was now called *joint MT-t'ing*, "MT" standing for "membership training." Each department in a university could hold an MT. Annually, at the beginning of the school year, all classes within a department would hold one together. Then each class by itself could hold them as often as it liked. MTs usually involved an overnighter. If they were for freshmen, the MT was called "orientation" and involved learning songs. When two departments from two universities participated together, it was called a *"joint MT."*

MT could be formal or informal. If formal, a professor might attend, although, according to one student, professors did not like to attend "because it is dangerous." Originally, joint MTs had a political agenda and were often used as a means for organizing student activism in days in the not too distant past when such activity was more rigidly suppressed by the government. Professors may not have liked to attend these MTs because they were held responsible by the government for their students' political activities. By the early 1990s, joint MTs were used less for political purposes than as a means of meeting and socializing with members of the opposite sex. An all-women's university often had joint MTs with a department from a co-ed university that had few women, such as engineering. *Joint MT-t'ing*, with the emphasis on socializing, generally involved an overnighter and may or may not have involve pairing off.

What happened to a relationship after a mit'ing? If a man was interested in continuing a relationship after an initial date arranged through mit'ing, he contacted the woman either by phone or by mail. If they got together a second time, that occasion was called an *aep'ŭtŏ*, or *"after."* "After" applied to a second date only if the couple did not know each other before the first and if they were introduced by chusŏnja or intermediaries of the same generation. A girl might be asked: "Did he ask you after?" ("[*Kŭ namja*] *tŏ hant'e after haenni?*"). If the couple continued to date, she might be asked: "*Sagwini?*" which literally means "Are you associating with him?" or "Are you going steady?"

Although it was usually the male who initiated subsequent contact after a meeting, the following anecdote reveals at least one young woman's frustration with that norm and her attempt to overcome the societal limits placed on her as a result of her gender.

Chang-mee had been to eight mit'ing. The first one, when she was a freshman, involved almost twenty people, the women from the math department to which she belonged at a women's university and the men from a prestigious co-educational university. They met at a disco. At first they all danced in a circle. She had her eyes on one man, but when they paired off, he asked a classmate, "a pretty one," to dance.

Later she asked her classmate if she was going steady with him. When she replied in the negative, Chang-mee decided to write a letter to him. Typically, Chang-mee explained to me, after a mit'ing, if the man was interested in a woman, he wrote her. (Chang-mee interjected that I might think her shameless for writing.) She, however, received no response from the man. She asked her second eldest brother about writing a second letter. Her brother advised her against it. So far she had not written again. She wanted to know and asked me how it would be in the States. These days Chang-mee was concentrating on studying for the entrance exam to graduate school. This was now her first priority. However, it was obvious she still longed for that young man who had caught her eye at her first mit'ing.

Male upperclassmen continued to resort to the use of intermediaries in arranging mit'ing in order to meet the incoming female freshmen. Mit'ing for female upperclassmen, however, tended not to be organized by intermediaries. Young-shil, a junior at a women's university, for example, participated in a mit'ing with two other girls from her university and three male students in medical school. The mit'ing was arranged by Young-shil's friend, who was one of the three female participants.

June-hee, another college junior, had been to several mit'ing as a freshman and sophomore, but now she preferred to organize them; she liked the power she had when serving as chusŏnja or intermediary. She had many opportunities to be involved in mit'ing because she lived in a dormitory at an all-women's university. Men from other universities frequently called the dorm and asked one of the women to help them put together a mit'ing. Mit'ing of this type are termed *pang-t'ing*, "*pang*" meaning "room," as in dorm room. In such cases, June-hee explained, the men usually came to the vicinity of the women's university for the mit'ing. Freshmen at her school also often approached June-hee and asked her to arrange mit'ing.

There was something called *sogae-t'ing* which was not normally classified as a type of mit'ing but which was related. Sogae-t'ing, which was derived from the Korean word *sogae* meaning "introduction," was an introduction of a single man and woman (rather than a group of men and women) made by a third party of the same generation. Sogae-t'ing often occurred among upperclassmen, as by then they felt less inhibited about meeting members of the opposite sex. However, underclassmen may also have first met this way.

Although one female university student I interviewed found mit'ing boring and uncomfortable, most university students seemed to enjoy them. Their older relatives, however, had other concerns. Chang-mee's brother-in-law, whom she thought was "too conservative," admonished her for participating in mit'ing, so she avoided telling him about them; she did tell her sister though. Many parents were concerned about their children meeting potential mates through mit'ing because such partners might be undesirable.

At least a few other parents of university-aged children were not even aware of the existence of mit'ing, or at least of the newly invented, less-conventional forms. One day while talking to Mrs. Baek, I brought up the topic of mit'ing. Mrs. Baek insisted such a thing did not exist in Korean society, and if it did exist, it was not a good thing. She was very adamant about the whole matter even after I had related to her what I had learned about mit'ing. So I called in her daughter, a recent university graduate, to confirm what I was saying. Sung-hee did support me, though she added, perhaps to reassure her mother, that mit'ing were mainly for fun rather than for the serious pursuit of a marriage partner.

Even if opportunities to meet members of the opposite sex may not have been the same or as casual as in the United States, there were spontaneous means. Memberships in a church or a club were two common ways to get acquainted with members of the opposite sex. One woman thought her involvement in various clubs (Bible study, music, and so on) allowed her to have contact with many men. One man told me he had much female companionship through the English circle in which he was an active participant. He did not feel the need to look elsewhere.

Marriages that resulted from meeting without the aid of parents (including the hiring of professional matchmakers) or without the help of relatives or friends of the parents' generation were what Koreans called "love" marriages (*yŏnae kyŏrhon*). Even though the emphasis in mit'ing was on fun and may have led to so-called love marriages, when one was getting serious about marriage as the desirable age to be married approached, more traditional means were often resorted to in finding a marriage partner. Marriages that were not so-called love marriage were either arranged (*chungmae*) or "half arranged, half love" (*pan chungmae pan yŏnae*). In the latter case, a couple may have met through the agency of chungmae (matchmaker or go-between) but may have decided to date before making a commitment to marry.

There were *chungmaejaeng'i*, professional matchmakers or marriage brokers who maintained lists of eligible men and women along with their qualifications and who charged a fee. Such a professional had delivered a business card to each of the mail boxes advertising her services in the apartment building I was living in. Matchmakers might also have been parents or relatives or friends of the parents' generation. In such cases, no fee was charged, though a gift was expected if the arrangement successfully led to a marriage.

Matchmakers arrange a formal interview between the two young people for the explicit purpose of coming to a marriage agreement. These interviews, often conducted in restaurants, were called *matsŏn*. Usually relatives (parents and sometimes siblings) of each side accompanied the young man and woman. A major difference between arranged marriages today and the majority of those arranged before the 1950s is that the young couple themselves met at these interviews, and they themselves could decide not to pursue the relationship.

Many young people today did not like matsŏn, considering them to be "artificial." One university woman said that her first matsŏn made her even more want to have a "natural," that is, a "love" marriage. Another university woman equated chungmae and matsŏn with a "man market" and did not like the idea. Many refused the offers of relatives to arrange matsŏn. Young people often thought that if a marriage was arranged through a matchmaker, it was because something was the matter with the individuals involved. I asked one unmarried male in his late twenties who expressed a strong dislike for matsŏn how people beyond the university years met potential marriage partners. Sheepishly, he answered: "Through matsŏn."

I found many other families who felt that employing a matchmaker, whether professional or not, was the best way of ensuring a good match. Mrs. Moon was a married woman in her mid-thirties. Her marriage was arranged through chungmae in the couple's mutual hometown. In her case, which was typical, the matchmaker was a person who knew both families rather than a professional broker. When asked what the advantage of a matchmaker was, Mrs. Moon replied that by using a matchmaker a person could be more secure in the knowledge about education, occupation, financial status, family background, and other characteristics of a potential marriage partner.

As mentioned earlier, it was the groom's family who typically provided the housing and the bride's the furnishings. Mrs. Moon emphasized that it was important that the bride's and groom's families were of equal economic status. "After all," she said in a very practical tone, "if the groom's family provided a house that was bigger than a bride's family could afford to furnish, that would not be right."

I received a variety of responses from university students when I asked when chungmae might be used to arrange matsŏn. They included the following: chungmae was used if you wanted certain conditions met. Someone that used chungmae considered economic status more important than personality, and thus was often used by the upper-middle class. A matchmaker was used if someone wanted to marry but did not have a partner. One student said she would consider using a go-between if she did not have a boyfriend because it could guarantee family background. Finally, a matchmaker was often resorted to when a man or a woman had reached an age when mit'ing were no longer possible and there was as yet no prospective partner. Whether a matchmaker was involved or not, many young adults also expressed the sense that they themselves might not know enough to choose a good mate; therefore they wanted and expected their parents' advice.

Because Koreans had become aware that marriage resulting from romantic love was a Western ideal and was associated with modernity, many younger married Koreans, on the one hand, did not like to admit that theirs was an arranged marriage. On the other hand, as we shall see, there were others, especially among the upper-middle class, who had negotiated their marriage from a strong position and who did not seem to mind in the least that their marriage had been arranged.

Thus, while mit'ing had become popular among the college crowd, the role of matsŏn, the interview arranged through a matchmaker, had far from disappeared. On the surface, mit'ing and matsŏn may seem similar: They were both first-time meetings of "eligible" young men and women; both used an intermediary for introductions; and both could lead to marriage. These similarities notwithstanding, in the minds of Koreans, mit'ing and matsŏn were very distinct.

When I was first trying to discern the difference between the significance of these two types of introductions, I suggested to Mr. Oh that mit'ing might have more relevance for the younger generation and matsŏn for the older generation. Mr. Oh, who has quite a sense of humor, laughed and replied: "Today, matsŏn are for those who don't succeed at mit'ing." More generally, I was told by others I asked that mit'ing were for fun, for making friends, though they could conceivably lead to marriage, whereas matsŏn were serious occasions for the explicit purpose of arranging a marriage.

I had the opportunity to witness various aspects of the matchmaking process in progress. I relate the following anecdotes, some of which show the randomness with which the actual process of matchmaking occurs.

While walking on the grounds of Kyŏngbok Palace my first week in Seoul, a twenty-four-year-old typist for a small firm who had been studying English at a hagwŏn in the evenings for the past year approached me to practice her English. We ended up exchanging information about each other for a couple of hours. One of the topics we discussed was marriage. When asked, she responded that she was not married and had no "lover" at this time, but expected that her parents would help find her a husband.

While the two of us were strolling about, a sixty-nine-year-old gentleman (who did not look that old, but that information was one of the first things he volunteered), approached me with his hand stretched out to shake. He motioned for us to sit down on a nearby bench. We complied. He then took hold of my palm and "read" it, saying that my fortune was good and that I was or would be successful. Although this man initially showed interest in talking to me, he soon launched into an intensive conversation with the young Korean woman.

I was unable to catch everything being so quickly passed between the two, but after a while the woman burst out in English, with a somewhat embarrassed laugh, that this man had a nephew he wanted her to meet. The elder gentleman was obviously no longer interested in me and, feeling that I might be in the way, I tried to take my leave. I did say goodbye and left these two to their business. A short time later, however, the woman caught up with me, and we talked a bit about what the man was saying. His nephew was a biology teacher. The gentleman asked her for her phone number so that he might call to arrange a matsŏn. She apparently did give the man her number and expected to hear from him. The woman appeared somewhat embarrassed but not too displeased with what had just transpired.

On another occasion, In-sook, a university student in her senior year who lived with her parents in Seoul, told me that she might have a matsŏn that weekend, her first. A neighbor living downstairs in the same high-rise apartment building in Kangnam had seen In-sook around the apartment complex and approached In-sook's mother in the elevator about arranging a matsŏn with a relative of hers. In-sook's mother agreed to the matsŏn without consulting her daughter.

At first In-sook was angry at her mother, but then she became a bit curious. The man was thirty-one and a Christian. It was the latter characteristic that attracted In-sook, who, unlike the rest of her family, was also Christian. In-sook finally agreed to the matsŏn, but only if she and the man met alone, unaccompanied by any relatives. The reason In-sook was not sure whether this matsŏn would take place was because the man's mother needed to check on the *kunghap*, or marital harmony as predicted by a fortune-teller based on the couple's four pillars, or *saju*, that is, on the year, month, date, and hour of birth. In-sook said that many of the older generation thought kunghap was important.

In-sook surmised that this man must be anxious to marry because he was already beyond the desirable age for men (past the age of thirty). She also thought she herself was too young to marry. Yet, she mused, it might be good for a woman to marry earlier rather than later so that a woman would still be young enough to return to the work world after having children. At a subsequent meeting, In-sook told me that the matsŏn did take place. However, she decided he was too old for her. "Besides," she explained, "a woman should not decide to marry after only one matsŏn; a woman should have many."

The same conclusion was reached by another young lady who was a recent university graduate. In fact, she is the daughter of Mrs. Baek, who did not believe in the existence of mit'ing. One evening I had plans to go out to dinner with the Baek family, including the mother, father, newly married son, and daughter-in-law. The unmarried daughter, Sung-hee, was going to be busy giving private music lessons and so could not join us. However, I was informed that the mother had to be back in time to accompany her daughter to a matsŏn at a nearby hotel restaurant at 8:30 that evening. After dinner, the father invited me to their apartment to wait for his wife and daughter to return from this matsŏn, saying it probably would not take long, perhaps twenty or thirty minutes. As it turned out I stayed at their apartment until after 10:30 that evening.

When we first arrived at the apartment after dinner, Sung-hee was getting ready for the matsŏn. The mother quickly changed clothes, although I am not sure why. Both dresses were, to me at least, equally dressy. I thought the daughter might be embarrassed in front of me over the ordeal. On the contrary, she did not seem to be at all uncomfortable. I did not think to ask how many matsŏn she had had before, but going on one seemed very natural for her.

Sung-hee's mother returned home alone a little more than an hour after leaving. The young couple were left to talk with each other free from the scrutiny of their mothers. Not wanting to express her own impressions of the matsŏn at the time, Sung-hee's mother said that we would have to wait to hear her daughter's reaction. The mother did offer, though, that her daughter asked the prospective groom if he could cook rice. The father elaborated, saying that it was asked half in jest every time she met a man, because she could not cook and wanted her husband to be able to. This was consistent with what Sung-hee herself had told me in a previous conversation.

While waiting for Sung-hee's return, I asked the family's new daughter-in-law how common these matsŏn were. She replied that many people had them. Earlier that evening, her husband, Sung-hee's older brother, related that his wife had ten such matsŏn before meeting him. "I turned out to be perfect!" he jokingly added.

I recalled the day in the not too distant past when Sung-hee's brother, wearing a grin that communicated he was extremely pleased about something, came running to catch up to me on the street as I was headed toward the subway. He wanted to announce his engagement. As I was to find out later from his mother, his mother knew both the bride's mother and the bride; they all belonged to the same church choir. Moreover, his father volunteered later that the bride came from a family of the same socioeconomic class. Obviously excited, this thirty-year-old man told me that the day of his wedding was scheduled to be exactly ninety days after the matsŏn. We separated, continuing on our ways. He was headed for the health club to lift weights.

Sung-hee returned home about forty-five minutes after her mother, much later than her parents had expected. While waiting, the mother appeared anxious, getting up several times, pacing, and looking out the window to see if her daughter was on her way back. At one point I mentioned that perhaps I had better be going since it was getting late and the mother was leaving for a trip to the States the next day. The father insisted that there was no problem with my being there and that if I had the time, I should wait around to hear a "report" from his daughter. Besides, he said, his wife would not go to sleep until after their daughter returned. While waiting, the father mentioned that if a young couple appeared seriously interested in each other, there was a point at which the fathers of the two would also meet. But, as he put it, "They don't participate in these early rounds."

When Sung-hee finally returned, the whole family gathered in the living room. The father told his daughter that I was waiting to hear a report. Before the daughter had much of a chance to change clothes and "report," however, the mother received a phone call from the mother of the potential groom. The mother took the call in the bedroom. The daughter went to listen through the crack in the door, leaning close with hand to ear.

The introduced man was expecting to go to the United States soon for study. His parents wanted to introduce him to Sung-hee before he left. The outcome of the matsŏn as far as the daughter was concerned was that the man "seemed like a nice enough person for a friend, but not a husband." "And besides," she finished, "I'm too young to get married yet."

When asked, the majority of Koreans told me that love marriages accounted for roughly 50 percent of marriages in Korea today, with arranged and half-arranged/half-love marriages making up the other half. This popular conception was corroborated by statistics. Quoting from the Korea Institute for Population and Health, Tsuya and Choe (1991:37) note that as late as the decade leading up to the Korean War (1940–1949), 96 percent of Korean marriages were arranged. During the 1950s and 1960s, the percentage remained high, 89 percent and 81 percent, respectively. It wasn't until the 1970s, when South Korea's economic advance was well on its way, that the rate of arranged marriages precipitously dropped to 55 percent. It was also in 1977 that the Korean civil code first permitted marriages without parental consent (Tsuya and Choe 1991:9).

For the period between 1980 and 1986, 45 percent of all marriages, regardless of class, were still arranged. For reasons discussed below, I would assert that the higher the class, the higher this percentage would be. According to the same Korea Institute for Population and Health statistics, among those considered "love marriages," almost half (26 percent of the total marriages) of the couples were introduced by friends, 16 percent met at work, 3 percent met at school (supporting the statement that mit'ing were mainly for fun), and another 3 percent were next-door neighbors. Statistically none met "by chance." The remaining 7 percent were listed as "other," and probably most of these were "half arranged and half love," that is, they were introduced by a matchmaker but decided to date before marrying. A survey, conducted in 1990 and reported in *Asia Week* (Dec. 13, 1991), similarly states that 55 percent of marriages were found to be "free," that is, "love marriages, " with the remaining 45 percent being broken down into those that were arranged (39 percent) and those that were "half arranged and half love" (6 percent).

In her survey of seventy-two upper-middle-class families living in an apartment complex in the Kangnam area of Seoul in 1990, Kim Myung-hye (1992:73) emphasized that more than three-quarters of her sample did not have arranged marriages. Kim, however, defined arranged marriages to be only those employing a professional matchmaker. Even traditionally, as discussed above, matchmakers were often not professionals. Thus I find the fact that 25 percent of the marriages were arranged professionally to be a significant percentage. Moreover, the high percentage of arranged marriages by professional matchmakers among these upper-middle-class families supports the argument that the higher one's social status was, the more concerned one was with securing an appropriate marriage partner. Perhaps the point is best made if contrasted with marriage arrangements among the lower classes.

As mentioned above, in writing about a village where no surname group claimed yangban ancestry, Yoon Hyungsook (1989) notes that traditionally, because of poverty, even though parents remained involved, "nonideal" patterns, such as child-bride, concubine, adopted son-in-law, and junior wife arrangements were often observed along with the more ideal forms of arranged marriages. With industrialization and easy access by regular transportation to Seoul, increased employment opportunities for young people loosened the control parents had over their children's marriage. Since the 1960s, the young people in Yoon's village study whose marriages were arranged had participated in the introduction arranged by the matchmaker and had had the opportunity to express their opinions. They may have also dated after the formal introduction before making up their minds, thus having a "half-arranged and half-love" marriage. Laurel Kendall has pointed out that children of urban professional families had been meeting at matsŏn from at least the 1940s, and even the 1930s. Seeing each other before marriage was becoming common in the 1960s and seems to have been widely accepted in the 1970s (Kendall, pers. comm.).

The first so-called love marriage in Yoon's village in 1953 was considered a scandal. By the 1970s love marriages occurred more frequently in the village, however, and began to be accepted. When Yoon conducted her fieldwork in 1986, love marriages were the most common practice. But because of financial circumstances, an actual wedding ceremony was often delayed and cohabitation without a ceremony became a common form of marriage.

Female migrant factory workers studied by Spencer (1988:148–157) during the 1970s tended inevitably to rely on go-betweens, whether parents, more distant relatives, or even landlords, to help arrange a marriage. In any case, the girls expected and wanted their parents to become involved, checking the status, background, and desirability of a potential mate. Cohabitation did not appear to be the norm. Many still held out for the real possibility that they might marry a man with a promising future.

This contrasts with the migrant factory women in Kim Eun-shil's (1993) comparative study of middle-class and working-class women in a satellite city of Seoul almost two decades later (1990–91). Kim (1993:205–223) reports that tonggŏ or cohabitation was the most common marriage strategy among this group of migrant factory women. Differences in social origins and the opportunity for social mobility between the two time periods may account for the differences in marriage arrangements. By 1990, single female migrants from rural middle-class families were not likely to engage in factory work but would more than likely come to Seoul to go to school. Unmarried women among the rural poor who migrated to Seoul, however, were more likely to work in low-class jobs.

Tonggŏ is defined literally as living together without having a wedding ritual or registering the marriage. "However," Kim Eun-shil (1993:210) reports, "many working-class women in the *Yaksan* area said, '*donggo* [*sic*] is not a bad idea for those of us who are poor at the time of marriage. For us, it is the same as marriage because we will have the marriage ceremony with our children's father some day, anyhow." Many, though not all, apparently did make the relationship legal later, usually by the time their children entered school, by registering the woman's name on the husband's household register. When financial circumstances allowed, a wedding ceremony may have also been performed according to both Kim Eun-shil and Kim Choong Soon. This difference of occurrence of legal versus common-law marriage on the basis of class standing is reminiscent of traditional times, as Tsuya and Choe (1991:56) note: "In Korea [during the Chosŏn dynasty], legality of marriage was primarily the concern of the *yangban* class owing to the importance attached to the legitimacy of an heir. It is thought that among commoners the legality of marriage was less important and marriage and divorce were performed mostly according to social or folklore customs."

Academics and the majority of Koreans in general may regard any marriage not arranged by elders as a love marriage. Regardless of class, however, a love match in Korea did not have the same significance as it did in the West. A "love marriage" simply meant that the young couple had met and dated without the formal intervention of the parents and relatives (see also Yoon Hyungsook 1989:23). As Kim Eun-shil's case studies demonstrate, marriage through cohabitation among the poor was born of economic necessity. Those women whose parents could not afford to pay for a wedding engaged in tonggŏ, for example, as the only way to become independent from their natal families and achieve the status of social adults, as full adult status was not achieved in Korea until one was married.

In the village study by Yoon Hyungsook in 1986, young people still felt that they needed their parents' approval of their "love marriage." Yoon cited the conflict between in-laws that would continue and create tension in the conjugal relationship if the young people got married despite strong disapproval from parents (1989:23). For these reasons and for the support that they could obtain from their parents, I found that even in the case of love marriages among members of the middle class, parental approval was often required or sought. Parents maintained a considerable authority over their children both with regard to selection of a marriage partner and even after the young couple was married.

Mr. Oh and his wife, for example, who had been married for about seven years, met without their parents' help while both were attending graduate school, but his mother-in-law-to-be made sure that it would be a harmonious union. As Mr. Oh told it: "My wife's mother was very scientific about it. She went to ten or so different fortune tellers to see if our four pillars [or saju], were compatible. Since the majority of fortune tellers determined they were, she figured it was probably safe for us to get married."

Furthermore, even though Mr. Oh's marriage was a love marriage, his parents still required that he and his wife live with them for a year before allowing the young couple to move into their own apartment. This was not at all uncommon. A love marriage among the middle class did not necessarily mean total independence of the conjugal pair from kin control. The following case, though extreme, illustrates this.

Mrs. Yim, forty and a high school graduate, has been married for twenty years. Her marriage was a so-called love marriage. Her husband-to-be and she met without a formal introduction or aid from their elders. Her husband's parents were opposed to their getting married. However, her husband, an eldest son, threatened to marry no one if they did not allow him to marry her, leaving his parents without a male heir to carry on the family line. The parents finally conceded.

For twenty years Mrs. Yim lived in a four-generation household, dutifully fulfilling the role of eldest daughter-in-law as she had been socialized to do. Her only social life was going to church on Sundays. Just a few months before I met Mrs. Yim, she, her husband, and their children were required to move out of her in-laws' house for one year to make room for her newly married, youngest brother-in-law and his wife to reside for that period with the parents. Until that time, isolated from the changes that were occurring in her country in the outside world, she had not realized how secluded and different from other women's lives hers was.

Mrs. Yim was still required to go to her in-laws' three days a week to help with housework. For the first time in twenty years, however, she experienced a freedom she had never known before. For the first time she saw how other women were living, how women's lives in South Korea had changed over the past two decades. In fact, that is how I was able to meet her. Mrs. Moon, one of the women who met with me regularly, arranged for the interview. Mrs. Moon tutored Mrs. Yim's middle-school-aged daughter in English. Mrs. Yim said if her mother-in-law knew of it, which she would if they had been living in the same house, she would not have allowed the girl to take private lessons. Mrs. Yim illustrated how conservative her family was and how much control her elders had by saying that her mother-in-law even forbade Mrs. Yim's daughter from going without wearing socks in the summertime even though that was the style among the girl's classmates.

Mrs. Yim confided that when she realized what the last twenty years of her life had been, she went to a public bath, turned on the shower, and cried. What made it worse, she added, was that after the year was up, she would be required to move back in with her in-laws. She did not know how she could possibly face that kind of life again. Although Mrs. Yim's case was extreme and not the norm, a certain degree of control was not unique. Whether a woman worked outside the home or not did not necessarily make a difference either, as the case of Professor Wang discussed earlier testifies.

For many Koreans the Western concept of love thus did not have the same relevance as it did in the West. More important than love in many cases was the family's status. Whether a couple met through a matchmaker or through such newly developed mechanisms as mit'ing, class endogamy, as among the yangban of the past, was observed among South Korea's middle class and family status was ensured.

Conclusion

Historical legacies frequently override industrial imperatives. . . . I believe it is more important to establish the particular forms taken by class in different societies than to establish some general model of class roughly applicable to all industrial societies. Thus the first task, as I see it, is to establish the *historical context* which determines the particular shape which class and class relationships will take place in a particular society.

—Arthur Marwick (1986:9)

With modernization, economies worldwide are changing in certain universal ways, urbanizing, industrializing, and commercializing. As the first non-Western country to reach a level of industrialization and urbanization on a par with the advanced countries of Europe and the United States, Japan was envisioned as a model for Third World development (Garon 1994:362). Vogel's seminal study *Japan's New Middle Class: The Salary Man and His Family in a Tokyo Suburb* (1963, 1991) seemed also to confirm theories that predicted the convergence of class structures and families toward patterns observed in North America and the industrialized countries of Western Europe (for example, Mills 1956; Goode 1963, 1982). Over thirty years later, Vogel's basic conclusions remained valid, and full-time, lifetime, large-organization employment as a salary man and a socially and physically nuclear family unit became part of the "model organization of New Middle Class Japan" (Kelly 1986:604).

South Korea, Japan's closest parallel geographically, historically, and culturally, has recently reached a level of urbanization and industrialization comparable to that of Japan's two to three decades earlier. A comparison with Japan is valid despite the difference in timing if in fact the convergence theories have validity. Yet, in contrast to the Japanese case, the conventional division of a modern industrial society's middle class into an "old middle class" and a "new middle class" based on occupation does not reflect the complexity of the class structure in contemporary South Korea. Nor has the South Korean middle-class family system become a conjugal one when one defines family in terms of economic interdependence rather than as a residential unit.

In contrast to the situations in Japan and the West, Korea did not experience the growth of commerce and manufacture over an extended period of time prior to industrialization. Thus, in Korea, the older social structure of estates, derived from Confucian ideas of social stratification, had barely begun to transform into a capitalist class system prior to industrialization as had occurred elsewhere (see also Marwick 1986:8). That is, because commercialization barely preceded industrialization in Korea, those classified as having "old middle-class" occupations did not appear on the scene much if at all before people with "new middle-class" occupations. Moreover, as South Korea industrialized, proletarianization did not lead to the predicted demise of self-employed business owners (compare Mills 1956). Rather, in contrast to Japan, the "old middle class" in South Korea grew along with the growth of manual production workers, urban professionals, and salaried, white-collar workers (Yoon In-Jin 1993:22; see also Koo and Hong 1980; E. Vogel 1991:273). Thus a middle class itself is new in Korea. When we speak of South Korea's new urban middle class, we include both the self-employed and the salaried who are living a middle-class lifestyle.

There are other differences in South Korea's class structure. Although there are those with "new middle class" occupations, there is no truly distinct "new middle class" that depends on occupation alone rather than on property for income (see also Mills 1956:65). Most families of South Korean salary men who were living a middle-class lifestyle in the 1990s also depended on some form of property, such as land, stocks, rentals, or a business run by the wife, if not also on another family member's salary, for additional income. Moreover, regardless of the size of the company he worked for, a salary man in South Korea did not enjoy the security of lifetime employment that until recently his Japanese counterpart did enjoy. Moreover, it was not uncommon for a salary man in South Korea to make a mid-life shift in careers and join the ranks of small businessmen.

Differences in lifestyle observed among the middle-class families in South Korea were thus not based primarily on the various middle-class occupations as in Japan (Vogel 1963:3–10, 1967; Kelly 1986; Bestor 1989, 1992). Even though the salary man's way of life observed in urban Japan in 1958 at the time of Vogel's original work has not only become, in the decades since, more affluent but also "the expected life-style of most Japanese" (E. Vogel 1991:272; S. H. Vogel 1991:286), a distinction between "old middle-class" and "new middle-class" lifestyles, in the conventional sense, still remains in Japan.

Bestor makes this point in his study of a predominantly "old middle-class" neighborhood in Tokyo:

Socially, if not numerically, Miyamoto-chō is dominated by the households of small merchants and other petty entrepreneurs, who set the tone for neighborhood interaction and local social life. In the central role assumed by entrepreneurs and in the plethora of institutions and associations that loom so large in Miyamoto-chō, the neighborhood resembles shitamachi, the older mercantile and artisanal districts of central Tokyo. The distinction between shitamachi and its opposite—*yamanote*, the nonmerchant more "modern" lifestyles—is one of the most fundamental social, subcultural, and geographic demarcations in contemporary Tokyo. This dichotomy is not only applied to Tokyo as a whole, but also is projected upon the social life of even so small a unit as Miyamoto-chō.

In the minds of most Japanese, class standing and involvement in neighborhood affairs are inextricably linked. Neighborhood social life is seen as an aspect of the lifestyle of the so-called old middle class, a lifestyle that persists because of the cultural conservatism thought to be inherent in shitamachi. . . .

Although no one is formally excluded from participating in the social life of Miyamoto-chō, members of the new middle class—*sarariiman*, salaried employees of large corporations and government bureaucrats—are excluded de facto, by their lack of time to assume leadership roles, by their involvement in other kinds of social institutions, and by their general social values; that is, they tend to look down on community involvement as parochial, feudal, and undemocratic. In this they share the standard outlook of yamanote Tokyo, the Tokyo of the new middle-class elite. (Bestor 1992:28)

Moreover, in Japan "most shopkeepers, craftspeople, factory owners, and even professionals, such as doctors, dentists, or accountants, conduct business in small shops, workshops, or offices attached to their homes" and "family members are often involved in all aspects of the household enterprise" (Bestor 1992:27).

Because most shopkeepers in South Korea did not earn enough to support a middle-class lifestyle and because of the primacy of the manual/nonmanual axis of division over profits or income in perceptions of social stratification, most shopkeepers and craftspeople were not even counted among the middle class in South Korea. Moreover, as mentioned earlier, the owners of the businesses surrounding the high-rise apartment complexes of the middle class did not in general reside in the apartment community, but rather commuted from without (see also Kim Kwang-ok 1993) or lived in low-rise, lower-cost housing near but not in the apartment complex. Those independent businessmen who earned enough to live a middle-class lifestyle, including doctors, dentists, and the like, lived among and shared a lifestyle similar to that of salaried employees. Although there was more than one middle-class life-style, occupation was not the primary determinant.

Differences in families were also not so much a function of occupation among South Korea's middle class. In his seminal study on Japan, Vogel wrote that a landowner was much more likely to turn to relatives in time of need than a salary man in the city: "Whatever their reason, most of these [salary man] families would undergo great sacrifices rather than call on relatives or friends for financial assistance" (Vogel 1963:15). Moreover, once a young man in Japan migrated from the countryside to the city, obtained a salaried position, married, and established a household, contact with relatives in the rural village became rare. From the time such a man and his bride married, the young couple's financial security was dependent on his company, not on kin. Thus, from the time of marriage, a Japanese couple was independent of kin control (Vogel 1967). For those Japanese whose parents were established in the city, visits to parents and grandparents may have been frequent (E. Vogel 1991:280). However, "although some parents do live with their grown children, it is because they are in need of care and companionship, not because they are part of an economic unit where the headship is passed on from one generation to the next" (S. H. Vogel 1991:295).

In South Korea, in contrast, exchanges among kin of middle-class families were necessary to maintain middle-class status regardless of occupation. Moreover, exchanges could be extensive, with the network extending into the countryside as well as among kin in the city (and even abroad to relatives living overseas). A salary man in South Korea, who also frequently owned some form of property, was as likely to be part of a stem family as a South Korean businessman. Birth order remained the primary determinant, as both by law and by custom the eldest son, whether he resided with his parents or not, was held responsible for his elderly parents and would succeed his father as household head upon his father's death. In Japan, where the corporate family had been abolished in 1945, a salary man was not likely to be part of a stem family, whereas an independent professional or small business owner who had a business to pass on might de facto be a part of a stem family.

Although the dynamics are complex, some of the differences observed between the Japanese and South Korean situations can be explained in terms of differences in traditional family systems and contemporary family law. The traditional Japanese system was such that one child, usually the eldest son, generally inherited all of the family property as well as the headship and ritual responsibilities when the father either formally retired or passed away. Other siblings, without a chance of inheriting property and without ritual or other responsibilities, were required to leave home by their early twenties at the latest, either being adopted as heirs in families with no sons or starting relatively independent "branch" lineages of their own (Vogel 1967:92, 94). With no economic ties to their kin, nonsuccessor children became relatively free from kin control. The employer often took on the role of family. Moreover, the Japanese practice of adoption of a son-in-law or of other nonkin to succeed a household head made it possible for the company-as-surrogate or adopted-family metaphor to be put into practice.

In Korea, in contrast, traditionally only a member of the patrilineage could be adopted as heir if a household had no sons. And under modernization, the employer-as-father-figure or company-as-family metaphor never took root. Moreover, while the eldest son succeeded his father and inherited a greater share of the property, younger sons were also entitled to their share. Correspondingly, although the eldest son inherited the primary responsibility of conducting ancestor worship for his ancestors, younger sons also had ritual obligations and were required to return to their parents' home, or their eldest brother's home if the father was deceased, in order to participate in these rites. Nor has the corporate, stem family system, though modified, been abolished in South Korea. The eldest son still by law succeeds his father as head of the household only upon his father's death and at that time inherits the responsibilities for ancestor worship, if the family continued to observe these rituals. Changes in South Korean family law that took effect during my tenure in Korea in the early 1990s provided for a more equal distribution of inheritance to all children, including daughters, which perhaps strengthened economic ties. Thus, while the nuclear form of the family as a residential unit had become the norm statistically in South Korea (Tsuya and Choe 1991:22), along with the corporate patrilineage, the corporate and stem family continues to exist legally and conceptually if not always residentially, dispelling any remaining notions of convergence not only toward predetermined class structure but also toward family forms.

South Korea's urban middle class differed from Japan's in yet another important way. Despite pursuing occupations conventionally classified as middle class (even if the division of the class into the conventional "old" and "new" middle class based on occupation is not as useful here), from at least three other perspectives, South Korea's contemporary urban middle class actually displayed characteristics that have more typically been associated with an upper rather than a middle class.

First, from a historical perspective, South Korea's new urban middle class emulates the elite yangban of yesteryear. In fact, it appears that a significant number of today's middle class are direct descendants of these traditional aristocratic yangban families; conversely, a significant number of descendants of yangban count themselves among the contemporary middle class. Second, in a Bourdieuian sense of "distinction," South Korea's contemporary urban middle class possesses the socioeconomic conditions and thus the dispositions and lifestyles of a dominant class (see also Bourdieu 1984). Third, South Korean middle-class families exhibit features that, according to Goode (1982), would be expected to be associated with upper-strata families.

What unites these tendencies toward upper-class characteristics, detailed below, is a strong desire on the part of Korean families to acquire high social status, itself a reflection of the status-conscious character of Korean society and the important role family plays in determining one's social status. Status assertion or this pursuit of status on the part of Korean families, in turn, has become an important element in both the formation and the definition of South Korea's new urban middle class.

The Yangban Legacy: A Historical Perspective

To briefly review, as South Korea industrialized, urbanized, commercialized, and, in general, modernized, the class structure during the course of the twentieth century gradually transformed from a Confucian-based estate system into a capitalist one "where social status comes more and more to reflect differences in wealth and to be expressed by differences in consumption standards" (Sorensen 1993b:144). The demise of the Confucian-based order and the rule of the yangban elite began at the end of the nineteenth century with the forced opening of Korea to trade with Japan and the West. The Chosŏn dynasty collapsed with Japanese annexation in 1910. Passing of civil service exams and being appointed to government office were no longer available means to achieving status. The landed aristocracy, however, still referred to as yangban, was allowed to keep its elite status vis-à-vis other Koreans. The basis of its status was landholding. But with Korean liberation from Japan in 1945, subsequent land reform, and the devastating effects of the Korean War, the yangban also lost landholding as a basis of their status. By the end of the Korean War in 1953, Korean society had become more egalitarian as well as poor.

Beginning with economic reforms in the 1960s, South Koreans again were presented with increased opportunities for social mobility. Over the next few decades, a new middle class, in the broad sense, whose seeds were planted during the Japanese occupation, emerged along with a proletariat or working class and a numerically insignificant bourgeoisie or capitalist class. The new middle class drew its membership from both former yangban and commoner families, if not also from families of lowborn origins. Those with yangban ancestry sought to regain their previous status; those with commoner backgrounds sought to acquire status (see also Kim Kwang-ok 1992:197). In the pursuit of status, I have argued, both groups, consciously or unconsciously, have capitalized on traditional ways of asserting high status, displaying certain elite traits, many of which are modeled after those of the yangban of times past.

During the Chosŏn dynasty, ancestry became the main basis of asserting high or yangban status. The maintenance of genealogies and the performance of lineage rituals conferred status "because they advertise[d] a lineage's existence" which was indicative of yangban status (Janelli and Janelli 1982:133). The fact that South Koreans have revived interest in keeping genealogies and in performing ancestor worship (Kim Kwang-ok 1992; Lee Kwang Kyu 1989), acts formerly indicative of elite status, and the fact that families of commoner background have retroactively published genealogies to "support" their claim to "a good family background," signify the importance that social origins and the yangban heritage have in defining status in the modern context. (Although not necessarily mutually exclusive, seeking leadership roles in the church rather than participating in ancestor worship has become an alternative means of asserting status for many Christians.)

But because ancestry no longer provides a legal basis for claiming high status in South Korea, concern with the production of family status in areas other than those related to ancestry, such as possession of status goods, have grown in relative importance. This is especially true among the middle class, where social mobility is most possible and most sought after (see also Papanek 1979). In the process, certain boundaries between the upper and middle classes have become blurred in recent years and contemporary South Korean society has become dichotomized, much like Chosŏn society, between those preoccupied with status, including members of the so-called middle class, and those too poor to assert status.

Although the boundary between lower- and middle-class occupations, for example, is quite well defined, that between middle and upper is much more blurred. And while the situation may change if wages for skilled labor continue to increase and blue-collar workers are able to attain a lifestyle similar to that of white-collar workers, to date, the dichotomy between manual and nonmanual workers remains as significant today as during the Chosŏn dynasty. As way of illustration, there is at least one case in the mid-1990s in which owners of upper-middle-class apartments demonstrated against the nearby construction by the government of high-rise apartments buildings for lower-income families. Although the individual units were very small, the outside appearance of the buildings did not seem to detract from the look of the neighborhood. Still, some of those living in the more expensive complexes instructed their children not to play with children in the lower-cost apartments. Although most of the children's parents may have been taxi drivers and the like, the wealthier people might have been surprised to find children of professors and professionals among those of lower-status occupations. Not only do educated middle- and upper-class South Koreans alike avoid blue-collar work but many are contemptuous of those who do such labor. Elitist attitudes displayed by South Korea's contemporary middle and upper classes, including a disdain for manual workers and a refusal to associate with them on equal terms, are part of the legacy inherited from the traditional land- and slave-owning estate of the past (see also Eckert 1993: 114).

While manual labor remains unthinkable for members of families concerned with status, attitudes toward commerce have been adapted to fit the requirements of a modern capitalist economy. The manual/nonmanual axis of differentiation remains primary. Businesses that require manual labor of their owners are generally considered lower class. Those businesses that are primarily nonmanual in nature can be considered middle class if the volume of business is sufficient to provide what South Koreans define as a middle-class lifestyle.

Except perhaps for positions at the highest levels of government, the civil servant and teaching positions that had once been reserved for the yangban elite would by today's conventions be classified as "middle class." Careers in government and in academia have retained much of the prestige of their historical antecedents. Whether a white-collar worker is considered middle or upper-middle class often depends on criteria other than the particular occupation itself. For government employees and corporate salary men, status is often a function of age and how far they have advanced on the career ladder. In the case of business owners, it may depend on volume of business. What differentiates the upper middle from the upper class may be a function of power. Thus the political and military elite and the economic elite (the owner-managers of the large business conglomerates or chaebŏl) have a certain power that the average government bureaucrat, business owner, or salary man lacks.

Typical of highly stratified societies and of labor forces highly segregated by sex, work appropriate for women, too, is circumscribed by class standing. Just as among the lower classes in the past, the economic situation of lower-class families today requires that women go out of the house and earn a living in order for the family to survive (see also Yoon In-Jin 1993:17; Kim Eun-shil 1993:173). In today's urban industrial setting, lower-class women often hold such low-status jobs as factory workers or low-level jobs in the service sector. While many college-educated women do office work until they marry or until after having their first child, only certain occupations have been open to married women whose families are concerned with status (see also Papanek 1979).

The majority of women in middle- and upper-class families are not employed in the formal sector but may contribute substantially to the family income through their activities in the informal sector.

Upper- and middle-class women are no longer secluded and segregated in the house as marks of status. The division of labor in these households is still highly segregated by sex, however, and much of a woman's unpaid labor is directed toward maintaining and enhancing the family's status (see also Papanek 1979; Moon Okpyo 1990; Kim Myung-hye 1993). The home is still considered the woman's domain, and she is still responsible for most of the housekeeping. Today, though, her housekeeping responsibilities, including status-production work, require involvement in the public domain. The family's status is maintained or enhanced by visiting a child's teacher at school and arranging for private tutors; marketing, including the purchasing of status consumer goods; banking; representing the family at the monthly neighborhood meetings; and even participating in such leisure activities as frequenting health clubs, doing volunteer work, and attending concerts. Although women's work now takes them into the public as well as the private domain and women enjoy much autonomy in those areas, the position of women nevertheless remains subordinate to that of men. Middle- and upper-class families remain largely patriarchal.

Regardless of occupation, just as the elite yangban of yesteryear depended on property and kin for support in addition to any occupation they might have had, so too do members of the modern-day middle (and upper) class rely on property and kin. Accompanying the commercialization of the economy, however, are new forms of property besides rural land (and formerly slaves) and new opportunities for capital accumulation. Likewise, though kin support remains critical to one's status, the form that support takes has been adapted to modern requirements. For example, children are dependent upon kin for their education, a university degree having become a marker of middle-class status. They are also dependent upon their parents for help with paying for their wedding and setting them up in a household. This is true for all sons and daughters, for the family remains corporate by law and now all children, including daughters, are entitled to their share of inheritance. (The probable lag between law and the realization of more equal inheritance, however, is another issue.) Whether an eldest son remains with his parents upon marriage or not, parents of middle-class families generally provide housing for both eldest and younger sons. Daughters as a rule receive dowries, which include furnishings for whatever housing is provided. Children may also depend on kin, including other siblings, for start-up money for a business or for other expenses.

Even though less tangible assets such as ancestry, officeholding, and appropriate family behavior were more important than displays of wealth for asserting status in the Confucian society of the past, a certain opulence and conspicuous consumption, such as in housing, dress, and ritual paraphernalia, was nevertheless part of a distinctive lifestyle associated with yangban status (see also Janelli and Janelli 1982:136; Deuchler 1992:11, 13; Bourdieu 1984). As discussed above, in modern-day South Korea, where status is no longer hereditary and where in large urban centers not everybody knows everybody else, conspicuous displays of wealth have become more important as status display and distinctive lifestyles have become associated with middle-class status. Moreover, even though I usually found it easy to distinguish features of a lower-class lifestyle from those of a middle-class lifestyle, differences between a middle-class and upper-class lifestyle were not so distinct. Although the gap between the rich and poor may have again been increasing, the middle class, especially since the mid-1980s, had become more affluent and members of the middle class were using their new wealth to close the gap between themselves and the upper class. Neighborhoods, high-rise apartments, Western-style houses, dress, places frequented for shopping and leisure activities, possession of certain material goods such as automobiles and air conditioners, maid service, and sometimes even chauffeurs, though not universal and sometimes differing in quality, were features shared by both the middle and the upper classes but generally not by the lower classes (see also Garon 1994:351). This is not to say that there were not economic gradations. The yangban too could be conceived of as having a range of assets, but nevertheless, all yangban shared a distinction from the lower classes.

With regard to the pursuit of education, there is no difference today between the middle and upper classes. During the Chosŏn dynasty, mastery of Chinese and the Confucian classics and passing the civil service exams and thereby earning a degree conferred high status. Now, it is the mastery of English and passing the university entrance exam in order to acquire a university degree that are marks of culture and high status. Although the substance of education has changed from Confucian to modern, the prestige value remains; many families have used education as a means of social mobility. As a result, in comparison with other countries, newly industrializing and industrialized alike, South Korea has tended to excel in most educational indicators (Amsden 1989:217; J. Robinson 1994; Sorensen 1994), and its highly educated labor force is often cited as a significant contributing factor in its rapid emergence as a major player in the global economy.

Just as education was equated with moral worth and conferred prestige in and of itself in the Confucian world order of days past, education today is being sought for its own sake or, rather, for the prestige it confers. This is reflected in the fact that higher education is still pursued even though the better the education one has in South Korea, the harder it is to find work in today's economic climate.

Finally, choosing a suitable marriage partner was another traditional strategy for maintaining social standing among the endogamous yangban (Deuchler 1977b:9–12, 1992: 239; Janelli and Janelli 1982:132). The contemporary, status-conscious, urban middle-class families in South Korea have continued to employ this basic strategy, though adapted to modern requirements. While today the young couple meets before the actual marriage and makes the final decision as to whether to marry, matchmaking is still a popular means among the middle and upper (though not the lower) classes of introducing potential partners and ensuring class endogamy. During the Chosŏn dynasty, there were certain lineages at the very top of society, the ones most powerful and influential in Korean society, who married only among themselves. This tendency is observed today among major chaebŏl families and between chaebŏl families and those of government elites (*Seoul Business Newspaper* 1991). During the Chosŏn dynasty, less powerful yangban married within lineages with similar socioeconomic standings. So is it today with South Korea's contemporary middle- and upper-class families. Thus, through choice of spouse, one's status is asserted.

We see that the contemporary middle class is essentially a convergence of yangban and commoner families (though not of all commoner families) and, though distinct from the lower classes, is difficult in certain areas of life to distinguish from the upper class. We also see that traditional ways of asserting high (yangban) status, including claiming a good family background (ancestry), performing rituals, pursuing a suitable occupation, living a distinctive lifestyle, acquiring an education, and marrying an appropriate mate, while adapted to modern requirements and interacting with Western models, are being used by members of the middle and upper classes to claim high status in the modern context.

Just as in the past, each family can advance its own assets and stress different criteria by which prestige is sought in an effort to raise its standing (see also Janelli and Janelli 1982:132; Dawnhee Yim Janelli 1984). A family with yangban ancestry who has not shared in the recent real estate and money market windfalls, on the one hand, might choose to emphasize more traditional criteria such as ancestry and education to assert its claim to superior status. A family of commoner background, on the other hand, might choose to assert status by the conspicuous display of recent wealth such as expensive housing, home furnishings, and trips abroad. However a family chooses to assert its status, status and thus status assertion are a family, rather than an individual, affair. But because ancestry is less important than in the past for asserting status, status assertion is more a matter of the individual family than of the corporate lineage.

Essentially, the growth of South Korea's middle class can be characterized as the yangbanization of Korean society in the modern context. Lee Kwang Kyu (1986:18) apparently first coined the word "yangbanization" in his article "Confucian Tradition in the Contemporary Korean Family":

Confucianism was monopolized by the upper class *yangban* in the past even though it was the state doctrine of the Yi dynasty. But in modern Korean society, it has become the ethic of all people. In this sense, Korean society is undergoing a *yangbanization* process. Whether it had low or high status in the past, every lineage tries to achieve a higher status. And if every lineage attains the status of *yangban* in the future, Confucian Puritanism will become the popular philosophy of all Koreans.

Suenari (1994:577–578) makes a finer distinction between "yangbanization" and "Confucianization," as I did above:

Yangbanization is a process by which the members of a kinship group . . . of lower rank raise their social ranking by making meticulous efforts to conform to the behaviour model of the upper *yangban*. Since this phenomenon covers not only non-*yangban* becoming *yangban* but also lower *yangban* raising their status, a more suitable word might be desirable. However, the alternative term, "Confucianization," does not fit the situation well, since Confucianism as an ideal norm infiltrated the whole society during the Yi dynasty, so much so that it was shared also by the non-*yangban* sectors by the end of the dynasty.

Yangbanization as a process of mobility in Korean social stratification has been likened to Sanskritization in India and its Hindu caste system in that in both, a unit of lower rank tries to raise its rank on the ladder of hierarchy (Suenari 1994:585; see also Srinivas 1989). There are some features that are unique to Korea, however. Among those enumerated by Suenari are that the unit of yangbanization is a kin group that is not endogamous, scholastic factors are more important in the value system than ritual purity, and the reaction against such upward mobility has been different, that is, when a lower kin group tries to raise its ranking, there are few open attempts to negate these efforts, for most of them are related to the observance of rules and rituals in the Confucian tradition. Criticism is rather directed toward their incompleteness and failure to follow the "right" example (Suenari 1994:585–587).

James Watson introduces the concept of gentrification as a pattern of elite formation observed in South China as a process comparable to Sanskritization and yangbanization but also drawing on European parallels, notably the process by which nouveaux riches have tried to emulate aristocratic lifestyles over the centuries (Watson, in press). Former tenants attempted to attain status by investing in public symbols that once brought status to their rivals in elite (gentry) lineages. Watson discerned a "lagging emulation," however, much as Srinivas (1989) found among the lower caste groups in India, as the subordinate groups tended to emulate cultural symbols that were no longer fashionable among the local elite. In contrast to Sanskritization and gentrification, such a "lagging emulation" phenomenon is not evident in Korea. Descendants of yangban and commoner families alike have revived traditional symbols of status to regain or acquire status. I have shown that in addition to keeping genealogies and performing ancestor rites, both groups have also asserted status in ways other than those related to ancestry, because yangban status no longer has a legal basis. Moreover, many of these other ways also have a historical basis.

Suenari (1994:588–590) conceptually distinguishes between two types of yangbanization: traditional and unconventional. Traditional yangbanization is that which occurred during the Chosŏn dynasty, "proceeding in the local scene within the confines of traditional norms and customs" (1994:588). Unconventional yangbanization refers to that process occurring in the modern context, after the demise of the Chosŏn dynasty and the legal yangban system, and therefore unable to satisfy all of the conventional standards. In this setting, one might choose or satisfy only some of the qualifications of yangban status. With regard to the question of how it is possible for yangbanization to occur in the modern setting when state support has collapsed, Suenari (1994:589) writes:

I think the presence of a group or grouping to give the sanction is the only important point to distinguish both types, that is, whether it is a game with a judge or one without a judge.

Even though the state had exerted much influence on the process of yangbanization through the national examination or through appointment of bureaucrats, it did not directly define who were *yangban* as a social class and who were not. It was the opinion of the circle of elite in the local society that decided the ranking of lineage. So, this explains why the *yangban* system did not disappear with the fall of the Yi dynasty and why it still survives as the core of yangbanization.

Suenari goes on to say that though the circle of local elites had been greatly damaged by the loss of institutions through which the state supported their status, a portion of them survived anyhow with some influence in the local scene, slowing down the traditional yangbanization of the whole population. "On the other hand, unconventional yangbanization occurs easily in urban areas and also in rural areas where the tradition of classical *yangban* is not so strong" (Suenari 1994:589). Suenari also notes that while yangbanization was the only legitimate way to raise one's ranking locally, it is only one of the choices South Koreans have recourse to in the modern situation. Yet it is a recourse still often taken. Suenari (1994:590) offers one explanation:

Possibly it retains a value as the ideal form not necessarily associated with an historical entity. It succeeded from the old counterpart, the ancestral cult and manners as essence. The ancestral cult provides an individual with a sense of stability, giving him a position in the highly developed patrilineal system. Some of *yangban* manners might be adopted to smooth the straightforward expression of conflicting views in social life.

Roger Janelli suggests the following regarding this matter:

In my opinion . . . continuities as well as changes deserve explanation. When you point to a specific continuity, you might also point out what has reproduced the phenomenon. When looking to explain why some ideas, attitudes, or prejudices have been reproduced, you might look to see who is responsible for that reproduction and how it serves their interests. For example, I tend to think that status assertion in the Chosŏn dynasty was encouraged by a measure of local autonomy: local elites were left more or less to run the affairs of their own villages, so it was important to demonstrate that one was entitled to elite status. In more recent times, status assertion seems to have been encouraged by the centralization of the government: it helps to have connections to obtain government approvals. Nowadays, it seems that status assertion helps one to establish that he or she is worth knowing. (R. Janelli, pers. comm.)

Janelli also notes that if we do not consider the practical benefits to be derived from status assertion in contemporary South Korea, "we are left with a seemingly unmotivated disposition: South Korea is said to be a status-conscious society in which status consciousness is 'deeply ingrained,' passed on from one generation to the next" (R. Janelli, pers. comm.). His point is well taken. Some insight into practical benefits may be gained from James Robinson's (1994) study "Social Status and Academic Success in South Korea." Robinson demonstrated that a teacher's expectation of a student on the basis of the student's family background translated into higher achievers among those coming from higher social backgrounds. Thus it was to a student's benefit for a family to assert status. Likewise, as I discussed earlier, asserting status is beneficial in the search for marriage partners; acquiring a good match assures one of having the contacts needed for further social mobility. Also, asserting status may prevent one from being disdained, as those with low status often are.

Without diminishing the importance of these and undoubtedly other benefits to the continuity of the process and without going so far as to say that unconventional yangbanization remains a self-satisfied act without positive sanction (see also Suenari 1994:589), I do maintain that part of the reason behind the continued recourse to the yangbanization process is an ingrained concern with status passed on from generation to generation. An excerpt from an unpublished article entitled "Yŏksa wa aeguksim ŭi kwang'gye" or "The Relationship of Patriotism to History" written by Sin Ch'ae-ho about 1910, translated by Clark Sorensen, captures this essence:

> From olden times in our country official families that have produced famous persons, if they merely come across another's secret burial among their family tombs, they think it is a stain on their family honor. . . . And though the family be ruined and have lost its fortune, they take this [insult] deeply to heart. . . . I personally suffer this shame. . . . I think of my grandfather, with the beautiful posthumous titles [given to eminent scholars and such]. . . . I would rather throw this body into the water of the Han River and be entombed in the stomach of a fish than receive their scorn and lower my family's reputation. . . . [F]or a person once termed "base" [ch'ŏnin], hard thrashing is never far from his back . . . they don't dare harbor a word of resentment, but only pitifully beg, kowtowing until hand and foot change places. . . . Though the grandfather dies at it, the father dies at it, the older brother dies at it, the younger brother dies at it, this is recognized as an ordinary thing. Perhaps someone says, "Thou, too, if thou didst strenuously cultivate thy studies and make a blood oath of vengence, shouldst certainly have a day of retaliation with these loftier than lofty ones," but even they reply, startled and unbelieving, "Could it be true? . . . My family has fallen into *sangnom* [commoner] status. Since this sort of shameful abuse is [an ordinary thing from ancient times], how could I dare hold such absurd thoughts?" . . . And he shrinks his head in like a turtle, and prostrates his body like a rolled up porcupine. He has no thought of even one step to transcend this hell of misery. The sons, alas, are the same. What is the reason that those, like their fathers, are elevated and lofty [kosang], so these, like their fathers, are lowly and base . . . ? No other reason than those families, having history (that is, genealogical records), always respect themselves; and these families, having no history, always abase themselves. Since those always respect themselves, they always love themselves, and since these abase themselves, they always despise themselves. Alas, if people already despise themselves, how can they not go on to lose?

The Dominant Class: A Bourdieuian Analysis

A Bourdieuian analysis supports this idea of the yangbanization of Korean society, or the notion that, in recent years, as South Korea's middle class has become more affluent, it has come to exhibit characteristics more typically associated with an upper rather than a middle class.

Theoretically, members of the middle class in industrialized societies have presented classification problems. The major problem is that they occupy conflicting positions on two different dimensions of social stratification (Burris 1986:330). In economic terms they are indistinguishable from the proletariat; that is, they are in the same relation to production as the wage earner. In terms of social status they form a separate group. Bourdieu resolves this problem of an opposition between class based on objective criteria and status groups based on subjective criteria by demonstrating a link between the two (1984:xi-xii, 483).

Rather than viewing the social hierarchy as one-dimensional, "reducing the social universe to a continuum of abstract strata" (upper class, upper middle class, lower middle class, and so on) according to a single criterion, Bourdieu suggests a multidimensional model of social space that takes both objective and subjective criteria into consideration (1984:125, 115). Bourdieu (1984:114–115) speaks in terms of assets, which are actually usable resources and powers, and include economic capital (stocks, shares, rural and urban property), cultural capital (measured primarily by educational qualifications, both formal and those inherited from family or dependent on social origins), and social capital ("connections"). Volume of capital, composition of capital, and change in these two properties over time ("manifested by past and potential trajectory in social space"; Bourdieu 1984:114) constitute three fundamental dimensions of social space.

The distribution of different classes runs from those most endowed with both economic and cultural capital, who aggregate to form the dominant or upper classes, to those who are least endowed with any sort of capital, who aggregate to form the dominated or lower classes. Those possessing a volume of capital intermediate between the two extremes form the middle classes.

Different class fractions are defined by different asset structures, that is, by their different distributions of their total capital among the different kinds of capital. In the dominant class, for example, we may find independent professionals who have high levels of income and education; that is, their economic and cultural capital are roughly equal. Industrial and commercial employers, however, may be endowed with much more economic than cultural capital, whereas the asset structures of professors may be structured in the opposite way.

Differences among classes, according to Bourdieu, are a function of overall capital volume. Both industrial and commercial employers of the dominant class and craftsmen and shopkeepers of the middle class (at least in the French case) may have more economic than cultural capital, but industrial and commercial employers have a higher volume of economic capital than craftsmen and shopkeepers. Likewise, professors and elementary school teachers generally both have more cultural than economic capital, but professors have a higher volume of capital and thus belong to the dominant class whereas elementary school teachers, who have a smaller volume of capital, form a fraction within the middle class.

Different asset structures lead to different lifestyles. More specifically, a particular class of economic and social conditions of existence (capital volume and composition, in both synchronic and diachronic aspects) produces a class *habitus* or a system of dispositions or preferences that generates a system of distinctive features or practices called a lifestyle (Bourdieu 1984:170). The main opposition by overall capital volume is between those practices requiring the most capital and designated as distinguished because of their rarity and those practices identified as vulgar because they are both easy and common. In between are those practices perceived as pretentious "because of the manifest discrepancy between ambition and possibilities" (Bourdieu 1984:176).

The "tastes" of the lower classes by definition are dominated by necessity and are different from those of the dominant or upper classes who are more richly endowed and free from necessity: "The true basis of the differences found in the area of consumption, and far beyond it, is the opposition between the tastes of luxury (or freedom) and the tastes of necessity. The former are the tastes of individuals who are the product of material conditions of existence defined by distance from necessity, by the freedoms or facilities stemming from possession of capital; the latter express, precisely in their adjustment, the necessities of which they are the product" (Bourdieu 1984:177). Thus one's class is defined as much by one's "tastes" or lifestyle as by one's relation to the mode of production, "even if it is true that the latter governs the former" (Bourdieu 1984:483). Furthermore, taste does not simply reflect social position but is also a means whereby those higher up on the economic and political scale restrict access to those lower down and thereby preserve political privilege and economic advantage.

I suggest that the status-conscious character of South Korea's urban middle class is, in Bourdieuian terms, its habitus. That is, status consciousness is not only the middle class's most important property but the principle that generates all of its properties, including its dispositions (embodied forms) and its goods, qualification, and so on (objectified forms), in short, its lifestyles (see also Bourdieu 1984:170,110). (This notion of habitus helps to explain how "taste" or lifestyle is used by elites without their necessarily being consciously aware of this process of exclusion [R. Janelli, pers. comm.].)

Because of the leveling of Korean society as a result of post-1945 land reforms and the devastating effects of the Korean War, even most of the traditional elite, the descendants of yangban, were not "free from necessity," that is, they were poor, lacking economic if not also cultural capital. With increased educational opportunities after liberation and the war, many families from all social backgrounds began to acquire educational capital, a type of cultural capital. With the economic reforms in the 1960s came increased economic opportunities as well. For those who were able to take advantage of them, material conditions of existence also began to improve and a new middle class, intermediate between that conditioned by necessity and that free from necessity, emerged (see also Bourdieu 1984:177).

Many families with commoner origins rose to middle-class status, through acquiring educational capital and then a middle-class job, through commerce, and more recently (in the mid-1980s) through economic windfalls associated with land speculation and the money market. Those families with social capital, or "connections," however, especially descendants of the traditional elite, were advantaged with regard to chances for social mobility. Yoon In-Jin (1993:26) reports that in a national survey (Institute of Social Sciences 1987:107), 70 percent of the respondents believed it was difficult to succeed if they did not have connections or a good family background. That families least endowed with social capital, that is, those with lower social backgrounds, were disadvantaged is reflected in the data that show that they make up the majority of the working class and the urban lower class of Seoul (Yoon In-Jin 1993:24, 25).

Disposition apparently has also played a role in social mobility. As Yoon In-Jin (1993:24) reports, a disproportionate number of the 1.2 million refugees fleeing from North Korea between 1945 and 1951 to escape from political persecution, economic hardship, and downward social mobility under communist rule were from the upper strata. Landlords, intellectuals, and government employees as well as Christians, they had to start from scratch without social support networks, which put them at a disadvantage in competing with South Koreans for wage employment in the private and public sectors. Despite their loss of social capital, many North Korean refugees, conditioned by their high social origins (see also Bourdieu 1984:151), sought ways to regain their status. Many North Korean refugees achieved middle-class status by electing to engage in commerce, in which their participation rate is higher than the national average, rather than compete with the South Koreans in wage labor (Yoon In-Jin 1993:24).

As recently as the early 1980s the material conditions of existence of the middle class were in accordance with Bourdieu's definition, in an intermediate position between that dominated by necessity and that free from necessity, that is, between the dominated or lower classes and the dominant or upper classes. Even though South Korean society by the early 1980s was becoming more affluent, cars and trips abroad, including overseas study, for example, were luxuries that usually only members of the upper class enjoyed (Brandt 1983). Since the mid-1980s, however, it has become increasingly difficult to distinguish an upper from a middle-class family in these consumption patterns. Much as with the yangban of the past, even those counted among the so-called middle class who do not have as much economic capital may still meet Bourdieu's criteria for dominant class status if they possess the necessary cultural and/or social capital.

According to Bourdieu, what distinguishes an upper or dominant class from all others is its possession of capital, economic, cultural, and social. However, the dominant class itself is composed of different fractions formed by different asset structures; that is, there are fractions richer in cultural capital and less rich in economic capital and fractions whose assets are structured in the opposite way (Bourdieu 1984:177). Different asset structures, in turn, lead to different lifestyles within the dominant class: "Different things differentiate themselves through what they have in common. Similarly, the different fractions of the dominant class distinguish themselves precisely through that which makes them members of the class as a whole, namely the type of capital which is the source of their privilege and the different manners of asserting their distinction which are linked to it" (Bourdieu 1984:258).

By choosing different lifestyles, individuals of the dominant class are essentially engaging in a struggle over the legitimate definition of culture, that is, over whether the dominant principle of domination should be economic, cultural, or social capital (Bourdieu 1984:57, 124, 254). By definition, only members of the dominant class have the ability, the socioeconomic conditions of existence, that is, sufficient capital, to make choices, to strategize, to engage in this "game of distinction" (Bourdieu 1984:57). We saw this struggle among the yangban during the Chosŏn dynasty. For example, among the local gentry there were sŏnbi whose lifestyle was defined primarily by their scholarship and some "unlettered" gentry whose lifestyle was defined more by their land- and slave-holding. A third fraction among the traditional dominant class were the career bureaucrats in Seoul, the scholar-officials, who perhaps had a more equal distribution of cultural, economic, and social capital. Some yangban had higher amounts of overall capital than others, and thus enjoyed higher status. Each of these fractions, though, participated in the struggle over the legitimate definition by living different lifestyles, by asserting their status according to their assets. It is because this struggle is currently occurring in South Korea's so-called middle class that I assert that this middle class has actually become part of the dominant class. In South Korea, this struggle is also one between tradition, where social and cultural capital defined the dominant principle of domination, and modernity, where economic capital tends to dominate.

The two women I met on my first day in Seoul provide concrete examples of this struggle over the legitimate definition of culture. The social trajectories of Mrs. Hwang and Professor Lee, now in their forties, coincided when they became undergraduate classmates at a prestigious university in Seoul. The trajectories they elected to pursue diverged from there. Mrs. Hwang went on to earn an MBA, acquiring more educational capital but in a field that had only recently gained acceptance in this traditional Confucian society which had held business in low esteem. She married a man in a "new middle-class" occupation, a salary man. Mrs. Hwang then converted social capital into economic capital by acquiring money from her family to start a business. The business proved successful, increasing the family's economic capital. When her husband resigned from his salaried position to take over management of the business, she could then devote all her time to other status-enhancing activities, such as the purchasing of status-enhancing goods, leisure activities, and volunteer work for the church, which in effect increased her social and cultural capital.

Mrs. Hwang's lifestyle reflects the family's wealth. She wore expensive and fashionable clothes. When she was not being chauffeured, she was driving around in a sporty red car. Her family had just recently bought a new apartment. Her husband played golf. Her son was sent to the United States with relatives for his education beginning as early as high school.

Mrs. Hwang's former classmate, Professor Lee, also possessed a significant amount of capital. However, she chose a much different way of asserting status. While Mrs. Hwang initially invested economic capital provided by her family in a business, Professor Lee had invested capital in pursuing an education in the United States. (It should be emphasized that a certain volume of capital, social, cultural, and economic, was also initially required to invest in such an education.) By earning a doctorate in the social sciences from an American university, she chose to increase her cultural rather than her economic capital. In addition to possessing the Ph.D. degree, in contrast to Mrs. Hwang, Professor Lee spoke fluent English and was quite at ease with foreigners, both attributes perceived as cultural capital.

As a result of her different asset structure, Dr. Lee lived a lifestyle quite different from that of Mrs. Hwang. Professor Lee's consumption patterns were much more modest. She dressed modestly, for example. Although the family had a car, she often rode public transportation. She and her husband had recently scraped enough money together by borrowing money from family and others to buy a small apartment. Up to that time, they had been renting. She herself said that economically they were not even middle class, but because she and her husband both had Ph.D.s, socially they were upper class. Home ownership is a major criterion used by many Koreans, including Professor Lee, to qualify as middle class. Although Dr. Lee did not live the same extravagant lifestyle as her friend, she nevertheless was accorded high prestige and shown much deference as a scholar, traditionally still the most prestigious of occupations in Korea.

I would argue that these two women, even though identified as among South Korea's so-called middle class, actually represent two fractions of the dominant or upper class. They both possessed enough capital of various sorts to participate in the "game of distinction." That is, they both enjoyed the freedom from necessity enjoyed, by definition, only by members of the dominant or upper class to make conscious, elective choices about lifestyles and, in so doing, to participate in the struggle over the legitimate definition of culture. In these cases, one of the women chose economic, the other cultural capital as the dominant principle determining her respective lifestyle (see also Bourdieu 1984:57, 93).

These two women were not pretentious; we see no "manifest discrepancy between ambition and possibilities" as Bourdieu describes the middle class (Bourdieu 1984:176). Furthermore, in the struggle over the legitimate definition of culture, both of these two women's definitions of culture currently enjoyed more legitimacy in South Korean society than that of South Korea's economic or political elite (though both may be gaining more legitimacy than they have enjoyed in the past [see also Eckert 1993; C. Eckert, pers. comm.]). Indeed, in an ironic twist in this struggle over the legitimate definition of culture, in a confrontation with students at Pusan National University in 1984 the founder of Hyundai, Chung Ju Yung, attempted to counter criticism of his concentration of wealth by downplaying his assets; he essentially claimed that, being an uneducated man of low social origins, if he had had the choice, he would have opted for educational capital over economic capital (Eckert 1990–1991:144).

Members of the lowest fractions of South Korea's urban so-called middle class, those least endowed with capital of any sort, may not have had sufficient capital to participate in this "game of distinction" and thus by definition would not be a part of the upper or dominant class. With time and investments, however, they could increase their capital and enter the ranks of the dominant class. A family whose male head had a university degree and a "new middle-class" occupation, that is, a salary man, but who otherwise had no other assets, would fall into this category. Depending on the nature of his business, so would a small business owner's family with no other assets. In the first case, because of his university degree, the man could claim middle-class status, though, owing to his lower standard of living he might not be recognized by others as such. In time, however, he could strengthen his claims to middle-class status if savings and investments allowed him to buy a home.

He could even eventually enter the dominant class if he advanced from junior to senior executive, a promotion that would lead to increases in both economic capital and social status.

In the second case, the small business owner could identify himself and be identified more with the lower than the middle class if one or more of the following conditions applied: he lacked a university degree; the nature of his business primarily involved his manual labor, that is, the modern-day equivalent of the traditionally despised occupation of craftsman; or his income was insufficient to maintain what South Koreans have come to identify as a middle-class lifestyle. In fact, if he lived a life "dominated by necessity," he would de facto be lower class in the Bourdieuian sense. He could increase his volume of capital and assert his claim to middle-class status, however, if he increased the volume of his business or if he, through sacrifice, managed to put a child through college.

In the conventional sense, both of these cases, the salary man and the self-employed businessman without other assets, are middle class. With respect to their occupations, one represents the conventional "new middle class" and the other the "old middle class." Either may fall into the intermediate position between being dominated by necessity and being free from necessity and thus in the Bourdieuian sense would also be classified as middle class. Although both of these cases either by conventional criteria or by Bourdieu's would be identified as middle class, they would only marginally be considered so in South Korea. They do not constitute what South Koreans conceive of as "Korea's urban middle class" or even a distinct group.

Conceptionally, South Koreans' standards for what constitutes middle-class status have become much higher than the conventional or Bourdieuian criteria. The assertion that South Korea's urban middle class exhibits characteristics more typically identified as those of an upper or dominant class is further supported by the upper-strata characteristics that South Korean urban middle-class families exhibit.

Upper-Strata Families: Modernization Theory

For all the attention, first in the form of acclamation and then in the form of criticism, given to Goode's theory (1963, 1982) positing a destruction of traditional extended family systems and a convergence toward a conjugal system as societies industrialize, little mention has been made of what he says regarding the points at which family systems may resist the pressures of industrialization. Upper-strata families are one case in point. Goode (1982:190) writes:

Although the data on this point are not secure, it seems likely that at upper-class levels in industrialized societies, more political-economic opportunities are determined through family-linked social connections than at lower-class levels. . . . This occurs in part because members of the upper class are in structural positions where substantial opportunities occur, and members of their kin network are the most easily available persons in command of enough resources to make exchanges worthwhile. (Goode 1982:190)

Goode adds: "Having an extended kinship network to call on, and often an extended household, [upper-strata families] are better able to put together the necessary capital for new types of enterprise, or help each other to get better jobs" (1982:106). Thus, "as the author [that is, Goode himself] noted over two decades ago, a key paradox in the apparently simple conflict between industrialization and family forces is that the most successful families and family networks in the industrial economy, the members of the upper class, very likely engage in more familistic behavior than almost any other stratum" (Goode 1982:190). We see this behavior among South Korea's contemporary urban middle-class families.

"Familism," generally attributed by definition to extended rather than conjugal family systems, refers to an extraordinary preoccupation with family solidarity and interests and involves heavy dependence on kin networks for various types of support. This in turn results in strong family control over its members. Goode (1982:179–181) suggests that traditionally the crux of family power was the family's control over economic resources, such as land, and the dependence of children on their elders for access to those resources and for other services. Where the extended family was the ideal, as it was during the Chosŏn dynasty, upper-strata families who had the requisite resources were the most likely to form extended families. The emergence of jobs not dependent on family resources (such as wage labor), the development of banking facilities as an alternate source of investment capital, the growth of public education, and the creation of impersonal services that could be obtained on the open market are processes associated with industrialization that weaken traditional family control. Not only do these developments allow individuals to live more adequately apart from the controls of the kin network, but they also undermine the controls of large-scale kin units over individual families.

Although South Korea has become industrialized, personal or small business loans from banking institutions have been extremely difficult if not impossible to obtain; the financial burden for education remains largely on families; services such as day care for children and care for the elderly remain for all intents and purposes unavailable outside of the family; and in the current economic climate in South Korea, the income from jobs is insufficient by itself for children in middle-class families to establish complete independence from their elders. Just as with their historical predecessors, among lower-class families who have no assets, where there is no corporate property, the corporateness of the family provided for in contemporary South Korean family law has little relevance and family control would be expected to be much less. In contrast, the dependence of middle-class children on their elders continues to remain strong, as does the control that elders have over their children. Dependence and control are both manifested in various ways.

During the Chosŏn dynasty, only the members of the yangban elite were able to realize the ideals of an extended family. Whether an extended family is considered ideal today or not, support from an extended kin network is vital to achieving and maintaining middle-class status in contemporary South Korea. It is true that with urbanization and industrialization the Korean family system has undergone some change. In conformance with general convergence theory (see also Goode 1982:179–181), we observe an increase in the number of both men and women holding jobs independent of the family; an increase in women's rights; an increased age at marriage for men and women; a decline in the birth rate; neolocal residence; and "love marriages." Nevertheless, in contrast to the general theory, we continue to observe such family patterns as corporate kin groups (including stem families and patrilineages); ancestor worship; dowries; arranged marriages (along with "love marriages"); and such characteristics as "filial piety, ancestor reverence, patriarchal authority, female subordination, respect for the elderly, intergenerational continuity, long-term planning and fear of collective dishonor" (Rozman 1991:30). Although these displays of familism among South Korea's urban middle class, indices of a heavy dependence on kin networks and strong family control, are inconsistent with the general theory of convergence toward a conjugal family system, they are consistent with what Goode suggests may be typical among upper-strata families in an industrialized society.

I have argued that South Korea's so-called contemporary middle class displays features more typically associated with an upper class. I supported this argument by demonstrating that: (1) the so-called middle class displays certain elite characteristics modeled after those traditionally exhibited by the aristocratic yangban; (2) the class displays the features of a dominant class in Bourdieuian terms; and (3) middle-class families exhibit features Goode associates with upper-strata families in industrialized societies. I also asserted that what ties all these tendencies toward upper-strata characteristics together is the deeply ingrained, status-conscious character of Korean society.

Status consciousness is in Bourdieuian terms the habitus of South Korea's contemporary middle class. That is, status consciousness is not only the middle class's most important property but the principle that generates all of its properties, including its dispositions and its lifestyles. Different lifestyles within the class result from different asset structures. Fractions richer in economic capital, for example, live lifestyles different from those richer in cultural capital. Nevertheless, the members of the class identified by South Koreans as middle class are united by its class habitus, namely, status consciousness.

Status consciousness is embodied in a need for status and a disposition toward pursuing status. Status consciousness is imposed and internalized by class conditions or by conditions of existence. Part of class conditioning is socially constituted. The need for status, as are all cultural needs, is a product of upbringing and education (see also Bourdieu 1984:1). Part of that upbringing among Koreans has been the transmittal and inheritance of traditional yangban dispositions toward status, including the notion that one's class status is largely a function of one's family status.

Status itself is not a rigidly fixed attribute. Dawnhee Yim Janelli's (1984) analysis of social stratification in traditional and contemporary rural Korea from a symbolic interactionist perspective is useful here because it strengthens the argument that traditional ways of asserting status continue to inform contemporary ones. According to this view (which is not inconsistent with Bourdieuian analysis), rather than assuming the existence of an objectively real social hierarchy where an individual, family, or lineage would be assigned a place on the hierarchy and where social mobility could be assessed according to movement up or down that hierarchy over time, Korea could be viewed as a stratifying rather than a stratified society. Rather than viewing social structure as a system of clearly definable statuses with specified rights and duties, Dawnhee Yim Janelli (1984:27,33) explains, the symbolic interactionist perspective views social stratification as a process whereby individuals constantly strive to maintain or enhance their respective social position in the eyes of one another:

In the real world, the rights of any individual to occupy a given status, as well as the privileges and obligations attached to that status, are often subject to opposing claims and counterclaims. In order to promote his or her own interests, an individual may seek to redefine the various statuses, the criteria by which they are attained, or their attendant rights and duties. Continual strategizing, manipulation, and attempts at persuasion are a reality of social life. Thus, statuses may be gained and lost neither by ascription nor achievement but by "negotiation." (Dawnhee Yim Janelli 1984:33)

To describe South Korea's contemporary class structure, I claim, one need only replace the term "yangban" with "middle class" or "upper class" in the following analysis of Korea's social structure in traditional times:

Some individuals are unquestionably *yangban*: whenever they claim *yangban* status, their claims are accepted. Other individuals are certainly not *yangban*: they never press claims to *yangban* status because such claims would be universally rejected. Yet other individuals do not belong to either category. These persons sometimes claim or imply their entitlement to *yangban* status, and their claims are rejected in only some situations or by only some members of Korean society. Their *yangban* identity is neither ascribed nor attained but continually renegotiated, for they qualify as yangban by some criteria but are disqualified by others. (Dawnhee Yim Janelli 1984:35–36)

The societies Bourdieu himself analyzed have been more stable than South Korea during the past few decades, and thus his emphasis is on maintaining class distinctions. But in his discussion of social space and its transformations, Bourdieu (1984:147) writes that, in times of change, "the strategies which one group may employ to try to escape downclassing and to return to their class trajectory, and those which another group employs to rebuild the interrupted path of a hoped-for trajectory, are now one of the most important factors in the transformation of social structures." One of the strategies employed by South Koreans involves selecting elements from Western models or models of modernity and assigning prestige value to them. Another strategy families of both yangban and commoner social origins are using to reclaim or attain status in South Korea today involves adapting and reasserting the value of certain qualifications formerly required to claim yangban status: families are acquiring those qualifications and thereby "obtaining the rewards [these qualifications] secured in an earlier state of the market" (Bourdieu 1984:147). In fact, these two strategies are interacting to bring about patterns that are neither traditional nor modern or foreign: "Even if, for a time, the foreign impact seems to be displacing more and more of the traditional behavior, a process of interaction is at work in which some elements of tradition may be reasserted and may guide modernization in new directions" (Rozman 1991:19–20).

In the Korean case, moreover, where exposure to modern or Western ideas did not begin until the end of the nineteenth century and change in many social areas did not begin in earnest until the second half of the twentieth century, it is highly plausible that intergenerational value transmission is playing a major role in the reassertion of traditional values and behaviors by contemporary Koreans when socioeconomic conditions have allowed: in the course of primary socialization, traditional cultural values and behavior norms associated with the yangban heritage have been passed on by the parental and grandparental generations, the family being the primary socialization agent (see also Light and Bonacich 1988:224, 287). There is no major "leap" between yangban society and contemporary South Korean middle-class society, even with the intrusion of the Japanese colonization.

The yangban, who enjoyed an elite position recognized as legitimate by other members of society, have provided a model of emulation not only for their contemporaries (see also Palais 1975:95) but for those aspiring to be middle class in South Korea today. In addition to inheriting from the yangban tradition the cultural need for status (see also Kim Kyong-dong 1994:102; Bourdieu 1984:1), in the pursuit of status, Koreans consciously or unconsciously are also capitalizing on traditional ways of asserting status. Certain traditionally recognized elite cultural characteristics of occupation, family, lifestyle, education, and marriage, though modified to fit modern requirements, are being emulated in order to substantiate claims to status in a modern context.

These modernized ways of asserting status not only constitute defining characteristics of South Korea's new urban middle class, but provide a model of emulation for contemporary South Korean society as a whole. Moreover, just as the ideology of the yangban had not only become the dominant ideology of its time but also the "common sense" of South Korean society as a whole, Korea's middle-class aspirations and ideals permeate all levels of South Korean society today. Furthermore, as these aspirations and ideals are derived at least in part from those of the traditional yangban (not to mention the fact that most descendants of the yangban are members of the middle class), I argue that in at least the sociocultural realm members of the middle class have become the historical successors to the yangban elite.

In the past, the only people who were able to obtain an education were members of yangban lineages. Now a much greater percentage of the South Korean population is able to pursue and obtain an education. These educated people feel they are entitled to the status traditionally conferred upon those with education. At the same time, because many records have been lost, it is possible to claim yangban ancestry without firm proof. As noted earlier, the pressure is so strong to make the claim of yangban ancestry that most do.

It is true that the South Korean new middle class lacks the elite and hegemonic character of the yangban. It is also true that because the term connotes elite status, most Koreans I asked did not consciously make a connection between the middle class and the yangban at an abstract level. Yet when I asked self-proclaimed members of the middle class about their family background, they invariably claimed yangban ancestry.

"But these days everybody claims to be yangban," Koreans will argue. But that is the point. Whether or not one can trace actual lineal descent from the yangban, members of the new middle class seek high status. The "game of distinction" played by the yangban of yesterday has become the "game" of contemporary middle-class Koreans. By choosing an elite model to emulate, albeit adapted to meet modern requirements, South Korea's middle class has acquired many elite characteristics. Among those characteristics is familistic behavior that Goode suggests may be typical among the most successful families in an industrial economy (1982:190).

Because one's class status is so very much a function of one's family status, not only has the class system affected the family system, but the overriding concern with family status has affected the class system as well. In the pursuit of status, when the political and economic climate has allowed, Korean families have not only taken advantage of opportunities to increase their status but have in the process contributed to the development of South Korea's middle class and of South Korea itself.

Reference Matter

References

Abelmann, Nancy. 1996. *Echoes of the Past, Epics of Descent: A South Korean Social Movement.* Berkeley: University of California Press.

Abu-Lughod, Lila. 1991. "Writing against Culture." In *Recapturing Anthropology: Working in the Present*, ed. R. G. Fox, 137–162. Santa Fe: School of American Research Press.

Amsden, Alice H. 1989. *Asia's Next Giant: South Korea and Late Industrialization.* New York: Oxford University Press.

Bae Chong-keun. 1991. "Education Top Reason behind Rapid Growth: Schooling for Economic Takeoff." *Koreana* 5(2):56–62.

Bartz, Patricia M. 1972. *South Korea.* Oxford: Clarendon Press.

Bestor, Theodore C. 1989. *Neighborhood Tokyo.* Stanford: Stanford University Press.

———. 1992. "Conflict, Legitimacy, and Tradition in a Tokyo Neighborhood." In *Japanese Social Organization*, ed. Takie Sugiyama Lebra, 23–47. Honolulu: University of Hawaii Press.

Bishop, Isabella Bird. 1970 [1898]. *Korea and Her Neighbors.* Reprint. Seoul: Yonsei University Press.

Bourdieu, Pierre. 1984, 1988. *Distinction.* Translated by Richard Nice. Cambridge: Harvard University Press.

Brandt, Vincent S. R. 1971. *A Korean Village between Farm and Sea.* Cambridge: Harvard University Press.

———. 1983. "South Korean Society in Transition." Paper no. 12. Elkins Park, Pa.: Phillip Jaisohn Memorial Foundation.

Burris, Val. 1986. "The Discovery of the New Middle Class." *Theory and Society* 15:317–349.

Chang, Sue. 1992. "Labor Pains: No End in Sight to Shortage of Workers." *Business Korea* 9(7):41–43.

Cho Eun and Cho Oakla. 1991. *Toshibinminŭi sam kwa kongkan: sadangdong chae-gaebaljiyŏk hyŏnjang yŏngu* [*The Urban Poor's Life and Space: Sadang-dong Redevelopment Zone Field Research*]. Seoul: Seoul National University Press.

Christian Institute for the Study of Justice and Development, ed. 1988. *Lost Victory: An Overview of the Korean People's Struggle for Democracy.* Seoul: Minjungsa.

Chun Kyung-soo. 1984. *Reciprocity and Korean Society: An Ethnography of Hasami.* Seoul: Seoul National University Press.

Chung, Young-Iob. 1984. "The Traditional Economy of Korea." *Journal of Modern Korean Studies* 1 (April):21–52.

Cohen, Anthony. 1983. *The Symbolic Construction of Community.* London: Tavistock.

Deuchler, Martina. 1977a. *Confucian Gentlemen and Barbarian Envoys: The Opening of Korea, 1875–1885.* Seattle: University of Washington Press.

———. 1977b. "The Tradition: Women during the Yi Dynasty." In *Virtues in Conflict: Tradition and the Korean Woman Today,* ed. Sandra Matelli, 1–47. Seoul: Royal Asiatic Society.

———. 1992. *The Confucian Transformation of Korea: A Study of Society and Ideology.* Harvard-Yenching Institute Monograph, no. 36. Cambridge: Council on East Asian Studies, Harvard University.

Ebrey, Patricia. 1991. "The Chinese Family and the Spread of Confucian Values." In *The East Asian Region: Confucian Heritage and Its Modern Adaptation,* ed. Gilbert Rozman, 45–83. Princeton: Princeton University Press.

Eckert, Carter. 1990–91. "The South Korean Bourgeoisie: A Class in Search of Hegemony." *Journal of Korean Studies* 7:115–48.

———. 1991. *Offspring of Empire: The Koch'ang Kims and the Colonial Origins of Korean Capitalism, 1876–1910.* Seattle: University of Washington Press.

———. 1993. "The South Korean Bourgeoisie: A Class in Search of Hegemony." In *State and Society in Contemporary Korea,* ed. Hagen Koo, 95–130. Ithaca: Cornell University Press.

Emerson, Tony. 1991. "Too Rich, Too Soon: Is South Korea Living beyond Its Means?" *Newsweek: The International Magazine.* November 11:15–16.

Gale, James S. 1975 [1898]. *Korean Sketches.* Published for the Royal Asiatic Society Korea Branch. Seoul: Kyung-In Publishing.

Garon, Sheldon. 1994. "Rethinking Modernization and Modernity in Japanese History: A Focus on State-Society Relations." *Journal of Asian Studies* 53(2):346–366.

Giddens, Anthony. 1981. *The Class Structure of Advanced Societies.* 2nd ed. London: Hutchinson.

Goode, William J. 1963. *World Revolution and Family Patterns.* New York: Free Press.

———. 1982 *The Family.* 2nd ed. Englewood Cliffs, N.J.: Prentice-Hall.

Gramsci, Antonio. 1971. *Selections from the Prison Notebooks.* Edited and translated by Quintin Hoare and Geoffrey Nowell Smith. New York: International Publishers.

Ha Tae Hung. 1958. *Folk Customs and Family Life.* Seoul: Yonsei University Press.

Haboush, JaHyun Kim. 1991. "The Confucianization of Korean Society." In *The East Asian Region: Confucian Heritage and Its Modern Adaptation*, ed. Gilbert Rozman, 84–110. Princeton: Princeton University Press.

Han Do Hyun. 1997. "Housing, Land Development Projects, and Land Speculation in Seoul." In *Contemporary Korea: Democracy, Economic Development, Social Change, Reunification Process*, ed. Ho-Youn Kwon, 287–305. Chicago: North Park College and Theological Seminary.

Han Sang-bok. 1977. *Korean Fishermen: Ecological Adaptation in Three Communities*. Seoul: Seoul National University Press.

Hong Chan-shik. 1991. "The Other Face of Seoul Not Exactly Appetizing: Growth Also Means Mounting Trouble." *Koreana* 5(1):76–82.

Hong Doo-Seung. 1990. "Occupation and Class: An Exploration of Classification by Cluster Analysis." *Korea Social Science Journal* 16:7–25.

Hong Doo-Seung and Kwan-Mo Surh. 1985. "The Current Status of Korean Class and Problems with Conceptual Reconstruction." *Studies of Korean Class*, vol. 1, 11–24. Seoul: Hanul Publishing.

Hong Sah-myung. 1991. "All about Koreans Studying Overseas." *Koreana* 5(2):80–85.

Hong Sun-hee. 1992. "In Addition to Silk and Ramie Clothes Accessories Distinguish Yangban's Hanbok." *Korea Times*, April 17:5.

Housing Administration Bureau, Korea National Housing Corporation (Chut'ae Kongsa Hut'aekkuk). 1987. *Ap'at'ŭ chugŏmunhwa palchŏn chonghap taech'aek— Ap'at'ŭ tanji-e taehan sahoemunhwajŏk chŏpkŭn*. Seoul: Ch'angjak-sa.

Hulbert, Homer B. 1969 [1906]. *The Passing of Korea*. Seoul: Yonsei University Press.

Hwang Keewon. 1991. "Kangnam: A Boomtown across the Han: What Price Urban Glories?" *Koreana* 5(1):27–33.

Institute of Social Sciences. 1987. *Korean Society in Transition*. Seoul: Korea Times Publishing Office.

Janelli, Dawnhee Yim. 1984. "Strategic Manipulation of Social Relationships in Rural Korea." *Korea Journal* 24 (June):27–39.

Janelli, Roger L., with Dawnhee Yim. 1993. *Making Capitalism: The Social and Cultural Construction of a South Korean Conglomerate*. Stanford: Stanford University Press.

Janelli, Roger L., and Dawnhee Yim Janelli. 1978. "Lineage Organization and Social Differentiation in Korea." *Man*, n.s., 13:272–289.

———. 1982. *Ancestor Worship and Korean Society*. Stanford: Stanford University Press.

Kang Yeoun-sun. 1992. "After-School Sessions Oppress Children." *Korea Herald*, May 22:W1, W4.

Kawashima, Fujiya. 1989. "The Way of the Sonbi: Local Yangban and the Korean Intellectual Tradition." *Korean Culture* 10(2) (Summer):4–14.

Kelly, William W. 1986. "Rationalization and Nostalgia: Cultural Dynamics of New Middle-Class Japan." *American Ethnologist* 13(4):603–617.

Kendall, Laurel. 1985a. *Shamans, Housewives, and Other Restless Spirits: Women in Korean Ritual Life*. Honolulu: University of Hawaii Press.

———. 1985b. "Ritual Silks and Kowtow Money: The Bride as Daughter-in-Law in Korean Wedding Rituals." *Ethnology* 24(4):253–267.

———. 1989. "A Noisy and Bothersome New Custom: Delivering the Gift Box to a Korean Bride." *Journal of Ritual Studies* 3(2):185–202.

———. 1996. *Getting Married in Korea: Of Gender, Morality, and Modernity*. Berkeley: University of California Press.

Kim Choong Soon. 1974. "The *Yŏn'jul-hon* or Chain-String Form of Marriage Arrangement in Korea." *Journal of Marriage and the Family* 36(3):575–579.

———. 1992. *The Culture of Korean Industry: An Ethnography of Poongsan Corporation*. Tuscon: University of Arizona Press.

Kim Eun-shil. 1993. "The Making of the Modern Female Gender: The Politics of Gender in Reproductive Practices in Korea." Ph.D. dissertation, University of California, Berkeley.

Kim Hyun Mee. 1995. "Labor, Politics, and the Woman Subject in Contemporary Korea." Ph.D. dissertation, University of Washington.

Kim Kwang-ok. 1992. *Socio-Political Implications of the Resurgence of Ancestor Worship in Contemporary Korea*. Studies in East Asian Society. Seoul: Centre for East Asian Cultural Studies.

———. 1993. "The Religious Life of the Urban Middle Class." *Korea Journal* 33(4) (Winter):5–33.

Kim Kyong-dong. 1994. "Confucianism and Capitalist Development in East Asia." In *Capitalism and Development*, ed. Leslie Sklair, 87–106.

Kim Myung-hye. 1992. "Late Industrialization and Women's Work in Urban South Korea: An Ethnographic Study of Upper-Middle-Class Families." *City and Society* 6(2):156–173.

———. 1993. "Transformation of Family Ideology in Upper-Middle-Class Families in Urban South Korea." *Ethnology* 32(1):69–85.

Kim Seung-Kyung. 1990. "Capitalism, Patriarchy, and Autonomy: Women Factory Workers in the Korean Economic Miracle." Ph.D. dissertation, City University of New York.

Koo, Hagen. 1987. "The Interplay of State, Social Class, and World System in East Asian Development: The Cases of South Korea and Taiwan." In *The Political Economy of the New Asian Industrialism*, ed. Frederic C. Deyo, 165–181. Ithaca: Cornell University Press.

Koo Hagen and Hong Doo-Seung. 1980. "Class and Income Inequality in Korea." *American Sociological Review* 45(August):610–626.

Korea Annual. 1992. *Korea Annual, 1992: A Comprehensive Handbook on Korea*. 29th annual ed. Seoul: Yonhap News Agency.

Korean Women's Development Institute (KWDI). 1991. *Status of Women in Korea*. Seoul: KWDI Reference on Women, 400–415.

Kuhn, Philip A. 1984. "Chinese Values of Social Stratification." In *Class and Social*

Stratification in Post-Revolution China, ed. James L. Watson, 16–28. Cambridge: Cambridge University Press.

Kwak Byong-sun. 1992. "Examination Hell in Korea Revisited." *Koreana* 5(2):45–55.

Kwak Young-sup. 1992. "Convenience Stores Popular." *Korea Newsreview* 221(5):30.

KWDI, *see* Korean Women's Development Institute

Lebra, Takie Sugiyama. 1993. *Above the Clouds: Status Culture of the Modern Japanese Nobility.* Berkeley: University of California Press.

Lee Chang-sup. 1997. "Underground Money Invested in Small, Venture Firms to See Temporary Tax Exemptions." *Korea Times*, March 27:9.

Lee Hyo-jae. 1971. *Life in Urban Korea.* Transactions, vol. 46. Royal Asiatic Society Korea Branch. Seoul: Taewon Publishing.

Lee Ki-baik. 1984. *A New History of Korea.* Trans. by Edward W. Wagner with Edward J. Schultz. Cambridge: Harvard University Press.

Lee Kwang Kyu. 1975. *Kinship Systems in Korea.* 2 vols. HRAFlex Books, AA1-002, Ethnography Series. New Haven, Conn.: Human Relations Area Files.

———. 1984. "Family and Religion in Traditional and Contemporary Korea." Reprint from George DeVos and Takao Sofue, eds., *Religion and Family in East Asia.* Senri Ethnological Studies 11. Osaka, Japan: National Museum of Ethnology.

———. 1986. "Confucian Tradition in the Contemporary Korean Family." Reprint from Walter H. Slote, ed., *The Psycho-Cultural Dynamics of the Confucian Family: Past and Present.* ICSK Forum Series no. 8. Seoul: International Cultural Society of Korea.

———. 1989. "The Practice of Traditional Family Rituals in Contemporary Urban Korea." *Journal of Ritual Studies* 3(2):167–183.

Lee Tae-Yong. 1991. *Kajokpŏp kaejŏng undong 37 nyŏnsa* [*History of Korean Family Law 37 Year Reform Movement*]. Seoul: Korean Legal Aid Center for Family Relations.

Lee Won-ho. 1991. "Modern System Came Hard Way to Korea." *Koreana* 5(2):23–29.

Li Mirok. 1986. *The Yalu Flows: A Korean Childhood.* Edited by Chung Kyu-Hwa and translated by H. A. Mammelman and Gertraud Gutensohn. Elizabeth, N.J.: Hollym International Corporation.

Light, Ivan, and Edna Bonacich. 1988. *Immigrant Entrepreneurs: Koreans in Los Angeles from 1965 to 1982.* Berkeley: University of California Press.

Macdonald, Donald Stone. 1990. *The Koreans: Contemporary Politics and Society.* 2nd ed. San Francisco: Westview Press.

Marwick, Arthur, ed. 1986. *Class in the Twentieth Century.* Sussex: Harvester Press.

Mason, Edward S., et al. 1980. *The Economic and Social Modernization of the Republic of Korea.* Cambridge: Harvard University Press.

McGrane, George A. 1973. *Korea's Tragic Hours: The Closing Years of Yi Dynasty.* Edited by Harold F. Cook and Alan M. MacDougall. Seoul: Taeown Publishing.

Mills, C. Wright. 1956. *White Collar: The American Middle Classes.* London: Oxford University Press.

Ministry of Labor, Republic of Korea. 1993. *Yearbook of Labor Statistics, 1992.* Seoul.

Moon Okpyo. 1990. "Urban Middle Class Wives in Contemporary Korea: Their Roles, Responsibilities, and Dilemma." *Korea Journal* 30 (Nov.–Dec.):30–43.

———. 1992. "Tosichugsanch'üngüi kajoksaenghwal kwa chupuüi yo'hwal" [The Family Lives of Urban Middle-Class and the Life of Housewives]. In *Tosichungsanch'üng'üi Saengwal Munwha* [*The Living Culture of Urban Middle Class*], 57–103. Songnam Korea: Academy of Korean Studies.

Moon Okpyo et al. 1992. *Tosichungsanch'üng'üi Saengwal Munwha* [*The Living Culture of Urban Middle Class*]. Sŏngnam, Korea: Hankukchopngsinmunhwaeo'kuwŏn.

Moose, J. Robert. 1911. *Village Life in Korea*. Nashville: Publishing House of the M.E. Church, South.

National Statistics Office. 1991. *Hankuku' i sahoe chip'yo* [*Social Indicators in Korea*]. Seoul: National Statistics Office.

Osgood, Cornelius. 1951. *The Koreans and Their Culture*. New York: Ronald Press.

Palais, James B. 1975. *Politics and Policy in Traditional Korea*. Cambridge: Harvard University Press.

———. 1996. *Confucian Statecraft and Korean Institutions: Yu Hyŏngwŏn and the Late Chosŏn Dynasty*. Seattle: University of Washington Press.

Papanek, Hanna. 1979. "Family Status Production Work: The 'Work' and 'Non-Work' of Women." *Signs* 4(4):775–781.

Park Chang-seok. 1992. "Housing Prices Continue Downward: Spurred by Massive Supply." *Korea Times*, May 29:1.

Passin, Herbert. 1955. "Untouchability in the Far East." *Monumenta Nipponica* 11:247–267.

———. 1956–57. "The Paekchŏng of Korea: A Brief Social History." *Monumenta Nipponica* 12:195–240.

Robinson, James. 1994. "Social Status and Academic Success in South Korea." *Comparative Education Review* 38(4) (November):506–530.

Robinson, Michael. 1991. "Perceptions of Confucianism in Twentieth-Century Korea." In *The East Asian Region: Confucian Heritage and Its Modern Adaptation*, ed. Gilbert Rozman, 204–225. Princeton: Princeton University Press.

Rozman, Gilbert, ed. 1991. *The East Asian Region: Confucian Heritage and Its Modern Adaptation*. Princeton: Princeton University Press.

Rutt, Richard. 1964 [1957–58]. *Korean Works and Days: Notes from the Diary of a Country Priest*. Seoul: Royal Asiatic Society Korea Branch.

Ryu Choon-soo. 1991. "For All Its Ancient Glories Seoul Defies Understanding: Cons and Pros about City of Seoul (1): An Architect's View." *Koreana* 5(1):45–48.

Seoul Business Newspaper [Seoul Kyŏngje Sinmun]. 1991. *Chaebŏl kwa kabŏl* [Chaebŏl and kabŏl]. Seoul: Chinsuk Sanŏp Sa.

Seoul Metropolitan Government. 1993. *Comparative Statistics of Major Cities*. Seoul.

Sorensen, Clark. 1983. "Women, Men, Inside, Outside: The Division of Labor in Rural Central Korea." In *Korean Women: View from the Inner Room*, ed. Laurel Kendall and Mark Peterson, 63–79. New Haven, Conn.: East Rock Press.

————. 1988. *Over the Mountains Are Mountains: Korean Peasant Households and Their Adaptations to Rapid Industrialization.* Seattle: University of Washington Press.

————. 1993a. "Asian Families: Domestic Group Formation." In *Asia's Cultural Mosaic: An Anthropological Introduction,* ed. Grant Evans, 89–117. New York: Prentice Hall.

————. 1993b. "Ancestors and In-Laws: Kinship beyond the Family." In *Asia's Cultural Mosaic: An Anthropological Introduction,* ed. Grant Evans, 118–151.

————. 1994. "Success and Education in South Korea." *Comparative Education Review* 38(1):10–35.

Spencer, Robert F. 1988. *Yŏgong: Factory Girl.* Seoul: Royal Asiatic Society Korea Branch.

Srinivas, M.N. 1989. *The Cohesive Role of Sanskritization and Other Essays.* Delhi: Oxford University Press.

Suenari, Michio. 1994. "The Yangbanization of Korean Society." In *The Universal and Particular Natures of Confucianism,* 575–595. Proceedings of the 8th International Conference on Korean Studies. Sŏngnam Academy of Korean Studies.

Thomas, James Philip. 1993. "Contested from Within and Without: Squatters, the State, the Minjung Movement, and the Limits of Resistance in a Seoul Shanty Town." Ph.D. dissertation, University of Rochester.

Tsuya, Noriko O., and Choe Minja Kim. 1991. "Changes in Intrafamilial Relationships and the Role of Women in Japan and Korea." NUPRI Research Paper Series no. 58.

Tu Weiming, Milan Hejtmanek, and Alan Wachman, eds. 1992. *The Confucian World Observed: A Contemporary Discussion of Confucian Humanism in East Asia.* Honolulu: Program for Cultural Studies, East-West Center.

Underwood, Horace G. 1991. "An American Boy in Yesterday's Seoul: 'Golden Days' Fondly Recalled." *Koreana* 5(1):19–26.

Underwood, Lillas Horton. 1987 [1904]. *Fifteen Years among the Top-Knots.* Seoul: Royal Asiatic Society Korea Branch.

Vogel, Ezra F. 1963. *Japan's New Middle Class: The Salaryman and His Family in a Tokyo Suburb.* Berkeley: University of California Press.

————. 1967. "Kinship Structure, Migration to the City, and Modernization." In *Aspects of Social Change in Modern Japan,* ed. Ronald P. Dore, 91–111. Princeton: Princeton University Press.

————. 1991 [1963]. *Japan's New Middle Class.* 2nd ed. Berkeley: University of California Press.

Vogel, Suzanne Hall. 1991. "Beyond Success: Mamachi Thirty Years Later." In Ezra Vogel, *Japan's New Middle Class,* 2nd ed., 282–311.

Wagner, Edward W. 1974. "The Ladder of Success in Yi Dynasty Korea." *Occasional Papers on Korea* 1:1–8.

Watson, James L. In press. "Yangbanization in Comparative Perspective: The View from South China." In *The Anthropology of Korea: East Asian Perspectives,* ed. Mutsuhiko Shima and Roger L. Janelli. Osaka: National Museum of Ethnology.

Wright, Edward Reynolds, and Man Sill Pai. 1984. *Korean Furniture: Elegance and Tradition.* Tokyo: Kodansha International.

Wright, Eric Olin, et al. 1989. *The Debate on Classes.* London:Verso.

Yi Eunhee Kim. 1993. "From Gentry to the Middle Class: The Transformation of Family, Community, and Gender in Korea." Ph.D. dissertation, University of Chicago.

Yoo Seung-won. 1988. "The Status System in the Early Chosŏn Period." *Seoul Journal of Korean Studies* 1:69–99.

Yoon Hyungsook. 1989. "Rethinking Traditional Marriage in Korea." *Korea Journal* 29(12):17–17.

Yoon In-Jin. 1993. *The Social Origins of Korean Immigration to the United States from 1965 to the Present.* Papers of the Program on Population. Honolulu: East-West Center.

Yu, Eui Young. 1983. "Korean Communities in America: Past, Present, and Future." *Amerasia Journal* 10:23–51.

Guide to Romanization

aep'ŭtŏ (after) 애프터
ajumŏni 아주머니
anch'ae 안채
an chuin 안주인
annil 안 일
anpang 안방
Apkujŏng-dong 압구정동 (押鳩亭洞)
araenmok 아랫목

car-t'ing 카팅
chaebŏl 재벌 (財閥)
chaein 재인
chaesusaeng 재수생 (再修生)
chagŭn chip 작은집
chagŭn manura 작은 마누라
chang ot 장옷
changsikchang 장식장 (裝飾欌)
ch'imat param 치맛바람
chokpo 족보 (族譜)
ch'ŏn 천 (賤)
ch'onji 촌지
ch'ŏnmin 천민 (賤民)
chŏnse 전세 (傳貰)
ch'ŏp 첩 (妾)
Chosŏn 조선 (朝鮮)
chubu 주부 (主婦)
chung'in 중인 (中人)
chungmae 중매 (仲媒)
chungmaejaeng'i 중매장이
chungsanch'ŭng 중산층 (中産層)

Chusŏk 추석 (秋夕)
chusŏnja 주선자 (周旋者)
counseling 카운셀링

elevator-t'ing 엘리베이터 팅

hagwŏn 학원 (學院)
hang'ari 항아리
hangnyŏk kosa-t'ing 학력고사 (學力考查) 팅
han'gŭl 한글
hansu ("hansoo") 한수
hoesawŏn 회사원 (會社員)
hwajangsil 화장실 (化粧室)
hwan'gap 환갑 (還甲)
hy'ŏn'gwan 현관 (玄關)
hyŏnjo 현조 (懸祖)

ibul 이불
Ich'on-dong 이촌동
imdae 임대 (賃貸)

James Bond-t'ing 제임스본드 팅
joint MT-t'ing 조인트 엠티 팅

kang 강 (江)
Kangnam-gu 강남구 (江南區)
kimch'i 김치
kisaeng 기생 (妓生)
kohyang 고향 (故鄉)

kŏlle 걸레
kongjang 공장 (工場)
kŏnnŏnbang 건넌방
kosang 고상 (高尚)
kŏsil 거실 (居室)
ku (-gu) 구 (區)
kŭ namja nŏ hant'e after haenni?
    그 남자 너한테 애프터했니?
k'ŭn chip 큰집
kunghap 궁합 (宮合)
kungmin chut'aek 국민주택 (國民住宅)
kwagŏ 과거 (科擧)
kye 계 (契)
kyosu 교수 (教授)

madang 마당
Map'o 마포 (麻浦)
maru 마루
matsŏn 맛선
minmyŏnŭri 민며느리
mit'ing 미팅
munkwa 문과 (文科)
myŏngbun 명분 (名分)

nam 남 (南)
noraebang 노래방

opistel (officetel) 오피스텔

paekchŏng 백정 (白丁)
pakkatch'ae 바깥채
pakkat chuin 바깥주인
pakkat-il 바깥일
paksa 박사 (博士)
panch'an 반찬 (飯饌)
pan chungmae pan yŏnae 반중매
    반연애 (半仲媒 半戀愛)
pang 방 (房)
pangmang'i 방망이
pangsŏk 방석 (方席)
pang-t'ing 방팅
pansanghoe 반상회 (班常會)
pegae 베개
peranda (verandah) 베란다

phone-t'ing 폰팅
pilla (villa) 빌라
pinil hausŭ 비닐하우스
pohak 보학 (譜學)
pon'gwan 본관 (本貫)
porich'a 보리차
pudongsan 부동산 (不動産)
puk (-buk) 북 (北)
punyang 분양 (分讓)
pu'ŏk 부엌
pyŏng 뼝 (炳)
p'yŏng 평 (坪)

sach'ae 사채 (私債)
sadaebu 사대부 (士大夫)
sae 새
sagwini? 사귀니?
saju 사주 (四柱)
samsusaeng 삼수생 (三修生)
sang 상 (床)
sang'in 상인 (常人)
sangnom 상놈
sarang 사랑
sarangbang 사랑방
"sarang'i mwogillae?" 사람이 뭐길래?
sihŏm chiok 시험지옥 (試驗地獄)
siktang 식당 (食堂)
sinbang 신방 (新房)
soban 소반 (小盤)
sŏdang 서당 (書堂)
sogae 소개 (紹介)
sogae-t'ing 소개 (紹介) 팅
sŏja 서자 (庶子)
soksem 속셈
sŏnbi 선비
ssijok 씨족 (氏族)
stop/go-t'ing 스톱/고 팅

tanji 단지 (團地)
tasaedae chut'aek 다세대주택 (多世
    帶住宅)
terilsawi 데릴사위
tok 독
toksŏsil 독서실 (讀書室)

tong (-dong) 동 (洞)
tonggŏ 동거 (同居)
ttŏk kap 떡값

uri chip saram 우리집사람

winmok 윗목
wŏn 원 (圓)

yang 양 (良)
yangban 양반 (兩班)

yehak 예학 (禮學)
yo 요
"yŏksa wa aeguksim ui kwangye"
    역사 (歷史) 와 애국심 (愛國心) 의
    관계 (關係)
yŏllip chut'aek 연립주택 (聯立住宅)
yŏnae kyŏrhon 연애결혼 (戀愛結婚)
yŏnjulhon 연줄혼
Yŏngdŭngp'o 영등포
yuhak 유학 (留學)

Index

Abu-Lughod, Lila, 7

Administrators, 6, 36, 45. *See also* Managers; Salary men; White-collar work and workers

Adoption, 88, 205; in Japan, 205

Adult children and parents: unmarried children, 81–83, 131, 142–143; married children, 83–87; elderly parents, 87–88. *See also* Daughters; Eldest sons; Sons; Younger sons

Adult status, 178, 197

Affines, *see* In-laws

Age: as an hierarchical principle, 23, 44, 51–52, 89, 133, 208; discrimination, 44; of marriage, 62, 65, 81–82, 189, 191, 193, 224

Aged, care of, 23, 84, 87–92 *passim*, 95, 113, 204. *See also* Eldest sons

Agnates, 13, 15–16, 19, 22, 30–31, 38, 54, 59, 98, 121, 205–206, 213, 217, 218, 227. *See also* Ancestry; Lineages

Agriculture and agrarian society, 3, 17–19, 33–37

Ancestor, distinguished (*hyonjo*), 32

Ancestor rites, 22, 23, 31, 80, 81, 88, 205. *See also* Ancestors; Ancestor worship

Ancestors, 13, 21, 30, 32, 38, 54, 224. *See also* Ancestor rites; Ancestor worship; Ancestry

Ancestor worship, 14, 40, 88, 124, 207, 224; and eldest son, 23, 38–40, 85, 88, 90–91, 96, 205; and younger sons, 23, 85, 88, 96, 124–125, 205; and status, 31, 38–40, 136, 207; and Christianity, 59, 88, 207; and women's role of, 88, 90, 91. *See also* Ancestor rites

Ancestry, 20, 205; yangban, 15–16, 32, 38, 40, 54, 165, 183, 195–196, 206, 207, 211, 227; and status, 20–23, 32, 41, 80, 138, 207, 210, 211–213; commoner, 21, 22, 23, 38, 40, 206, 207. *See also* Genealogies; Lineages; Yangban

Anpang (inner room), 25, 26, 27, 118–125 *passim*, 128–135 *passim*, 145

Apartment complexes, 7, 8, 57, 102, 107–116 *passim*, 139, 149, 151, 152, 153, 195, 203, 207; for low-income families, 112–113, 207–208. *See also* Apartments

Apartment dwellers, 8, 115, 122, 135, 207

Apartment guards, 8, 10, 115, 151, 157

Apartments (condominiums), 8, 10, 59, 98, 100, 109, 111, 157, 158, 207, 210; cost and financing of, 59, 69, 72, 73, 79, 84, 85, 86, 89, 109–113 *passim*; as investments, 68–70, 74, 75, 77–78, 84, 86, 156; layout, furnishings, and use of space within, 100, 118, 122–125, 126 (fig.), 127 (fig.), 128–139; preference

Harvard East Asian Monographs

44. Benjamin I. Schwartz, ed., *Reflections on the May Fourth Movement.: A Symposium*

45. Ching Young Choe, *The Rule of the Taewŏngun, 1864–1873: Restoration in Yi Korea*

46. W. P. J. Hall, *A Bibliographical Guide to Japanese Research on the Chinese Economy, 1958–1970*

47. Jack J. Gerson, *Horatio Nelson Lay and Sino-British Relations, 1854–1864*

48. Paul Richard Bohr, *Famine and the Missionary: Timothy Richard as Relief Administrator and Advocate of National Reform*

49. Endymion Wilkinson, *The History of Imperial China: A Research Guide*

50. Britten Dean, *China and Great Britain: The Diplomacy of Commercial Relations, 1860–1864*

51. Ellsworth C. Carlson, *The Foochow Missionaries, 1847–1880*

52. Yeh-chien Wang, *An Estimate of the Land-Tax Collection in China, 1753 and 1908*

53. Richard M. Pfeffer, *Understanding Business Contracts in China, 1949–1963*

54. Han-sheng Chuan and Richard Kraus, *Mid-Ching Rice Markets and Trade: An Essay in Price History*

55. Ranbir Vohra, *Lao She and the Chinese Revolution*

56. Liang-lin Hsiao, *China's Foreign Trade Statistics, 1864–1949*

57. Lee-hsia Hsu Ting, *Government Control of the Press in Modern China, 1900–1949*

58. Edward W. Wagner, *The Literati Purges: Political Conflict in Early Yi Korea*

59. Joungwon A. Kim, *Divided Korea: The Politics of Development, 1945–1972*

60. Noriko Kamachi, John K. Fairbank, and Chūzō Ichiko, *Japanese Studies of Modern China Since 1953: A Bibliographical Guide to Historical and Social-Science Research on the Nineteenth and Twentieth Centuries, Supplementary Volume for 1953–1969*

61. Donald A. Gibbs and Yun-chen Li, *A Bibliography of Studies and Translations of Modern Chinese Literature, 1918–1942*

62. Robert H. Silin, *Leadership and Values: The Organization of Large-Scale Taiwanese Enterprises*

63. David Pong, *A Critical Guide to the Kwangtung Provincial Archives Deposited at the Public Record Office of London*

64. Fred W. Drake, *China Charts the World: Hsu Chi-yü and His Geography of 1848*

65. William A. Brown and Urgrunge Onon, translators and annotators, *History of the Mongolian People's Republic*

66. Edward L. Farmer, *Early Ming Government: The Evolution of Dual Capitals*

135. Parks M. Coble, *Facing Japan: Chinese Politics and Japanese Imperialism, 1931–1937*

136. Jon L. Saari, *Legacies of Childhood: Growing Up Chinese in a Time of Crisis, 1890–1920*

137. Susan Downing Videen, *Tales of Heichū*

138. Heinz Morioka and Miyoko Sasaki, *Rakugo: The Popular Narrative Art of Japan*

139. Joshua A. Fogel, *Nakae Ushikichi in China: The Mourning of Spirit*

140. Alexander Barton Woodside, *Vietnam and the Chinese Model.: A Comparative Study of Vietnamese and Chinese Government in the First Half of the Nineteenth Century*

141. George Elision, *Deus Destroyed: The Image of Christianity in Early Modern Japan*

142. William D. Wray, ed., *Managing Industrial Enterprise: Cases from Japan's Prewar Experience*

143. T'ung-tsu Ch'ü, *Local Government in China under the Ching*

144. Marie Anchordoguy, *Computers, Inc.: Japan's Challenge to IBM*

145. Barbara Molony, *Technology and Investment: The Prewar Japanese Chemical Industry*

146. Mary Elizabeth Berry, *Hideyoshi*

147. Laura E. Hein, *Fueling Growth: The Energy Revolution and Economic Policy in Postwar Japan*

148. Wen-hsin Yeh, *The Alienated Academy: Culture and Politics in Republican China, 1919–1937*

149. Dru C. Gladney, *Muslim Chinese: Ethnic Nationalism in the People's Republic*

150. Merle Goldman and Paul A. Cohen, eds., *Ideas Across Cultures: Essays on Chinese Thought in Honor of Benjamin L Schwartz*

151. James Polachek, *The Inner Opium War*

152. Gail Lee Bernstein, *Japanese Marxist: A Portrait of Kawakami Hajime, 1879–1946*

153. Lloyd E. Eastman, *The Abortive Revolution: China under Nationalist Rule, 1927–1937*

154. Mark Mason, *American Multinationals and Japan: The Political Economy of Japanese Capital Controls, 1899–1980*

155. Richard J. Smith, John K. Fairbank, and Katherine F. Bruner, *Robert Hart and China's Early Modernization: His Journals, 1863–1866*

156. George J. Tanabe, Jr., *Myōe the Dreamkeeper: Fantasy and Knowledge in Kamakura Buddhism*

157. William Wayne Farris, *Heavenly Warriors: The Evolution of Japan's Military, 500–1300*